LIVESTOCK FARMING

By

Parameshwar Hegde

M.Sc., M.A.

DISCOVERY PUBLISHING HOUSE PVT. LTD.

NEW DELHI-110 002

Published by:
Tilak Wasan
DISCOVERY PUBLISHING HOUSE PVT. LTD.
4383/4B, Ansari Road, Darya Ganj
New Delhi-110 002 (India)
Phone : +91-11-23279245, 23253475, 43596065
E-mail : discoverypublishinghouse@gmail.com
namitwasan9@gmail.com
sales@discoverypublishinggroup.com
web : www.discoverypublishinggroup.com

***Edition:* 2020**

ISBN: 978-93-5056-276-5

Livestock Farming

Printed at:
Infinity Imaging Systems
Delhi

Preface

Livestock farming is raising animals for food or to sell. Some of these animals might be: cattle/dairy cows, chickens, Goats, Hogs/pigs, Sheep, Horses.

There are other kinds of livestock animals that you might not think about. These are: donkeys, mules, and rabbits. Bees are raised for their honey. All kinds of fish are raised on fish farms. Livestock gives us our meat, eggs and milk. We also use the skins [leather] and hair of some animals for blankets, clothing, shoes, and brushes. Some livestock organs are used for medicines like insulin. Hoofs and horns are used for buttons, combs, glue and knives. Manure from these animals will be used to make plants grow better. When we talk about livestock, we will include beef cattle, hogs/pigs, goats, sheep and horses. Dairy cows can be found in the Dairy Farm area and chickens can be found on the Poultry Farming page. They were separated because they are a large part of livestock and needed more space.

We were surprised to see that livestock farming is well planned. We didn't know that farmers 'design' their herds of animals by deciding which characteristics are good ones. To make it easier to understand, we will use an example. Let's say that Ginny is the best cow that the farmer has because she is from a good family and has given birth to other great cows. The farmer will take the best things about Ginny and pair them with Hector, the bull. Hector will be chosen because he has other qualities like a good family and good beef. The combination will make a calf that has qualities from Ginny and Hector. The farmer will even have another cow be pregnant with Ginny and Hector's calf if Ginny has had her limit or needs time off from being pregnant. This is selective breeding. There is much more planning and thought in cattle production than we ever knew.

Livestock can be mated in three ways:

1. *Randomly*—by putting a few males and a few females of one species in a pen and allowing them to mate with whichever one they want.
2. *Inbreeding*—by mating animals that are closely related. They pick two that are related and have really good genes so that the baby will have them, too.
3. *Crossbreeding*—by mating unrelated animals. Sometimes these animals are of different breeds.

Farmers feed livestock with grazing and giving them feed. When a farmer feeds his livestock, he tries very hard to feed them things that help them grow. He adds vitamins, minerals, and protein so that the animals stay healthy. Farmers will figure out how much of each ingredient the livestock should have. Sometimes cereal grains are added so that the livestock produce better or more beef. Cattle have bodies that can take grazing food and make it into the protein it needs.

Livestock (also cattle) refers to one or more domesticated animals raised in an agricultural setting to produce commodities such as food, fibre and labour. The term "livestock" as used does not include poultry or farmed fish; however the inclusion of these, especially poultry, within the meaning of "livestock" is common.

Livestock generally are raised for subsistence or for profit. Raising animals (animal husbandry) is an important component of modern agriculture. It has been practised in many cultures since the transition to farming from hunter-gather lifestyles.

–Author

Contents

CHAPTER 1
Introduction

Livestock farming is raising animals for food or to sell. Some of these animals might be:

Cattle/dairy cows, Chickens, Goats, Hogs/pigs, Sheep, Horses.

There are other kinds of livestock animals that you might not think about. These are: donkeys, mules, and rabbits. Bees are raised for their honey. All kinds of fish are raised on fish farms. Livestock gives us our meat, eggs and milk. We also use the skins [leather] and hair of some animals for blankets, clothing, shoes, and brushes. Some livestock organs are used for medicines like insulin. Hoofs and horns are used for buttons, combs, glue and knives. Manure from these animals will be used to make plants grow better. When we talk about livestock, we will include beef cattle, hogs/pigs, goats, sheep and horses. Dairy cows can be found in the Dairy Farm area and chickens can be found on the Poultry Farming page. They were separated because they are a large part of livestock and needed more space.

We were surprised to see that livestock farming is well planned. We didn't know that farmers 'design' their herds of animals by deciding which characteristics are good ones. To make it easier to understand, we will use an example. Let's say that Ginny is the best cow that the farmer has because she is from a good family and has given birth to other great cows. The farmer will take the best things about Ginny and pair them with Hector, the bull. Hector will be chosen because he has other qualities like a good family and good beef. The combination will make a calf that has qualities from Ginny and Hector. The farmer will even have another cow be pregnant with Ginny and Hector's calf if Ginny has had her limit or needs time off from being pregnant. This is selective breeding. There is much more planning and thought in cattle production than we ever knew.

Livestock can be mated in three ways:

Randomly — By putting a few males and a few females of one species in a pen and allowing them to mate with whichever one they want.

Inbreeding — By mating animals that are closely related. They pick two that are related and have really good genes so that the baby will have them, too.

Crossbreeding— By mating unrelated animals. Sometimes these animals are of different breeds.

Farmers feed livestock with grazing and giving them feed. When a farmer feeds his livestock, he tries very hard to feed them things that help them grow. He adds vitamins, minerals, and protein so that the animals stay healthy. Farmers will figure out how much of each ingredient the livestock should have. Sometimes cereal grains are added so that the livestock produce better or more beef. Cattle have bodies that can take grazing food and make it into the protein it needs.

Depending on what kind of livestock it is, farmers give them places to live. Sometimes it is in a building that has its temperature controlled and sometimes it is just a place where they can get out of the rain. Since farmers began to 'design' their herds, the animals have become a little weaker and can't take very bad weather conditions like they used to years ago.

Livestock (also cattle) refers to one or more domesticated animals raised in an agricultural setting to produce commodities such as food, fiber and labour. The term "livestock" as used does not include poultry or farmed fish; however the inclusion of these, especially poultry, within the meaning of "livestock" is common.

Livestock generally are raised for subsistence or for profit. Raising animals (animal husbandry) is an important component of modern agriculture. It has been practised in many cultures since the transition to farming from hunter-gather lifestyles.

Animal-rearing has its origins in the transition of cultures to settled farming communities rather than hunter-gatherer lifestyles. Animals are 'domesticated' when their breeding and living conditions are controlled by humans. Over time, the collective behaviour, life-cycle, and physiology of livestock have changed radically. Many modern farm animals are unsuited to life in the wild. Dogs were domesticated in East Asia about 15,000 years ago, Goats and sheep were domesticated around 8000 BCE in Asia. Swine or pigs were domesticated by 7000 BCE in the Middle East and China. The earliest evidence of horse domestication dates to around 4000 BCE.

Older English sources, such as the King James Version of the Bible, refer to livestock in general as "cattle", as opposed to the word "deer", which then was used for wild animals which were not owned. The word *cattle* is derived from Middle English *chatel*, which meant all kinds of moveable personal property, including of course livestock, which was differentiated from non-moveable real-estate. In later English, sometimes smaller livestock was called "small cattle" in that sense of movable property on land, which was not automatically bought or sold with the land. Today, the modern meaning of "cattle", without a qualifier, usually refers to domesticated bovines . Other species of the genus *Bos* sometimes are called wild cattle.

The term "livestock" is nebulous and may be defined narrowly or broadly. On a broader view, livestock refers to any breed or population of animal kept by humans for a useful, commercial purpose. This can mean domestic animals, semi-domestic animals, or captive wild animals. Semi-domesticated refers to animals which are only lightly domesticated or of disputed status. These populations may also be in the process of domestication. Some people may use the term livestock to refer just to domestic animals or even just to red meat animals.

'Livestock' are defined, in part, by their end purpose as the production of food, fibre and/or labour.

The economic value of livestock includes:

Meat

The production of a useful form of dietary protein and energy.

Dairy Products

Mammalian livestock can be used as a source of milk, which can in turn easily be processed into other dairy products, such as yogurt, cheese, butter, ice cream, kefir, and kumis. Using livestock for this purpose can often yield several times the food energy of slaughtering the animal outright.

Fibre

Livestock produce a range of fiber/textiles. For example, sheep and goats produce wool and mohair; cows, deer, and sheep skins can be made into leather; and bones, hooves and horns of livestock can be used.

Fertilizer

Manure can be spread on fields to increase crop yields. This is an important reason why historically, plant and animal domestication have been intimately linked. Manure is also used to make plaster for walls and floors, and can be used as a fuel for fires. The blood and bone of animals are also used as fertilizer.

Labour

Animals such as horses, donkey, and yaks can be used for mechanical energy. Prior to steam power, livestock were the only available source of non-human labour. They are still used for this purpose in many places of the world, including ploughing fields, transporting goods, and military functions.

Land Management

The grazing of livestock is sometimes used as a way to control weeds and undergrowth. For example, in areas prone to wild fires, goats and sheep are set to graze on dry scrub which removes combustible material and reduces the risk of fires.

During the history of animal husbandry, many secondary products have arisen in an attempt to increase carcass utilization and reduce waste. For example, animal offal and non-edible parts may be transformed into products such as pet food and fertilizer. In the past, such waste products were sometimes also fed to livestock as well. However, intra-species recycling poses a disease risk, threatening animal and even human health. Due primarily to BSE (Bovine Spongiform Encephalopathy) (mad cow disease), feeding animal scraps to animals has been banned in many countries, at least in regards to ruminants and pigs.

Farming practices vary dramatically worldwide and between types of animals. Livestock are generally kept in an enclosure, are fed by human-provided food and are intentionally bred, but some livestock are not enclosed, or are fed by access to natural foods, or are allowed to breed freely, or any combination thereof. Livestock raising historically was part of a nomadic or pastoral form of material culture. The herding of camels and reindeer in some parts of the world remains unassociated with sedentary agriculture. The transhumance form of herding in the Sierra Nevada Mountains of California still continues, as cattle, sheep or goats are moved from winter pasture in lower elevation valleys to spring pasture and summer pasture in the foothills and alpine regions, as the seasons progress. Cattle were raised on the open range in the Western United States and Canada, on the Pampas of Argentina, and other prairie and steppe regions of the world.

The enclosure of livestock in pastures and barns is a relatively new development in the history of agriculture. When cattle are enclosed, the type of 'enclosure' may vary from a small crate, a large fenced pasture or a paddock. The type of feed may vary from natural growing grass, to highly sophisticated processed feed. Animals are usually intentionally bred through artificial insemination or through supervised mating. Indoor production systems are generally used only for pigs and poultry, as well as for veal cattle. Indoor animals are generally farmed intensively, as large space requirements would make indoor farming unprofitable and impossible. However, indoor farming systems are controversial due to the waste they produce, odour problems, the potential for groundwater contamination and animal welfare concerns.

Other livestock are farmed outside, although the size of enclosure and level of supervision may vary. In large open ranges animals may be only occasionally inspected or yarded in "round-ups" or a muster (livestock). Working dogs such as sheep dogs and cattle dogs may be used for mustering livestock as are cowboys, stockmen and jackaroos on horses, or with vehicles and also by helicopters. Since the advent of barbed wire (in the 1870s) and electric fence technology, fencing pastures has become much more feasible and pasture management simplified. Rotation of pasturage is a modern technique for improving nutrition and health while avoiding environmental damage to the land. In some cases very large numbers of animals may be kept in indoor or outdoor feeding operations (on feedlots), where the animals' feed is processed, offsite or onsite, and stored on site then fed to the animals.

Livestock — especially cattle — may be branded to indicate ownership and age, but in modern farming identification is more likely to be indicated by means of ear tags than branding. Sheep are also frequently marked by means of ear marks and/or ear tags. As fears of mad cow disease and other epidemic illnesses mount, the use of microchip identification to monitor and trace animals in the food production system is increasingly common, and sometimes required by governmental regulations.

Modern farming techniques seek to minimize human involvement, increase yield, and improve animal health. Economics, quality and consumer safety all play a role in how animals are raised. Drug use and feed supplements (or even feed type) may be regulated, or prohibited, to ensure yield is not increased at the expense of consumer health, safety or animal welfare. Practices vary around the world, for example growth hormone use is permitted in the United States, but not in stock to be sold to the European Union. The improvement of health, using modern farming techniques, on the part of animals has come into question. Feeding corn to cattle, which have historically eaten grasses, is an example; where the cattle are less adapted, the rumen pH changes to more acidic, leading to liver damage and other difficulties. The USFDA still allows feedlots to feed nonruminant animal proteins to cattle. For example, feeding chicken manure and poultry meal is acceptable for cattle, and beef or pork meat and bone meal is being fed to chickens.

Predation

Livestock farmers had suffered from wild animal predation and theft by rustlers. In North America, gray wolf, grizzly bear, cougar, black bear, and coyote are sometimes considered a threat to livestock. In Eurasia and Africa, wolf, brown bear, leopard, tiger, lion, dhole, black bear, spotted hyena, and others caused livestock deaths. In Australia, the dingo, foxes, wedge-tailed eagles, hunting and domestic dogs (especially) cause problems for graziers because they often kill for fun. In Latin America, feral dogs cause livestock deaths in nightfall.

Livestock diseases compromise animal welfare, reduce productivity, and can infect humans. Animal diseases may be tolerated, reduced through animal husbandry, or reduced through antibiotics and vaccines. In developing countries, animal diseases are tolerated in animal husbandry, resulting in considerably reduced productivity, especially given the low health-status of many developing country herds. Disease management for gains in productivity is often the first step taken in implementing an agriculture policy.

Disease management can be achieved through changes in animal husbandry. These measures may aim to control spread using biosecurity measures, such as controlling animal mixing, controlling entry to farm lots and the use of protective clothing, and quarantining sick animals. Diseases also may be controlled by the use of vaccines and antibiotics. Antibiotics in sub-therapeutic doses may also be used as a growth-promoter, increasing growth by 10-15 per cent. The issue of antibiotic resistance has limited the practices of preventative dosing such as antibiotic-laced feed. Countries will often require the use of veterinary certificates before transporting, selling or showing animals. Disease-free areas often rigorously enforce rules for entry of potentially diseased animals, including quarantine.

Since many livestock are herd animals, they were historically driven to market "on the hoof" to a town or other central location. During the period after the American Civil War, the abundance of Longhorn cattle in Texas, and the demand for beef in Northern markets, led to the implementation of the Old West cattle drive. The method is still used in some parts of the world. Truck transport is now common in developed countries. Local and regional livestock auctions and commodity markets facilitate trade in livestock. In other areas, livestock may be bought and sold in a bazaar, such as may be found in many parts of Central Asia, or a flea market type setting.

Stock shows and fairs are events where people bring their best livestock to compete with one another. Organisations like 4-H, Block & Bridle, and FFA encourage young people to raise livestock for show purposes. Special feeds are purchased and hours may be spent prior to the show grooming the animal to look its best. In cattle, sheep, and swine shows, the winning animals are frequently auctioned off to the highest bidder, and the funds are placed into a scholarship fund for its owner.

The issue of raising livestock for human benefit raises the issue of the relationship between humans and animals, in terms of the status of animals and obligations of people. Animal welfare is the viewpoint that animals under human care should be treated in such a way that they do not suffer unnecessarily. What is 'unnecessary' suffering may vary. Generally, though, the animal welfare perspective is based on an interpretation of scientific research on farming practices. By contrast, animal rights is the viewpoint that using animals for human benefit is, by its nature, generally exploitation, regardless of the farming practices used. Animal rights activists would generally be vegan or vegetarian, whereas it is consistent with the animal welfare perspective to eat meat, depending on production processes.

Animal welfare groups generally seek to generate public discussion on livestock raising practices and secure greater regulation and scrutiny of livestock industry practices. Animal rights groups usually seek the abolition of livestock farming, although some groups may recognise the necessity of achieving more stringent regulation first. Animal welfare groups, such as the RSPCA, are often, in first world countries, given a voice at governmental level in the development of policy. Animal rights groups find it harder to find methods of input, and may go further and advocate civil disobedience or violence.

A number of animal husbandry practices have been the subject of campaigns in the 1990s and 2000s and have led to legislation in some countries. Confinement of livestock in small and unnatural spaces is often done for economic or health reasons. Animals may be kept in the minimum size of cage or pen with little or no space to exercise. Where livestock are used as a source of power, they may be pushed beyond their limits to the point of exhaustion. The public visibility of this abuse meant it was one of the first areas to receive legislation in the nineteenth century in European countries, but it still goes on in parts of Asia. Broiler hens may be de-beaked, pigs may have deciduous teeth pulled, cattle may be de-horned and branded, dairy cows and sheep may have tails cropped, merino sheep may be mulesed, and many types of male animals are castrated. Animals may be transported long distances to market and slaughter. Overcrowded conditions, heat from tropical-area shipping and lack of food, water and rest breaks have been subject to legislation and protest. Slaughter of livestock was an early target for legislation. Campaigns continue to target *Halal* and *Kosher* religious ritual slaughter.

At first reports like the United Nations report "Livestock's Long Shadow" cast a pall over the livestock sector (primarily cattle, chickens, and pigs) for 'emerging as one of the top two or three most significant contributors to our most serious environmental problems'. The United Nations controversially included emissions from deforestation as part of its methodology. Rather than the 18 per cent figure that placed on the sector as major contributor to emissions, the real figure, less deforestation is actually 12 per cent. In April 2008, the [United States Environmental Protection Agency] released a major stocktake of emissions in the United States entitled *Inventory of U.S. Greenhouse Gas Emissions and Sinks: 1990-2006*. On 6.1 it found "In 2006, the agricultural sector was responsible for emissions of 454.1 teragrams of CO_2 equivalent (Tg CO_2 Eq.), or six per cent of total U.S. greenhouse gas emissions." By way of comparison, transportation in the US produces more than 25 per cent of all emissions.

The issue of livestock as a major policy focus remains, especially when dealing with problems of deforestation in neotropical areas, land degradation, climate change and air pollution, water shortage and water pollution, and loss of biodiversity. A research team at Obihiro University of Agriculture and Veterinary Medicine in Hokkaido found that supplementing the animals' diet with cysteine, a type of amino acid, and nitrate can reduce the methane gas produced, without jeopardising the cattle's productivity or the quality of their meat and milk.

Researchers in Australia are looking into the possibility of reducing methane from cattle and sheep by introducing digestive bacteria from kangaroo intestines into livestock.

Research from the University of Botswana in 2008 has found that farmers' common practice of overstocking cattle to cope with drought losses made ecosystems more vulnerable and risked long term damage to cattle herds, in turn, by actually depleting scarce biomass. The study of the Kgatleng district of Botswana predicted that by 2050, the cycle of mild drought is likely to become shorter for the region (18 months instead of two years) due to climate change.

United States federal legislation sometimes more narrowly defines the term to make specified agricultural commodities either eligible, or ineligible, for a programme or activity. For example, the Livestock Mandatory Reporting Act of 1999 (P.L. 106-78, Title IX) defines livestock only as cattle, swine, and lambs. However, 1988 disaster assistance legislation defined the term as "cattle, sheep, goats, swine, poultry (including egg-producing poultry), equine animals used for food or in the production of food, fish used for food, and other animals designated by the Secretary".

CHAPTER 2
Domestication

Domestication (from Latin *domesticus*) or taming is the process whereby a population of animals or plants, through a process of selection, becomes accustomed to human provision and control. A defining characteristic of domestication is artificial selection by humans. Humans have brought these populations under their control and care for a wide range of reasons: to produce food or valuable commodities (such as wool, cotton, or silk), for help with various types of work (such as transportation, protection, and warfare), scientific research, or simply to enjoy as companions or ornaments.

Plants domesticated primarily for aesthetic enjoyment in and around the home are usually called *house plants* or *ornamentals*, while those domesticated for large-scale food production are generally called *crops*. A distinction can be made between those domesticated plants that have been deliberately altered or selected for special desirable characteristics and those domesticated plants that are essentially no different from their wild counterparts (assuming domestication does not necessarily imply physical modification). Likewise, animals domesticated for home companionship are usually called *pets* while those domesticated for food or work are called *livestock* or *farm animals*.

There is debate within the scientific community over how the process of domestication works. Some researchers give credit to natural selection, where mutations outside of human control make some members of a species more compatible to human cultivation or companionship. Others have shown that carefully controlled selective breeding is responsible for many of the collective changes associated with domestication. These categories are not mutually exclusive and it is likely that natural selection and selective breeding have both played some role in the processes of domestication throughout history. Either way, a process of selection is involved. The domestication of wheat is an example of this. Wild wheat falls to the ground to reseed itself when it is ripe, but domesticated wheat stays on the stem when it is ripe. There is evidence that this critical change came about as a result of a random mutation near the beginning of wheat's cultivation. Wheat with this mutation was the only wheat harvested and became the seed for the next crop. This wheat was much more useful to farmers and became the basis for the various strains of domesticated wheat that have since been developed.

The example of wheat has led some to speculate that mutations may have been the basis for other early instances of domestication. It is speculated that a mutation made some wolves less wary of humans. This allowed these wolves to start following humans to scavenge for food in their garbage dumps. Presumably something like a symbiotic relationship developed between humans and this population of wolves. The wolves benefited from human food scraps, and humans may have found that the wolves could warn them of approaching enemies, help with hunting, carry loads, provide warmth, or supplement their food supply. As this relationship evolved, humans eventually began to raise the wolves and breed the types of dogs that we have today.

Some researchers maintain that selective breeding rather than mutation or natural selection best explains how the process of domestication typically worked. Some of the most well-known evidence in support of selective breeding comes from an experiment by Russian scientist, Dmitri K. Belyaev, in the 1950s. His team spent many years breeding the Silver Fox (*Vulpes vulpes*) and selecting only those individuals that showed the least fear of humans. Eventually, Belyaev's team selected only those that showed the most positive response to humans. He ended up with a population of grey-coloured foxes whose behavior and appearance was significantly changed. They no longer showed any fear of humans and often wagged their tails and licked their human caretakers to show affection. More importantly, these foxes had floppy ears, smaller skulls, rolled tails and other traits commonly found in dogs.

Despite the success of this experiment, some scientists believe that selective breeding cannot always achieve domestication. They point out that known attempts to domesticate several kinds of wild animals in this way have failed repeatedly. The zebra is one example. Despite the fact that four species of zebra are interbreedable with and part of the same genus as the horse and the donkey, attempts at domestication have failed. The factors which influence 'domesticatability' of large animals are discussed in some detail in. Surprisingly only 14 species of large animal seem to be capable of domestication. In approximate order of their earliest domestication these are: dog, sheep, goat, pig, cow, horse, donkey, water buffalo, llama/alpaca, bactrian camel, and Arabian camel.

According to evolutionary biologist Jared Diamond, animal species must meet six criteria in order to be considered for domestication:

Hereford Cattle, Domesticated for Beef Production

Flexible diet—Creatures that are willing to consume a wide variety of food sources and can live off less cumulative food from the food pyramid (such as corn or wheat), particularly food that is not utilized by humans (such as grass and forage) are less expensive to keep in captivity. Carnivores by definition feed primarily or only on animal tissue, which requires the expenditure of many animals, though they may exploit sources of meat not utilized by humans, such as scraps and vermin.

Reasonably fast growth rate—Fast maturity rate compared to the human life span allows breeding intervention and makes the animal useful within an acceptable duration of caretaking. Large animals such as elephants require many years before they reach a useful size.

Ability to be bred in captivity—Creatures that are reluctant to breed when kept in captivity do not produce useful offspring, and instead are limited to capture in their wild state. Creatures such as the panda, antelope and giant forest hog are territorial when breeding and cannot be maintained in crowded enclosures in captivity.

Pleasant disposition—Large creatures that are aggressive toward humans are dangerous to keep in captivity. The African buffalo has an unpredictable nature and is highly dangerous to humans; similarly, although the American bison is raised in enclosed ranges in the US West, it is much too dangerous to be regarded as truly domesticated. Although similar to the domesticated pig in many ways, the American peccary and Africa's warthog and bushpig are also dangerous in captivity.

Temperament which makes it unlikely to panic—A creature with a nervous disposition is difficult to keep in captivity as it may attempt to flee whenever startled. The gazelle is very flighty and it has a powerful leap that allows it to escape an enclosed pen. Some animals, such as the Domestic sheep, still have a strong tendency to panic when their flight zone is crossed. However, most sheep also show a flocking instinct, whereby they stay close together when pressed. Livestock with such an instinct may be herded by people and dogs.

Modifiable social hierarchy—Social creatures that recognize a hierarchy of dominance can be raised to recognize a human as the pack leader.

Plants

The earliest human attempts at plant domestication occurred in Asia. There is early evidence for conscious cultivation and trait selection of plants by pre-Neolithic groups in Syria: grains of rye with domestic traits have been recovered from Epi-Palaeolithic (c. 11,050 BP) contexts at Abu Hureyra in Syria, but this appears to be a localised phenomenon resulting from cultivation of stands of wild rye, rather than a definitive step towards domestication.

By 10,000 BC the bottle gourd (*Lagenaria siceraria*) plant, used as a container before the advent of ceramic technology, appears to have been domesticated. The domesticated bottle gourd reached the Americas from Asia by 8000 BC, most likely due to the migration of peoples from Asia to America.

Cereal crops were first domesticated around 9000 BC in the Fertile Crescent in the Middle East. The first domesticated crops were generally annuals with large seeds or fruits. These included pulses such as peas and grains such as wheat.

The Middle East was especially suited to these species; the dry-summer climate was conducive to the evolution of large-seeded annual plants, and the variety of elevations led to a great variety of species. As domestication took place humans began to move from a hunter-gatherer society to a settled agricultural society. This change would eventually lead, some 4000 to 5000 years later, to the first city states and eventually the rise of civilization itself.

Domestication was gradual, a process of trial and error that occurred slowly. Over time perennials and small trees began to be domesticated including apples and olives. Some plants were not domesticated until recently such as the macadamia nut and the pecan.

In different parts of the world very different species were domesticated. In the Americas squash, maize, beans, and perhaps manioc (also known as cassava) formed the core of the diet. In East Asia millet, rice, and soy were the most important crops. Some areas of the world such as Southern Africa, Australia, California and Southern South America never saw local species domesticated.

Over the millennia many domesticated species have become utterly unlike their natural ancestors. Maize ears are now dozens of times the size of those of wild teosinte. A similar change occurred between wild strawberries and domesticated strawberries.

Domesticated plant species often differ from their wild relatives in predictable ways. These differences are called the domestication syndrome, and include:

- Higher germination rates.
- More predictable and synchronous germination.
- Increased size of reproductive organs.
- A tendency for ripe seeds to stay on the plant, rather than breaking off and falling to the ground.
- Reduced physical and chemical defences.
- Change in biomass allocation (more in fruits, roots, or stems, depending on human)

Due to elephants' slow growth, the boundaries between surviving wild populations and domestic clades can be vague. Similar problems of definition arise when domesticated cats go feral. A classification system that can help solve this confusion surrounding animal populations might be set up on a spectrum of increasing domestication:

Wild

These populations experience their full life cycles without deliberate human intervention.

Raised in Captivity/Captured from Wild

These populations are nurtured by humans but (except in zoos) not normally bred under human control. They remain as a group essentially indistinguishable in appearance or behaviour from their wild counterparts. Examples include Asian elephants, animals such as sloth bears and cobras used by showmen in India, and animals such as Asian black bears (farmed for their bile), and zoo animals, kept in captivity as examples of their species. (It should be noted that zoos and botanical gardens sometimes exhibit domesticated or feral animals and plants such as camels, mustangs, and some orchids.)

Raised Commercially

These populations are ranched or farmed in large numbers for food, commodities, or the pet trade, commonly breed in captivity, but as a group are not substantially altered in appearance or behavior from their wild cousins. Examples include the ostrich, various deer, alligator, cricket, pearl oyster, and ball python. (These species are sometimes referred to as *partially domesticated*).

Domesticated

These populations are bred and raised under human control for many generations and are substantially altered as a group in appearance or behaviour. Examples include pigs, ferrets, turkeys, canaries, domestic pigeons, budgerigars, goldfish, silkworms, dogs, cats, sheep, cattle, chickens, llamas, guinea pigs, laboratory mice, goats and (silver) foxes.

This classification system does not account for several complicating factors: genetically modified organisms, feral populations, and hybridization. Many species that are farmed or ranched are now being genetically modified. This creates a unique category because it alters the organisms as a group but in ways unlike traditional domestication. Feral organisms are members of a population that was once raised under human control, but is now living and multiplying outside of human control. Examples include mustangs. Hybrids can be wild, domesticated, or both: a liger is a hybrid of two wild animals, a mule is a hybrid of two domesticated animals, and a beefalo is a cross between a wild and a domestic animal.

A great difference exists between a tame animal and a domesticated animal. The term "domesticated" refers to an entire species or variety while the term "tame" can refer to just one individual within a species or variety. Humans have tamed many thousands of animals that have never been truly domesticated. These include the elephant, giraffes, and bears. There is debate over whether some species have been domesticated or just tamed. Some state that the elephant has been domesticated, while others argue the cat has never been. Dividing lines include whether a specimen born to wild parents would differ in appearance or behavior from one born to domesticated parents. For instance a dog is certainly domesticated because even a wolf (genetically the origin of all dogs) raised from a pup would be very different from a dog, in both appearance and behaviour.

Limits

Selection of animals for visible "desirable" traits may make them unfit in other, unseen, ways. The consequences for the captive and domesticated animals were reduction in size, piebald colour, shorter faces with smaller and fewer teeth, diminished horns, weak muscle ridges, and less genetic variability. Poor joint definition, late fusion of the limb bone epiphyses with the diaphyses, hair changes, greater fat accumulation, smaller brains, simplified behavior patterns, extended immaturity, and more pathology are a few of the defects of domestic animals, All of these changes have been documented in direct observations of the rat in the 19th century, by archaeological evidence, and confirmed by animal breeders in the 20th century.

One side effect of domestication has been zoonotic diseases. For example, cattle have given humanity various viral poxes, measles, and tuberculosis; pigs and ducks have given influenza; and horses have given the rhinoviruses. Humans share over sixty diseases with dogs. Many parasites also have their origins in domestic animals. The advent of domestication resulted in denser human populations which provided ripe conditions for pathogens to reproduce, mutate, spread, and eventually find a new host in humans.

Since the process of domestication inherently takes many generations over a long period of time, and the spread of breed and husbandry techniques is also slow, it is not meaningful to give a single "date of domestication". However, it is believed that the first attempt at domestication of both animals and plants were made in the Old World by peoples of the Mesolithic Period. The tribes that took part in hunting and gathering wild edible plants, started to make attempts to domesticate dogs, goats, and possibly sheep, which was as early as 9000 BC. However, it was not until the Neolithic Period that primitive agriculture appeared as a form of social activity, and domestication was well under way. The great majority of domesticated animals and plants that still serve humans were selected and developed during the Neolithic Period, a few other examples appeared later. The rabbit for example, was not domesticated until the Middle Ages, while the sugar beet came under cultivation as a sugar-yielding agricultural plant in the 19th century. As recently as the 20th century, mint became an object of agricultural production, and animal breeding programmes to produce high-quality fur were started in the same time period.

The methods available to estimate domestication dates introduce further uncertainty, especially when domestication has occurred in the distant past. So the dates given here should be treated with caution; in some cases evidence is scanty and future discoveries may alter the dating significantly.

Dates and places of domestication are mainly estimated by archaeological methods, more precisely archaeozoology. These methods consist of excavating or studying the results of excavation in human prehistorical occupation sites. Animal remains are dated with archaeological methods, the species they belong to is determined, the age at death is also estimated, and if possible the form they had, that is to say a possible domestic form. Various other clues are taken advantage of, such as slaughter or cutting marks. The aim is to determine if they are game or raised animal, and more globally the nature of their relationship with humans. For example the skeleton of a cat found buried close to humans is a clue that it may have been a pet cat. The age structure of animal remains can also be a clue of husbandry, in which animals were killed at the optimal age.

New technologies and especially mitochondrial DNA, which are simple DNA found in the mitochondria that determine its function in the cell provide an alternative angle of investigation, and make it possible to reestimate the dates of domestication based on research into the genealogical tree of modern domestic animals.

It is admitted for several species that domestication occurred in several places distinctly. For example, research on mitochondrial DNA of the modern cattle Bos taurus supports the archaeological assertions of separate domestication events in Asia and Africa. This research also shows that *Bos taurus* and *Bos indicus* haplotypes are all descendants of the extinct wild ox Bos primigenius. However, this does not rule out later crossing inside a species; therefore it appears useless to look for a separate wild ancestor for each domestic breed.

The first animal to be domesticated appears to have been the dog, in the Upper Paleolithic era. This preceded the domestication of other species by several millennia. In the Neolithic a number of important species such as the goat, sheep, pig and cow were domesticated, as part of the spread of farming with characterises this period. The goat, sheep and pig in particular were domesticated independently in the Levant and Asia.

There is early evidence of beekeeping, in the form of rock paintings, dating to 13,000 BC.

The archaeological evidence from Cyprus indicates domestication of a type of cat by perhaps 9500 BC.

The earliest secure evidence of horse domestication, bit wear on horse molars at Dereivka in Ukraine, dates to around 4000 BC. The *unequivocal* date of domestication and use as a means of transport is at the Sintashta chariot burials in the southern Urals, c. 2000 BC. Local equivalents and smaller species were domesticated from the 2500s BC.

The availability of both domesticated vegetable and animal species increased suddenly following the voyages of Christopher Columbus and the contact between the Eastern and Western Hemispheres. This is part of what is referred to as the Columbian Exchange.

Some species are said to have been domesticated, but are not any more, either because they have totally disappeared, or since their domestic form no longer exists. Examples include the Jaguarundi, the Kakapo, the Ring-tailed Cat, Cheetah, Caracal and Bos aegyptiacus.

Hybrid Domestic Animals

- Alpaca: DNA evidence shows that alpacas are a llama/vicuña hybrid
- Beefalo-Bengal cat
- Cama (animal)
- Chausie
- Cheetoh
- Coydog
- Dzo
- Sheep-goat hybrid
- Hinny

- Huarizo
- Iron Age Pig
- Mule
- Savannah (cat)
- Tiglon
- Wolfdog
- Wolphin
- Yakalo
- Zeedonk
- Zetland
- Zorse
- Zony
- Zubron

Animals of domestic origin and feral ones sometimes can produce fertile hybrids with native, wild animals which leads to genetic pollution in the naturally evolved wild gene pools, many a times threatening rare species with extinction. Cases include the mallard duck, wildcat, wild boar, the rock dove or pigeon, the Red Junglefowl (Gallus gallus) (ancestor of all chickens), carp, and more recently salmon. Another example is the dingo, itself an early feral dog, which hybridizes with dogs of European origin. On the other hand, genetic pollution seems not to be noticed for rabbits. There is much debate over the degree to which feral hybridization compromises the purity of a wild species. In the case of the mallard, for example, some claim there are no populations which are completely free of any domestic ancestor.

CHAPTER 3
Sheep Husbandry

Sheep husbandry is a subcategory of animal husbandry specifically dealing with the raising and breeding of domestic sheep. Sheep farming is primarily based on raising lambs for meat, or raising sheep for wool. Sheep may also be raised for milk or to sell to other farmers.

Sheep are kept in mobs in paddocks, in pens, or in a barn. In cold climates, sheep may need shelter if they are freshly shorn or have baby lambs. Freshly shorn hoggets can be very susceptible to wet, windy weather and can quickly succumb to exposure. Sheep have to be kept dry for one to two days before shearing so that the fleece is dry enough to be pressed and to protect the health of the shearers.

Healthcare

Sheep, particularly those kept inside, are vaccinated after they are born. The lambs receive their first antibodies via their mother's colostrum in the first few hours of life, then a vaccination booster every six weeks for next three months, and then by booster every six months thereafter.

Weaning is a critical period in the life of young sheep. Sheep of this age need careful observation to find any weaners that are hollow, have a pale skin, or are falling behind the mob. Weaners are very susceptible to the deadly Barbers Pole worm (*Haemonchus contortus*), fly strike (Myiasis), scabby mouth, mycotic dermatitis, pneumonia, fluctuations in feed availability, and general ill thrift.

Farmers work with animal nutritionists and veterinarians to keep sheep healthy and to manage health problems. Lambs may be castrated and have their tails docked for easier shearing, cleanliness, and to help protect them from fly strike. Shearers or farmers need to remove wool from the hindquarters around the anus so that droppings do not adhere. In the southern hemisphere this is called *dagging* or crutching.

Sheep need fresh water from troughs or ponds, except in some countries, such as New Zealand, where there is enough moisture in the grass to satisfy this requirements.

Upon being weaned from ewe's milk, they eat hay, grains, and grasses. The lambs are weaned due to increasing competition between the lamb and ewe for food. Sheep are active grazers where such feed is available at ground or low levels. They are usually given feed twice a day from troughs or are allowed to graze in a pasture.

Sheep are most comfortable when the temperature is moderate, so fans may be needed for fresh air if sheep are kept in barns during hot weather. In Australia, sheep in pasture are often subjected to temperatures of 40°C (104 °F) and higher without deleterious effects. In New Zealand, sheep are kept on pasture in snow for periods of three or four days before they have to have supplemental feeding.

Flock Management Styles

There are four general styles of sheep husbandry to serve the varied aspects of the sheep industry and the needs of a particular shepherd. Commercial sheep operations supplying meat and wool are usually either "range band flocks" or "farm flocks". Range band flocks are those with large numbers of sheep (often 1000 to 1500 ewes) cared for by a few full-time shepherds . The pasture—which must be large to accommodate the number of sheep—can either be fenced or open. Range flocks sometimes require the shepherds to live with the sheep as they move throughout the pasture, as well as the use of sheepdogs and means of transport such as horses or motor vehicles. As range band flocks move within a large area in which it would be difficult to supply a steady source of grain, almost all subsist on pasture alone. This style of sheep raising accounts for most of the sheep operations in the U.S., South America, and Australia.

Farm flocks are slightly smaller than range bands, and are kept on a more confined, fenced pasture land. Farm flocks may also be a secondary population on a larger farm, used by farmers who raise a surplus of crops to finish market lambs on or those with untillable land they wish to exploit. However, farm flocks account for many farms focused on sheep as primary income in the U.K. and New Zealand (due to the more limited land available in comparison to other sheep-producing nations). The farm flock is a common style of flock management for those who wish to supplement grain feed for meat animals.

An important corollary form of flock management to the aforementioned styles are specialized flocks raising purebred sheep. Many commercial flocks, especially those producing sheep meat, utilize cross-bred animals. Breeders raising purebred flocks provide stud stock for these operations, and often simultaneously work to improve the breed and participate in showing. Excess lambs are often sold to 4-H groups. The last type of sheep keeping is that of the hobbyist. This type of flock is usually very small compared to commercial operations, and may be considered pets. Those hobby flocks, which are raised with production in mind, may be for subsistence purposes or to provide a very specialized product, such as wool for handspinners. Quite a few people, especially those who emigrated to rural areas from urban or suburban enclaves, begin with hobby flocks or a 4-H lamb before eventually expanding to farm or range flocks.

A sheep farmer is concerned with keeping the correct ratio of male to female sheep , selecting traits for breeding, and controlling under-/over-breeding based on the size and genetic diversity of the flock. Other tasks include sheep shearing, crutching, and lambing the sheep.

Sheep breeders look for such traits in their flocks as high wool quality, consistent muscle development, quick conception rate (for females), multiple births, and quick physical development.

Sheep farmers also need to protect their livestock. Sheep have many natural enemies, such as coyotes (North America), foxes (Europe), dingoes (Australia), and dogs. Newborn lambs in pasture are particularly vulnerable, also falling prey to crows, eagles, and ravens. In addition, they are susceptible in some areas to flystrike which in itself has led to invention of practices such as mulesing.

Sheep may be kept in a fenced-in field or paddock. The farmer must ensure that the fences are maintained in order to prevent the sheep from wandering onto roads or neighbours' property. Alternatively, they may be "heafed" (trained to stay in a certain area without the need for fences). The hardy Herdwick breed is particularly known for its affinity for being heafed.

A shepherd and a livestock guardian dog may be employed for protection of the flock . On large farms, dogs and riders on horseback or motorcycles may muster sheep.

Marking of sheep for identification purposes is often done by means of ear tags or ear marks. In some areas sheep are still identified through the use of notches cut in the ear known as ear marking, using either specially designed tools (ear marking pliers) or other cutting implements.

Lambing is term for the management of birth in domestic sheep. In agriculture it often requires assistance from the farmer or shepherd because of breeding, climate, or the individual physiology of the ewe.

Australian farmers generally arrange for all the ewes in a mob to give birth (the *lambing season*) within a period of a few weeks. As ewes sometimes fail to bond with newborn lambs, especially after delivering twins or triplets, it is important to minimize disturbances during this period.

In order to more closely manage the births, vaccinate lambs, and protect them from predators, shepherds will often have the ewes give birth in "lambing sheds"; essentially a barn (sometimes a temporary structure erected in the pasture) with individual pens for each ewe and her offspring.

Life Cycle

Ewes are pregnant for just under five months before they lamb, and may have anywhere from one to three lambs per birth. Some ewes can have seven or eight lambs .Twin and single lambs are most common, triplets less common. A ewe may lamb once or twice a year. Lambs are weaned at three months. Sheep are full grown at two years and can weigh between 60 and 125 kilograms. Sheep can live to eleven or twelve years of age.

China actually has the greatest number of sheep in terms of number of livestock. While New Zealand rates number 2 on the list of total quantity of "indigenous sheep meat" produced, it has the highest number of sheep per-capita (outside of the Falkland Islands). Simon McCorkindale of Christchurch, New Zealand holds the current Guinness World Record for number of sheep owned by one man (384,143) and was named Royal ovis Aires Breed Board of Indigenous Territories (Rabbit) breeder for 12 consecutive years.

Sheep (*Ovis aries*) are quadrupedal, ruminant mammals typically kept as livestock. Like all ruminants, sheep are members of the order Artiodactyla, the even-toed ungulates. Although the name "sheep" applies to many species in the genus *Ovis*, in everyday usage it almost always refers to *Ovis aries*. Numbering a little over one billion, domestic sheep are also the most numerous species of sheep.

Sheep are most likely descended from the wild mouflon of Europe and Asia. One of the earliest animals to be domesticated for agricultural purposes, sheep are raised for fleece, meat (lamb, hogget or mutton) and milk. A sheep's wool is the most widely used animal fiber, and is usually harvested by shearing. Ovine meat is called lamb when from younger animals and mutton when from older ones. Sheep continue to be important for wool and meat today, and are also occasionally raised for pelts, as dairy animals, or as model organisms for science.

Sheep husbandry is practised throughout the majority of the inhabited world, and has been fundamental to many civilizations. In the modern era, Australia, New Zealand, the southern and central South American nations, and the British Isles are most closely associated with sheep production.

Sheep-raising has a large lexicon of unique terms which vary considerably by region and dialect. Use of the word *sheep* began in Middle English as a derivation of the Old English word *sceap*; it is both the singular and plural name for the animal. A group of sheep is called a flock, herd or mob. Adult female sheep are referred to as ewes, intact males as rams or occasionally tups, castrated males as wethers, and younger sheep as lambs. Many other specific terms for the various life stages of sheep exist, generally related to lambing, shearing, and age.

Being a key animal in the history of farming, sheep have a deeply entrenched place in human culture, and find representation in much modern language and symbology. As livestock, sheep are most-often associated with pastoral, Arcadian imagery. Sheep figure in many mythologies—such as the Golden Fleece—and major religions, especially the Abrahamic traditions. In both ancient and modern religious ritual, sheep are used as sacrificial animals.

Domestic sheep are relatively small ruminants, usually with a crimped hair called wool and often with horns forming a lateral spiral. Domestic sheep differ from their wild relatives and ancestors in several respects, having become uniquely neotenic as a result of selective breeding by humans. A few primitive breeds of sheep retain some of the characteristics of their wild cousins, such as short tails. Depending on breed, domestic sheep may have no horns at all (polled), or horns in both sexes (as in wild sheep), or in males only. Most horned breeds have a single pair, but a few breeds may have several.

Another trait unique to domestic sheep (as compared to wild ovines, not other livestock) is their wide variation in color. Wild sheep are largely variations of brown hues, and variation with species is extremely limited. Colors of domestic sheep range from pure white to dark chocolate brown and even spotted or piebald. Selection for easily dyeable white fleeces began early in sheep domestication, and as white wool is a dominant trait it spread quickly. However, colored sheep do appear in many modern breeds, and may even appear as a recessive trait in white flocks. While white wool is desirable for large commercial markets, there is a niche market for colored fleeces, mostly for handspinning. The nature of the fleece varies widely among the breeds, from dense and highly crimped, to long and hair-like. There is variation of wool type and quality even among members of the same flock, so wool classing is a step in the commercial processing of the fibre.

Depending on breed, sheep show a range of heights and weights. Their rate of growth and mature weight is a heritable trait that is often selected for in breeding. Ewes typically weigh between 45 and 100 kilograms (99 and 220 lb), and rams between 45 and 160 kilograms (99 and 350 lb). Mature sheep have 32 teeth. As with other ruminants, the front teeth in the lower jaw bite against a hard, toothless pad in the upper jaw. These are used to pick off vegetation, then the rear teeth grind it before it is swallowed. There are eight lower front teeth in ruminants, but there is some disagreement as to whether these are eight incisors, or six incisors and two incisor-shaped canines. This means that the dental formula for sheep is either I:0/4 C:0/0 P:3/3 M:3/3, or I:0/3 C:0/1 P:3/3 M:3/3. There is a large toothless gap between the front "biting" teeth and the rear "grinding" teeth.

For the first few years of life it is possible to calculate the age of sheep from their front teeth, as a pair of milk teeth is replaced by larger adult teeth each year, the full set of eight adult front teeth being complete at about four years of age. The front teeth are then gradually lost as sheep age, making it harder for them to feed and hindering the health and productivity of the animal. For this reason, domestic sheep on normal pasture begin to slowly decline from four years on, and the average life expectancy of a sheep is 10 to 12 years, though some sheep may live as long as 20 years.

Sheep have good hearing, and are sensitive to noise when being handled. Sheep have horizontal slit-shaped pupils, possessing excellent peripheral vision; with visual fields of approximately 270° to 320°, sheep can see behind themselves without turning their heads. However, sheep have poor depth perception; shadows and dips in the ground may cause sheep to baulk. In general, sheep have a tendency to move out of the dark and into well-lit areas, and prefer to move uphill when disturbed. Sheep also have an excellent sense of smell, and, like all species of their genus, have scent glands just in front of the eyes, and interdigitally on the feet. The purpose of these glands is uncertain, but those on the face may be used in breeding behaviours. The foot glands might also be related to reproduction, but alternative reasons, such as secretion of a waste product or a scent marker to help lost sheep find their flock, have also been proposed.

Sheep and goats are closely related as both are in the subfamily Caprinae. However, they are separate species, so hybrids rarely occur, and are always infertile. A hybrid of a ewe and a buck (a male goat) is called a sheep-goat hybrid (only a single such animal has been confirmed), and is not to be confused with the genetic chimera called a geep. Visual differences between sheep and goats include the beard and divided upper lip unique to goats. Sheep tails also hang down, even when short or docked, while the short tails of goats are held upwards. Sheep breeds are also often naturally polled (either in both sexes or just in the female), while naturally polled goats are rare (though many are polled artificially). Males of the two species differ in that buck goats acquire a unique and strong odor during the rut, whereas rams do not.

The domestic sheep is a multi-purpose animal, and the more than 200 breeds now in existence were created to serve these diverse purposes. Some sources give a count of a thousand or more breeds, but these numbers cannot be verified. Almost all sheep are classified as being best suited to furnishing a certain product: wool, meat, milk, hides, or a combination in a dual-purpose breed. Other features used when classifying sheep include face color (generally white or black), tail length, presence or lack of horns, and the topography for which the breed has been developed. This last point is especially stressed in the U.K., where breeds are described as either upland (hill or mountain) or lowland breeds. A sheep may also be of a fat-tailed type, which is a dual-purpose sheep common in Africa and Asia with larger deposits of fat within and around its tail.

Breeds are also grouped based on how well they are suited to producing a certain type of breeding stock. Generally, sheep are thought to be either "ewe breeds" or "ram breeds". Ewe breeds are those that are hardy, and have good reproductive and mothering capabilities—they are for replacing breeding ewes in standing flocks. Ram breeds are selected for rapid growth and carcase quality, and are mated with ewe breeds to produce meat lambs. Lowland and upland breeds are also crossed in this fashion, with the hardy hill ewes crossed with larger, fast-growing lowland rams to produce ewes called mules, which can then be crossed with meat-type rams to produce prime market lambs. Many breeds, especially rare or primitive ones, fall into no clear category.

Breeds are categorized by the type of their wool. Fine wool breeds are those that have wool of great crimp and density, which are preferred for textiles. Most of these were derived from Merino sheep, and the breed continues to dominate the world sheep industry. Downs breeds have wool between the extremes, and are typically fast growing meat and ram breeds with dark faces. Some major medium wool breeds, such as the Corriedale, are dual-purpose crosses of long and fine-wooled breeds and were created for high-production commercial flocks. Long wool breeds are the largest of sheep, with long wool and a slow rate of growth. Long wool sheep are most valued for crossbreeding to improve the attributes of other sheep types. For example: the American Columbia breed was developed by crossing Lincoln rams (a long wool breed) with fine-wooled Rambouillet ewes.

Coarse or carpet wool sheep are those with a medium to long length wool of characteristic coarseness. Breeds traditionally used for carpet wool show great variability, but the chief requirement is a wool that will not break down under heavy use (as would that of the finer breeds). As the demand for carpet-quality wool declines, some breeders of this type of sheep are attempting to use a few of these traditional breeds for alternative purposes. Others have always been primarily meat-class sheep.

A minor class of sheep are the dairy breeds. Dual-purpose breeds that may primarily be meat or wool sheep are often used secondarily as milking animals, but there are a few breeds that are predominantly used for milking. These sheep do produce a higher quantity of milk and have slightly longer lactation curves. In the quality of their milk, fat and protein content percentages of dairy sheep vary from non-dairy breeds but lactose content does not.

A last group of sheep breeds is that of fur or hair sheep, which do not grow wool at all. Hair sheep are similar to the early domesticated sheep kept before woolly breeds were developed, and are raised for meat and pelts. Some modern breeds of hair sheep, such as the Dorper, result from crosses between wool and hair breeds. For meat and hide producers, hair sheep are cheaper to keep, as they do not need shearing. Hair sheep are also more resistant to parasites and hot weather.

With the modern rise of corporate agribusiness and the decline of localized family farms, many breeds of sheep are in danger of extinction. The Rare Breeds Survival Trust of the U.K. lists 22 native breeds as having only 3000 registered animals (each), and the American Livestock Breeds Conservancy lists 14 as having fewer than 10000. Preferences for breeds with uniform characteristics and fast growth have pushed heritage (or heirloom) breeds to the margins of the sheep industry. Those that remain are maintained through the efforts of conservation organisations, breed registries, and individual farmers dedicated to their preservation.

Sheep are exclusively herbivorous mammals. Most breeds prefer to graze on grass and other short roughage, avoiding the taller woody parts of plants that goats readily consume. Both sheep and goats use their lips and tongues to select parts of the plant that are easier to digest or higher in nutrition. Sheep, however, graze well in monoculture pastures where most goats fare poorly. Like all ruminants, sheep have a complex digestive system composed of four chambers, allowing them to break down cellulose from stems, leaves, and seed hulls into simpler carbohydrates. When sheep graze, vegetation is chewed into a mass called a bolus, which is then passed into the first chamber: the rumen. The rumen is a 19 to 38-liter (5 to 10 gal) organ in which feed is fermented via a symbiotic relationship with the bacteria, protozoa, and yeasts of the gut flora. The bolus is periodically regurgitated back to the mouth as cud for additional chewing and salivation. Cud chewing is an adaptation allowing ruminants to graze more quickly in the morning, and then fully chew and digest feed later in the day. This is beneficial as grazing, which requires lowering the head, leaves sheep vulnerable to predators, while cud chewing does not.

During fermentation, the rumen produces gas that must be expelled; disturbances of the organ, such as sudden changes in a sheep's diet, can cause the potentially fatal condition of bloat, when gas becomes trapped in the rumen. After fermentation in the rumen, feed passes in to the reticulum and the omasum; special feeds such as grains may bypass the rumen altogether. After the first three chambers, food moves in to the abomasum for final digestion before processing by the intestines. The abomasum is the only one of the four chambers analogous to the human stomach (being the only one that absorbs nutrients for use as energy), and is sometimes called the "true stomach".

Sheep follow a diurnal pattern of activity, feeding from dawn to dusk, stopping sporadically to rest and chew their cud. Ideal pasture for sheep is not lawn-like grass, but an array of grasses, legumes and forbs. Types of land where sheep are raised vary widely, from pastures that are seeded and improved intentionally to rough, native lands. Common plants toxic to sheep are present in most of the world, and include (but are not limited to) oak and acorns, tomato, yew, rhubarb, potato, and rhododendron.

Sheep are largely grazing herbivores, unlike browsing animals such as goats and deer that prefer taller foliage. With a much narrower face, sheep crop plants very close to the ground and can overgraze a pasture much faster than cattle. For this reason, many shepherds use managed intensive rotational grazing, where a flock is rotated through multiple pastures, giving plants time to recover. Paradoxically, sheep can both cause and solve the spread of invasive plant species. By disturbing the natural state of pasture, sheep and other livestock can pave the way for invasive plants. However, sheep also prefer to eat invasives such as cheatgrass, leafy spurge, kudzu and spotted knapweed over native species such as sagebrush, making grazing sheep effective for conservation grazing. Research conducted in Imperial County, California compared lamb grazing with herbicides for weed control in seedling alfalfa fields. Three trials demonstrated that grazing lambs were just as effective as herbicides in controlling winter weeds. Entomologists also compared grazing lambs to insecticides for insect control in winter alfalfa. In this trial, lambs provided insect control as effectively as insecticides.

Other than forage, the other staple feed for sheep is hay, often during the winter months. The ability to thrive solely on pasture (even without hay) varies with breed, but all sheep can survive on this diet. Also included in some sheep's diets are minerals, either in a trace mix or in licks.

Naturally, a constant source of potable water is also a fundamental requirement for sheep. The amount of water needed by sheep fluctuates with the season and the type and quality of the food they consume. When sheep feed on large amounts of new growth and there is precipitation (including dew, as sheep are dawn feeders), sheep need less water. When sheep are confined or are eating large amounts of cured hay, more water is typically needed. Sheep also require clean water, and may refuse to drink water that is covered in scum or algae.

Sheep are one of the few livestock animals raised for meat today that have never been widely raised in an intensive, confined animal feeding operation (CAFO). Although there is a growing movement advocating alternative farming styles, a large percentage of beef cattle, pigs, and poultry are still produced under such conditions. In contrast, only some sheep are regularly given high-concentration grain feed, much less kept in confinement. Especially in industrialized countries, sheep producers may fatten market lambs before slaughter (called "finishing") in feedlots. Many sheep breeders flush ewes and rams with a daily ration of grain during breeding to increase fertility. Ewes are also flushed during pregnancy to increase birth weights, as 70 per cent of a lamb's growth occurs in the last five to six weeks of gestation. Otherwise, only lactating ewes and especially old or infirm sheep are commonly provided with grain. Feed provided to sheep must be specially formulated, as most cattle, poultry, pig, and even some goat feeds contain levels of copper that are lethal to sheep. The same danger applies to mineral supplements such as salt licks.

Sheep are prey animals with a strong gregarious instinct, and a majority of sheep behaviours can be understood in these terms. The dominance hierarchy of *Ovis aries* and its natural inclination to follow a leader to new pastures were the pivotal factors in it being one of the first domesticated livestock species. All sheep have a tendency to congregate close to other members of a flock, although this behaviour varies with breed. Farmers exploit this behaviour to keep sheep together on unfenced pastures and to move them more easily. Shepherds may also use herding dogs in this effort, whose highly bred herding ability can assist in moving flocks. Sheep are also extremely food-oriented, and association of humans with regular feeding often results in sheep soliciting people for food. Those who are moving sheep may exploit this behaviour by leading sheep with buckets of feed, rather than forcing their movements with herding.

In regions where sheep have no natural predators, none of the native breeds of sheep exhibit a strong flocking behaviour. Sheep can also become hefted to one particular local pasture (heft) so they do not roam freely in unfenced landscapes. Ewes teach the heft to their lambs, and if whole flocks are culled it must be retaught to the replacement animals.

Escaped sheep being led back to pasture with the enticement of food. This method of moving sheep works best with smaller flocks.

Flock dynamics in sheep are, as a rule, only exhibited in a group of four or more sheep. Fewer sheep may not react as normally expected when alone or with few other sheep. For sheep, the primary defense mechanism is simply to flee from danger when their flight zone is crossed. Secondly, cornered sheep may charge or threaten to do so through hoof stamping and aggressive posture. This is particularly true for ewes with newborn lambs.

In displaying flocking, sheep have a strong lead-follow tendency, and a leader often as not is simply the first sheep to move. However, sheep do establish a pecking order through physical displays of dominance. Dominant animals are inclined to be more aggressive with other sheep, and usually feed first at troughs. Primarily among rams, horn size is a factor in the flock hierarchy. Rams with different size horns may be less inclined to fight to establish pecking order, while rams with similarly sized horns are more so.

Sheep can become stressed when separated from their flock members. Sheep can recognize individual human and ovine faces, and remember them for years. Relationships in flocks tend to be closest among related sheep: in mixed-breed flocks same-breed subgroups tend to form, and a ewe and her direct descendants often move as a unit within large flocks.

Sheep are frequently thought of as extremely unintelligent animals. A sheep's herd mentality and quickness to flee and panic in the face of stress often make shepherding a difficult endeavor for the uninitiated. Despite these perceptions, a University of Illinois monograph on sheep found them to be just below pigs and on par with cattle in IQ, and some sheep have shown problem-solving abilities; a flock in West Yorkshire, England allegedly found a way to get over cattle grids by rolling on their backs, although documentation of this has relied on anecdotal accounts. In addition to long-term facial recognition of individuals, sheep can also differentiate emotional states through facial characteristics. If worked with patiently, sheep may learn their names, and many sheep are trained to be led by halter for showing and other purposes. Sheep have also responded well to clicker training. Very rarely, sheep are used as pack animals. Tibetan nomads distribute baggage equally throughout a flock as it is herded between living sites.

Sheep follow a similar reproductive strategy to other herd animals. A group of ewes is generally mated by a single ram, who has either been chosen by a breeder or has established dominance through physical contest with other rams (in feral populations). Most sheep are seasonal breeders, although some are able to breed year-round. Ewes generally reach sexual maturity at six to eight months of age, and rams generally at four to six months. Ewes have estrus cycles about every 17 days, during which they emit a scent and indicate readiness through physical displays towards rams. A minority of sheep display a preference for homosexuality (8% on average) or are freemartins (female animals that are behaviourally masculine and lack functioning ovaries).

In feral sheep, rams may fight during the rut to determine which individuals may mate with ewes. Rams, especially unfamiliar ones, will also fight outside the breeding period to establish dominance; rams can kill one another if allowed to mix freely. During the rut, even normally friendly rams may become aggressive towards humans due to increases in their hormone levels.

After mating, sheep have a gestation period of about five months, and normal labour take one to three hours. Although some breeds regularly throw larger litters of lambs, most produce single or twin lambs. During or soon after labour, ewes and lambs may be confined to small lambing jugs, small pens designed to aid both careful observation of ewes and to cement the bond between them and their lambs.

Ovine obstetrics can be problematic. By selectively breeding ewes that produce multiple offspring with higher birth weights for generations, sheep producers have inadvertently caused some domestic sheep to have difficulty lambing; balancing ease of lambing with high productivity is one of the dilemmas of sheep breeding In the case of any such problems, those present at lambing may assist the ewe by extracting or repositioning lambs. After the birth, ewes ideally break the amniotic sac (if it is not broken during labour), and begin licking clean the lamb. Most lambs will begin standing within an hour of birth. In normal situations, lambs nurse after standing, receiving vital colostrum milk. Lambs that either fail to nurse or that are rejected by the ewe require aid to live, such as bottle-feeding or fostering by another ewe.

After lambs are several weeks old, lamb marking (the process of ear tagging, docking, and castrating) is carried out. Vaccinations are usually carried out at this point as well. Ear tags with numbers are attached, or ear marks are applied for ease of later identification of sheep. Castration is performed on ram lambs not intended for breeding, although some shepherds choose to avoid the procedure for ethical, economic or practical reasons. Ram lambs that will either be slaughtered or separated from ewes before sexual maturity are not usually castrated. Docking, which is the shortening of a lamb's tail, is practised for health reasons. Objections to all these procedures have been raised by animal rights groups, but farmers defend them by saying they solve many practical and veterinary problems, and inflict only temporary pain.

Sheep may fall victim to poisons, infectious diseases, and physical injuries. As a prey species, a sheep's system is adapted to hide the obvious signs of illness, to prevent being targeted by predators. However, there are some obvious signs of ill health, with sick sheep eating little, vocalizing excessively, and being generally listless. Throughout history, much of the money and labour of sheep husbandry has aimed to prevent sheep ailments. Historically, shepherds often created remedies by experimentation on the farm. In some developed countries, including the United States, sheep lack the economic importance for drugs companies to perform expensive clinical trials required to approve drugs for ovine use. In such instances, shepherds resort to illegal, extra-label usage of drugs approved for other animals. In the 20th and 21st centuries, a minority of sheep owners have turned to alternative treatments such as homeopathy, herbalism and even traditional Chinese medicine to treat sheep veterinary problems. Despite some favorable anecdotal evidence, the effectiveness of alternative veterinary medicine has been met with skepticism in scientific journals. The need for traditional anti-parasite drugs and antibiotics is widespread, and is the main impediment to certified organic farming with sheep.

Many breeders take a variety of preventive measures to ward off problems. The first is to ensure that all sheep are healthy when purchased. Many buyers avoid outlets known to be clearing houses for animals culled from healthy flocks as either sick or simply inferior. This can also mean maintaining a closed flock, and quarantining new sheep for a month. Two fundamental preventive programmes are maintaining good nutrition and reducing stress in the sheep. Handling sheep in loud, erratic ways causes them to produce cortisol, a stress hormone. This can lead to a weakened immune system, thus making sheep far more vulnerable to disease. Signs of stress in sheep include: excessive panting, teeth grinding, restless movement, wool eating, and wood chewing. Avoiding poisoning is also important; common poisons are pesticide sprays, inorganic fertilizer, motor oil, as well as radiator coolant (the ethylene glycol antifreeze is sweet-tasting).

Common forms of preventive medication for sheep are vaccinations and treatments for parasites. Both external and internal parasites are the most prevalent malady in sheep, and are either fatal, or reduce the productivity of flocks. Worms are the most common internal parasites. They are ingested during grazing, incubate within the sheep, and are expelled through the digestive system (beginning the cycle again). Oral anti-parasitic medicines, known as drenches, are given to a flock to treat worms, sometimes after worm eggs in the feces has been counted to assess infestation levels. Afterwards, sheep may be moved to a new pasture to avoid ingesting the same parasites. External sheep parasites include: lice (for different parts of the body), sheep keds, nose bots, sheep itch mites, and maggots. Keds are blood-sucking parasites that cause general malnutrition and decreased productivity, but are not fatal. Maggots are those of the bot fly and the blow-fly. Fly maggots cause the extremely destructive condition of flystrike. Flies lay their eggs in wounds or wet, manure-soiled wool; when the maggots hatch they burrow into a sheep's flesh, eventually causing death if untreated.

In addition to other treatments, crutching (shearing wool from a sheep's rump) is a common preventive method. Nose bots are flies that inhabit a sheep's sinuses, causing breathing difficulties and discomfort. Common signs are a discharge from the nasal passage, sneezing, and frantic movement such as head shaking. External parasites may be controlled through the use of backliners, sprays or immersive sheep dips.

A wide array of bacterial diseases affect sheep. Diseases of the hoof, such as foot rot and foot scald may occur, and are treated with footbaths and other remedies. These painful conditions cause lameness and hinder feeding. Ovine Johne's disease is a wasting disease that affects young sheep. Bluetongue disease is an insect-borne illness causing fever and inflammation of the mucous membranes. Ovine rinderpest (or *peste des petits ruminants*) is a highly contagious and often fatal viral disease affecting sheep and goats.

A few sheep conditions are transmissible to humans. Orf (also known as scabby mouth, contagious ecthyma or soremouth) is a skin disease leaving lesions that is transmitted through skin-to-skin contact. Cutaneous anthrax is also called woolsorter's disease, as the spores can be transmitted in unwashed wool. More seriously, the organisms that can cause spontaneous enzootic abortion in sheep are easily transmitted to pregnant women. Also of concern are the prion disease scrapie and the virus that causes foot-and-mouth disease (FMD), as both can devastate flocks. The latter poses a slight risk to humans. During the 2001 FMD pandemic in the UK, hundreds of sheep were culled and some rare British breeds were at risk of extinction due to this.

Predation

Other than parasites and disease, predation is a threat to sheep and the profitability of sheep raising. Sheep have little ability to defend themselves, compared with other species kept as livestock. Even if sheep survive an attack, they may die from their injuries, or simply from panic. However, the impact of predation varies dramatically with region. In Africa, Australia, the Americas, and parts of Europe and Asia predators are a serious problem. In the United States, for instance, over one third of sheep deaths in 2004 were caused by predation. In contrast, other nations are virtually devoid of sheep predators, particularly islands known for extensive sheep husbandry. Worldwide, canids—including the domestic dog—are responsible for most sheep deaths. Other animals that occasionally prey on sheep include: felines, bears, birds of prey, ravens and feral hogs.

Sheep producers have used a wide variety of measures to combat predation. Pre-modern shepherds used their own presence, livestock guardian dogs, and protective structures such as barns and fencing. Fencing (both regular and electric), penning sheep at night and lambing indoors all continue to be widely used. More modern shepherds used guns, traps, and poisons to kill predators, causing significant decreases in predator populations. In the wake of the environmental and conservation movements, the use of these methods now usually falls under the purview of specially designated government agencies in most developed countries.

The 1970s saw a resurgence in the use of livestock guardian dogs and the development of new methods of predator control by sheep producers, many of them non-lethal. Donkeys and guard llamas have been used since the 1980s in sheep operations, using the same basic principle as livestock guardian dogs. Interspecific pasturing, usually with larger livestock such as cattle or horses, may help to deter predators, even if such species do not actively guard sheep. In addition to animal guardians, contemporary sheep operations may use non-lethal predator deterrents such as motion-activated lights and noisy alarms.

Sheep were among the first animals to be domesticated by humankind; sources provide a domestication date between nine and eleven thousand years ago in Mesopotamia. Their wild relatives have several characteristics—such as a relative lack of aggression, a manageable size, early sexual maturity, a social nature, and high reproduction rates—which made them particularly suitable for domestication. Today, *Ovis aries* is an entirely domesticated animal that is largely dependent on man for its health and survival. Feral sheep do exist, but exclusively in areas devoid of large predators (usually islands) and not on the scale of feral horses, goats, pigs, or dogs, although some feral populations have remained isolated long enough to be recognized as distinct breeds.

The exact line of descent between domestic sheep to their wild ancestors is presently unclear. The most common hypothesis states that *Ovis aries* is descended from the Asiatic (*O. orientalis*) species of mouflon. It has been proposed that the European mouflon (*O. musimon*) is an ancient breed of domestic sheep turned feral rather than an ancestor, despite it commonly being cited as ancestor in past literature. A few breeds of sheep, such as the Castlemilk Moorit from Scotland, were formed through crossbreeding with wild European mouflon.

The urial (*O. vignei*) was once thought to have been a forebear of domestic sheep, as they occasionally interbreed with mouflon in the Iranian part of their range. However, the urial, argali (*O. ammon*), and snow sheep (*O. nivicola*) have a different number of chromosomes than other Ovis species, making a direct relationship implausible, and phylogenetic studies show no evidence of urial ancestry. Further studies comparing European and Asian breeds of sheep showed significant genetic differences between the two. Two explanations for this phenomenon have been posited. The first is that there is a currently unknown species or subspecies of wild sheep that contributed to the formation of domestic sheep. A second hypothesis suggests that this variation is the result of multiple waves of capture from wild mouflon, similar to the known development of other livestock.

Initially, sheep were kept solely for meat, milk and skins. Archaeological evidence from statuary found at sites in Iran suggests that selection for woolly sheep may have begun around 6000 BC, but the earliest woven wool garments have only been dated to two to three thousand years later. By that span of the Bronze Age, sheep with all the major features of modern breeds were widespread throughout Western Asia. However, one chief difference between ancient sheep and modern breeds is the technique by which wool could be collected. Primitive sheep cannot be shorn, and must have their wool plucked out by hand in a process called "rooing". This is because fibers called kemps are still longer than the soft fleece. The fleece may also be collected from the field after it falls out. This trait survives today in unrefined breeds such as the Soay and many Shetlands. Indeed, the Soay, along with other Northern European breeds with short tails, unshearable fleece, diminutive size, and horns in both sexes, are closely related to ancient sheep. Originally, weaving and spinning wool was a handicraft practiced at home, rather than an industry. Babylonians, Sumerians, and Persians all depended on sheep; and although linen was the first fabric to be fashioned in to clothing, wool was a prized product. The raising of flocks for their fleece was one of the earliest industries, and flocks were a medium of exchange in barter economies. Numerous biblical figures kept large flocks, and subjects of the king of Israel were taxed according to the number of rams they owned.

In Africa

Sheep entered the African continent not long after their domestication in western Asia. A minority of historians once posited a contentious African theory of origin for *Ovis aries*. This theory is based primarily on rock art interpretations, and osteological evidence from Barbary sheep. The first sheep entered North Africa via Sinai, and were present in ancient Egyptian society between eight and seven thousand years ago. Sheep have always been part of subsistence farming in Africa, but today the only country that keeps an influential number of commercial sheep is South Africa. South African sheep producers, in an attempt to deal with the numerous predators of Africa, invented the livestock protection collar, which holds poison at the jugular to sicken or kill predators.

Sheep Husbandry Spread Quickly in Europe

Excavations show that In about 6000 BC, during the Neolithic period of prehistory, the Castelnovien people, living around Chateauneuf-les-Martigues near present-day Marseille in the south of France, were among the first in Europe to keep domestic sheep. Practically from its inception, ancient Greek civilization relied on sheep as primary livestock, and were even said to name individual animals. Scandinavian sheep of a type seen today—with short tails and multi-colored fleece—were also present early on. Later, the Roman Empire kept sheep on a wide scale, and the Romans were an important agent in the spread of sheep raising throughout the continent. Pliny the Elder, in his Natural History (*Naturalis Historia*), speaks at length about sheep and wool. Declaring "Many thanks, too, do we owe to the sheep, both for appeasing the gods, and for giving us the use of its fleece", he goes on to detail the breeds of ancient sheep and the many colors, lengths and qualities of wool. Romans also pioneered the practice of blanketing sheep, in which a fitted coat (today usually of nylon) is placed over the sheep to improve the cleanliness and luster of its wool.

During the Roman occupation of the British Isles, a large wool processing factory was established in Winchester, England in about AD 50 AD. By AD 1000, England and Spain were recognized as the twin centres of sheep production in the Western world. As the original breeders of the fine-wooled merino sheep that have historically dominated the wool trade, the Spanish gained great wealth. Wool money largely financed Spanish rulers and thus the voyages to the New World by conquistadors. The powerful *Mesta* (its full title was *Honrado Concejo de la Mesta*, the Honorable Council of the Mesta) was a corporation of sheep owners mostly drawn from Spain's wealthy merchants, Catholic clergy and nobility that controlled the merino flocks. By the 17th century, the *Mesta* held in upwards of two million head of merino sheep.

Mesta flocks followed a seasonal pattern of transhumance across Spain. In the spring, they left the winter pastures (*invernaderos*) in Extremadura and Andalusia to graze on their summer pastures (*agostaderos*) in Castile, returning again in the autumn. Spanish rulers eager to increase wool profits gave extensive legal rights to the *Mesta*, often to the detriment of local peasantry. The huge merino flocks had a lawful right of way for their migratory routes (*cañadas*). Towns and villages were obliged by law to let the flocks graze on their common land, and the Mesta had its own sheriffs that could summon offending individuals to its own tribunals.

Exportation of merinos without royal permission was also a punishable offense, thus ensuring a near-absolute monopoly on the breed until the mid-18th century. After the breaking of the export ban, fine wool sheep began to be distributed worldwide. The export to Rambouillet by Louis XVI in 1786 formed the basis for the modern Rambouillet (or French Merino) breed. After the Napoleonic Wars and the global distribution of the once-exclusive

Spanish stocks of Merinos, sheep raising in Spain reverted to hardy coarse-wooled breeds such as the Churra, and was no longer of international economic significance.

The sheep industry in Spain was an instance of migratory flock management, with large homogenous flocks ranging over the entire nation. The management model used in England was quite different but had a similar importance to economy of the British Empire. Up until the early 20th century, owling (the smuggling of sheep or wool out of the country) was a punishable offense, and to this day the Lord Speaker of the House of Lords sits on a cushion known as the Woolsack.

The high concentration and more sedentary nature of shepherding in the U.K. allowed sheep especially adapted to their particular purpose and region to be raised, thereby giving rise to an exceptional variety of breeds in relation to the land mass of the country. This greater variety of breeds also produced a valuable variety of products to compete with the superfine wool of Spanish sheep. By the time of Elizabeth I's rule, sheep and wool trade was the primary source of tax revenue to the Crown of England and the country was a major influence in the development and spread of sheep husbandry.

An important event not only in the history of domestic sheep, but of all livestock, was the work of Robert Bakewell in the 18th century. Before his time, breeding for desirable traits was often based on chance, with no scientific process for selection of breeding stock. Bakewell established the principles of selective breeding—especially line breeding—in his work with sheep, horses and cattle; his work later influenced Gregor Mendel and Charles Darwin. His most important contribution to sheep was the development of the Leicester Longwool, a quick-maturing breed of blocky conformation that formed the basis for many vital modern breeds. Today, the sheep industry in the UK has diminished significantly, though pedigreed rams can still fetch around 100,000 Pounds sterling at auction.

In the Americas

No ovine species native to the Americas has ever been domesticated, despite being closer genetically to domestic sheep than many Asian and European species. The first domestic sheep in North America—most likely of the Churra breed—arrived with Christopher Columbus' second voyage in 1493. The next transatlantic shipment to arrive was with Hernán Cortés in 1519, landing in Mexico. No export of wool or animals is known to have occurred from these populations, but flocks did disseminate throughout what is now Mexico and the Southwest United States with Spanish colonists. Churras were also introduced to the Navajo tribe of Native Americans, and became a key part of their livelihood and culture. The modern presence of the Navajo-Churro breed is a result of this heritage.

North America

The next transport of sheep to North America was not until 1607, with the voyage of the *HMS Susan Conant* to Virginia. However, the sheep that arrived in that year were all slaughtered because of a famine, and a permanent flock was not to reach the colony until two years later in 1609. In two decades time, the colonists had expanded their flock to a total of 400 head. By the 1640s there were about 100,000 head of sheep in the 13 colonies, and in 1662, a woolen mill was built in Watertown, Massachusetts. Especially during the periods of political unrest and civil war in Britain spanning the 1640s and 50s which disrupted maritime trade, the colonists found it pressing to produce wool for clothing. Many islands off the coast were cleared of predators and set aside for sheep: Nantucket, Long Island, Martha's Vineyard and small islands in Boston Harbor were notable examples. There remain some rare breeds of American sheep—such as the Hog Island sheep—that were the result of island flocks. Placing semi-feral sheep and goats on islands was common practice in colonization during this period. Early on, the British government banned further export of sheep to the Americas, or wool from it, in an attempt to stifle any threat to the wool trade in the British Isles. One of many restrictive trade measures that precipitated the American Revolution, the sheep industry in the Northeast grew despite the bans.

Gradually, beginning in the 19th century, sheep production in the U.S. moved westward. Today, the vast majority of flocks reside on Western range lands. During this westward migration of the industry, competition between sheep (sometime called "range maggots") and cattle operations grew more heated, eventually erupting into range wars. Other than simple competition for grazing and water rights, cattlemen believed that the secretions of the foot glands of sheep made cattle unwilling to graze on places where sheep had stepped. As sheep production centreed on the U.S. western ranges, it became associated with other parts of Western culture, such as the rodeo. In modern America, a minor event in rodeos is mutton busting, in which children compete to see who can stay atop a sheep the longest before falling off. Another effect of the westward movement of sheep flocks in North America was the decline of wild species such as Bighorn sheep (*O. canadesis*). Most diseases of domestic sheep are transmittable to wild ovines, and such diseases, along with overgrazing and habitat loss, are named as primary factors in the plummeting numbers of wild sheep. Sheep production peaked in North America during 1940s and 50s at more than 55 million head. Henceforth and continuing today, the number of sheep in North America has steadily declined with wool prices and the lessening American demand for sheep meat.

South America

In South America, especially in Patagonia, there is an active modern sheep industry. Sheep keeping was largely introduced through immigration to the continent by Spanish and British peoples, for whom sheep were a major industry during the period. South America has a large number of sheep, but the highest-producing nation (Brazil) kept only just over 15 million head in 2004, far fewer than most centres of sheep husbandry. The primary challenges to the sheep industry in South America are the phenomenal drop in wool prices in the late 20th century and the loss of habitat through logging and overgrazing. The most influential region internationally is that of Patagonia, which has been the first to rebound from the fall in wool prices. With few predators and almost no grazing competition (the only large native grazing mammal is the guanaco), the region is prime land for sheep raising. The most exceptional area of production is surrounding the La Plata river in the Pampas region. Sheep production in Patagonia peaked in 1952 at more than 21 million head, but has steadily fallen to fewer than ten today. Most operations focus on wool production for export from Merino and Corriedale sheep; the economic sustainability of wool flocks has fallen with the drop in prices, while the cattle industry continues to grow.

In Australia and New Zealand

Australia and New Zealand are crucial players in the contemporary sheep industry, and sheep are an iconic part of both countries' culture and economy. New Zealand has the highest density of sheep per capita (sheep outnumber the human population 12 to 1), and Australia is the world's indisputably largest exporter of sheep and cattle. In 2007, New Zealand even declared 15 February their official National Lamb Day to celebrate the country's history of sheep production.

The First Fleet brought the initial population of 70 sheep from the Cape of Good Hope to Australia in 1788. The next shipment was of 30 sheep from Calcutta and Ireland in 1793. All of the early sheep brought to Australia were exclusively used for the dietary needs of the penal colonies. The beginnings of the Australian wool industry were due to the efforts of Captain John Macarthur. At Macarthur's urging 16 Spanish merinos were imported in 1797, effectively beginning the Australian sheep industry. By 1801 Macarthur had 1,000 head of sheep, and in 1803 he exported 111 kilograms (245 lb) of wool to England. Today, Macarthur is generally thought of as the father of the Australian sheep industry.

The growth of the sheep industry in Australia was explosive. In 1820, the continent held 100,000 sheep, a decade later it had one million. By 1840, New South Wales alone kept 4 million sheep; flock numbers grew to 13 million in a decade. While much of the growth in both nations was due to the active support of Britain in its desire for wool, both worked independently to develop new high-production breeds: the Corriedale, Coolalee, Coopworth, Perendale, Polwarth, Booroola Merino, Peppin Merino, and Poll Merino were all created in New Zealand or Australia. Wool production was a fitting industry for colonies far from their home nations. Before the advent of fast air and maritime shipping, wool was one of the few viable products that was not subject to spoiling on the long passage back to British ports. The abundant new land and milder winter weather of the region also aided the growth of the Australian and New Zealand sheep industries.

Flocks in Australia have always been largely range bands on fenced land, and are aimed at production of medium to superfine wool for clothing and other products as well as meat. New Zealand flocks are kept in a fashion similar to English ones, in fenced holdings without shepherds. Although wool was once the primary income source for New Zealand sheep owners (especially during the New Zealand wool boom), today it has shifted to meat production for export.

Animal Welfare Concerns

The Australian sheep industry is the only sector of the industry to receive international criticism for its practices. Sheep stations in Australia are cited in *Animal Liberation*, the seminal book of the animal rights movement, as the author's primary evidence in his argument against retaining sheep as a part of animal agriculture. The practice of mulesing, in which skin is cut away from an animal's perineal area to prevent cases of the fatal condition flystrike, has been condemned by PETA as being painful and unnecessary. In response, a programme of phasing out mulesing is currently being implemented, and some mulesing operations are being carried out with the use of anaesthetic. The Animal Welfare Advisory Committee to the New Zealand Ministry of Agriculture *Code of recommendations and minimum standards for the welfare of Sheep*, considers mulesing a "special technique" which is performed on some Merino sheep at a small number of farms in New Zealand.

Most of the sheep meat exported from Australia is either frozen carcases to the U.K. or is live export to the Middle East. Shipped on livestock carriers in what has been called crowded, unsafe conditions by critics, live sheep are desired by Middle Eastern nations to meet the requirements of ritual halal slaughter. Opponents of the export—such as PETA—say that sheep exported to countries outside the jurisdiction of Australia's animal cruelty laws are treated with horrendous brutality and that halal facilities exist in Australia to make export of live animals redundant. A few celebrities and companies have pledged to boycott all Australian sheep products in protest.

Sheep are an important part of the global agricultural economy. However, their once-vital status has been largely replaced by other livestock species, especially the pig, chicken, and cow. China, Australia, India, and Iran have the largest modern flocks, and serve both local and exportation needs for wool and mutton. Other countries such as New Zealand have smaller flocks but retain a large international economic impact due to their export of sheep products. Sheep also play a major role in many local economies, which may be niche markets focused on organic or sustainable agriculture and local food customers. Especially in developing countries, such flocks may be a part of subsistence agriculture rather than a system of trade. Sheep themselves may be a medium of trade in barter economies.

Domestic sheep provide a wide array of raw materials. Wool was one of the first textiles, although in the late 20th century wool prices began to fall dramatically as the result of the popularity and cheap prices for synthetic fabrics. For many sheep owners, the cost of shearing is greater than the possible profit from the fleece, making subsisting on wool production alone practically impossible without farm subsidies. Fleeces are used as material in making alternative products such as wool insulation. In the 21st century, the sale of meat is the most profitable enterprise in the sheep industry, even though far less sheep meat is consumed than chicken, pork or beef.

Sheepskin is like wise used for making clothes, footwear, rugs, and other products. Byproducts from the slaughter of sheep are also of value: sheep tallow can be used in candle and soap making, sheep bone and cartilage has been used to furnish carved items such as dice and buttons as well as rendered glue and gelatin. Sheep intestine can be formed into sausage casings, and lamb intestine has been formed into surgical sutures, as well as strings for musical instruments and tennis rackets. Sheep droppings, which are high in cellulose, have even been sterilized and mixed with traditional pulp materials to make paper. Of all sheep byproducts, perhaps the most valuable is lanolin: the water-proof, fatty substance found naturally in sheep's wool and used as a base for innumerable cosmetics and other products.

Some farmers who keep sheep also make a profit from live sheep. Providing lambs for youth programmes such as 4-H and competition at agricultural shows is often a dependable avenue for the sale of sheep. Farmers may also choose to focus on a particular breed of sheep in order to sell registered purebred animals, as well as provide a ram rental service for breeding. The most valuable sheep ever sold to date was a purebred Texel ram that fetched £231,000 at auction. The previous record holder was a Merino ram sold for £205,000 in 1989. A new option for deriving profit from live sheep is the rental of flocks for grazing; these "mowing services" are hired in order to keep unwanted vegetation down in public spaces and to lessen fire hazard.

Despite the falling demand and price for sheep products in many markets, sheep have distinct economic advantages when compared with other livestock. They do not require the expensive housing, such as that used in the intensive farming of chickens or pigs. They are an efficient use of land; roughly six sheep can be kept on the amount that would suffice for a single cow or horse. Sheep can also consume plants, such as noxious weeds, that most other animals will not touch, and produce more young at a faster rate. Also, in contrast to most livestock species, the cost of raising sheep is not necessarily tied to the price of feed crops such as grain, soybeans and corn. Combined with the lower cost of quality sheep, all these factors combine to equal a lower overhead for sheep producers, thus entailing a higher profitability potential for the small farmer. Sheep are especially beneficial for independent producers, including family farms with limited resources, as the sheep industry is one of the few types of animal agriculture that has not been vertically integrated by agribusiness.

Sheep meat and milk were one of the earliest staple proteins consumed by human civilization after the transition from hunting and gathering to agriculture. Sheep meat prepared for food is known as either mutton or lamb. "Mutton" is derived from the Old French *moton*, which was the word for sheep used by the Anglo-Norman rulers of much of the British Isles in the Middle Ages. This became the name for sheep meat in English, while the Old English word *sceap* was kept for the live animal. Throughout modern history, "mutton" has been limited to the meat of mature sheep usually at least two years of age; "lamb" is used for that of immature sheep less than a year.

In the 21st century, the nations with the highest consumption of sheep meat are the Persian Gulf States, New Zealand, Australia, Greece, Uruguay, the United Kingdom and Ireland. These countries eat 14–40 lbs (3–18 kg) of sheep meat per capita, per annum. Sheep meat is also popular in France, Africa (especially the Maghreb), the Caribbean, the rest of the Middle East, India, and parts of China. This often reflects a past history of sheep production. In these countries in particular, dishes comprising alternative cuts and offal may be popular or traditional. Sheep testicles—called animelles or lamb fries—are considered a delicacy in many parts of the world. Perhaps the most unusual dish of sheep meat is the Scottish haggis, composed of various sheep innards cooked along with oatmeal and chopped onions inside its stomach. In comparison, countries such as the U.S. consume only a pound or less (under 0.5 kg), with Americans eating 50 pounds (22 kg) of pork and 65 pounds (29 kg) of beef. In addition, such countries rarely eat mutton, and may favor the more expensive cuts of lamb: mostly lamb chops and leg of lamb.

Though sheep's milk may be drunk rarely in fresh form, today it is used predominantly in cheese and yogurt making. Sheep have only two teats, and produce a far smaller volume of milk than cows. However, as sheep's milk contains far more fat, solids, and minerals than cow's milk, it is ideal for the cheese-making process. It also resists contamination during cooling better because of its much higher calcium content. Well-known cheeses made from sheep milk include the Feta of Bulgaria and Greece, Roquefort of France, Manchego from Spain, the Pecorino Romano (the Italian word for sheep is *pecore*) and Ricotta of Italy. Yogurts, especially some forms of strained yogurt, may also be made from sheep milk. Many of these products are now often made with cow's milk, especially when produced outside their country of origin. Sheep milk contains 4.8 per cent lactose, which may affect those who are intolerant.

Sheep are generally too large and reproduce too slowly to make ideal research subjects, and thus are not a common model organism. They have, however, played an influential role in some fields of science. In particular, the Roslin Institute of Edinburgh, Scotland used sheep for genetics research that produced groundbreaking results. In 1995, two ewes named Megan and Morag were the first mammals cloned from differentiated cells. A year later, a Finnish Dorset sheep named Dolly, dubbed "the world's most famous sheep" in Scientific American, was the first mammal to be cloned from an adult somatic cell. Following this, Polly and Molly were the first mammals to be simultaneously cloned and transgenic. As of 2008, the sheep genome has not been fully sequenced, although a detailed genetic map has been published, and a draft version of the complete genome produced by assembling sheep DNA sequences using information given by the genomes of other mammals.

In the study of natural selection, the population of Soay sheep that remain on the island of Hirta have been used to explore the relation of body size and coloration to reproductive success. Soay sheep come in several colors, and researchers investigated why the larger, darker sheep were in decline; this occurrence contradicted the rule of thumb that larger members of a population tend to be more successful reproductively. The feral Soays on Hirta are especially useful subjects because they are isolated.

Sheep are one of the few animals where the molecular basis of the diversity of male sexual preferences has been examined. However, this research has been controversial, and much publicity has been produced by a study at the Oregon Health and Science University that investigated the mechanisms that produce homosexuality in rams. Organisations such as PETA campaigned against the study, accusing scientists of trying to cure homosexuality in the sheep. OHSU and the involved scientists vehemently denied such accusations.

Domestic sheep are sometimes used in medical research, particularly for researching cardiovascular physiology, in areas such as hypertension and heart failure. Pregnant sheep are also a useful model for human pregnancy, and have been used to investigate the effects on fetal development of malnutrition and hypoxia. In behavioural sciences, sheep have been used in isolated cases for the study of facial recognition, as their mental process of recognition is qualitatively similar to humans.

Cultural Impact

Sheep have had a strong presence in many cultures, especially in areas where they form the most common type of livestock. In the English language, to call someone a sheep or ovine may allude that they are timid and easily led, if not outright stupid. In contradiction to this image, male sheep are often used as symbols of virility and power, such as for the St. Louis Rams and the Dodge Ram. Sheep are key symbols in fables and nursery rhymes like *The Wolf in Sheep's Clothing, Little Bo Peep, Baa, Baa, Black Sheep*, and *Mary Had a Little Lamb*. Novels such as George Orwell's *Animal Farm*, Haruki Murakami's *A Wild Sheep Chase*, Thomas Hardy's *Far from the Madding Crowd* and *Three Bags Full: A Sheep Detective Story* utilize sheep as characters or plot devices. Poems like William Blake's "The Lamb", songs such as Pink Floyd's *Sheep* and Bach's aria *Sheep may safely graze* (*Schafe können sicher weiden*) use sheep for metaphorical purposes. In more recent popular culture, the 2007 film *Black Sheep* exploits sheep for horror and comedic effect, ironically turning them into blood-thirsty killers.

Counting sheep is popularly said to be an aid to sleep, and some ancient systems of counting sheep persist today. Sheep also enter in colloquial sayings and idiom frequently with such phrases as "black sheep". To call an individual a black sheep implies that they are an odd or disreputable member of a group. This usage derives from the recessive trait that causes an occasional black lamb to be born in to an entirely white flock. These black sheep were considered undesirable by shepherds, as black wool is not as commercially viable as white wool. Citizens who accept overbearing governments have been referred to by the Portmanteau neologism of sheeple. Somewhat differently, the adjective "sheepish" is also used to describe embarrassment.

In antiquity, symbolism involving sheep cropped up in religions in the ancient Near East, the Mideast, and the Mediterranean area: Çatalhöyük, ancient Egyptian religion, the Cana'anite and Phoenician tradition, Judaism, Greek religion, and others. Religious symbolism and ritual involving sheep began with some of the first known faiths: skulls of rams (along with bulls) occupied central placement in shrines at the Çatalhöyük settlement in 8000 BCE. In Ancient Egyptian religion, the ram was the symbol of several gods: Khnum, Heryshaf and Amun (in his incarnation as a god of fertility). Other deities occasionally shown with ram features include: the goddess Ishtar, the Phoenician god Baal-Hamon, and the Babylonian god Ea-Oannes. In Madagascar, sheep were not eaten as they were believed to be incarnations of the souls of ancestors.

There are also many ancient Greek references to sheep: that of Chrysomallos, the golden-fleeced ram, continuing to be told through into the modern era. Astrologically, *Aries*, the ram, is the first sign of the classical Greek zodiac and the sheep is also the eighth of the twelve animals associated with the 12-year cycle of in the Chinese zodiac, related to the Chinese calendar. In Mongolia, shagai are an ancient form of dice made from the cuboid bones of sheep that are often used for fortunetelling purposes.

Sheep play an important role in all the Abrahamic faiths; Abraham, Isaac, Jacob, Moses, King David and the Islamic prophet Muhammad were all shepherds. According to the Biblical story of the Binding of Isaac, a ram is sacrificed as a substitute for Isaac after an angel stays Abraham's hand (in the Islamic tradition, Abraham was about to sacrifice Ishmael). Eid al-Adha is a major annual festival in Islam in which sheep (or other animals) are sacrificed in remembrance of this act. Sheep are also occasionally sacrificed to commemorate important secular events in Islamic cultures. Greeks and Romans also sacrificed sheep regularly in religious practice, and Judaism also once sacrificed sheep as a *Korban* (sacrifice), such as the Passover lamb. Ovine symbols—such as the ceremonial blowing of a shofar—still find a presence in modern Judaic traditions. Followers of Christianity are collectively often referred to as a flock, with Christ as the Good Shepherd, and sheep are an element in the Christian iconography of the birth of Jesus. Some Christian saints are considered patrons of shepherds, and even of sheep themselves. Christ is also portrayed as the Sacrificial lamb of God (*Agnus Dei*) and Easter celebrations in Greece and Romania traditionally feature a meal of Paschal lamb.

Domestic Sheep Reproduction

As with other mammals, domestic sheep reproduction occurs sexually. Their reproductive strategy is very similar to other domestic herd animals. A flock of ewes is generally mated by a single ram, which has either been chosen by a farmer or has established dominance through physical contest with other rams (in feral populations). Most sheep have a breeding season (*tupping*) in the autumn, though some are able to breed year-round.

Largely as a result of the influence of humans in sheep breeding, ewes often produce multiple lambs. This increase in the lamb births, both in number and birth weight, may cause problems in delivery and lamb survival, requiring the intervention of shepherds.

Ewes generally reach sexual maturity at six to eight months of age, and rams generally at four to six (ram lambs have occasionally been known to impregnate their mothers at two months). Ewes enter in to estrus cycles about every 17 days, which last for approximately 30 hours. In addition to emitting a scent, they indicate readiness through physical displays towards rams. Sheep may display homosexuality, which occurs in about eight per cent of rams. Its occurrence does not seem to be related to flock hierarchy (as some homosexual behaviour is in mammals), rather the ram's typical motor pattern for intercourse is directed at rams instead of ewes. The phenomenon of the freemartin, a female bovine that is behaviourally masculine and lacks functioning ovaries, is commonly associated with cattle, but does occur to some extent in sheep. The instance of freemartins in sheep may be increasing in concert with the rise in twinning (freemartins are the result of male-female twin combinations).

Rutting

Without human intervention, rams may fight during the rut to determine which individuals may mate with ewes. Rams, especially unfamiliar ones, will also fight outside the breeding period to establish dominance; rams can kill one another if allowed to mix freely. During the rut, even normally friendly rams may become aggressive towards humans due to increases in their hormone levels.

Historically, especially aggressive rams were sometimes blindfolded or hobbled. Today, those who keep rams typically prefer softer preventative measures, such as moving within a clear line to an exit, never turning their back on a ram, and possibly dousing with water or a diluted solution of bleach or vinegar to dissuade charges.

Without ultrasound or other special tools, determining if a sheep is pregnant is difficult. Ewes only begin to visibly show a pregnancy about six weeks before giving birth, so shepherds often rely on the assumption that a ram will impregnate all the ewes in a flock. However, by fitting a ram with a chest harness called a *marking harness* that holds a special crayon (or *raddle*, sometimes spelled *reddle*), ewes that have been mounted are marked with a color. Dye may also be directly applied to the ram's brisket. This measure is not used in flocks where wool is important, since the color of a raddle contaminates it.

After mating, sheep have a gestation period of around five months. Within a few days of the impending birth, ewes begin to behave differently. They may lie down and stand erratically, paw the ground, or otherwise act out of sync with normal flock patterns. A ewe's udder will quickly fill out, and her vulva will swell. Vaginal, uterine or anal prolapse may also occur, in which case either stitching or a physical retainer can be used to hold the orifice in if the problem persists.

Artificial Insemination

In addition to natural insemination by rams, artificial insemination and embryo transfers have been used in sheep breeding programmes for many years. However, ovine AI is a relatively complicated procedure compared to other livestock. Unlike cattle or goats, which have straight services that can be vaginally inseminated, ewes have a curved cervix which is more difficult to access. Additionally, breeders were until recently unable to control their ewe's estrus cycles.

Historically, vaginal insemination of sheep only produced 40-60 per cent success rates, and was thus called a "shot in the dark" (SID). In the 1980s, Australian researchers developed a laparoscopic insemination procedure which, combined with the use of progestogen and pregnant mare's serum gonadotropin (PMSG), yielded much higher success rates (50-80% or more), and has become the standard for artificial insemination of sheep in the 21st century.

Using a minor surgical procedure with almost no risk of injury or infection when performed properly, sheep laparoscopy allows the importation of improved genetics, even of breeds which may otherwise be non-existent in certain countries due to the regulation of live animal imports.

Lambing

When birth is imminent, contractions begin to take place, and the fitful behaviour of the ewe may increase. A normal labour may take one to several hours, depending on how many lambs are present, the age of the ewe, and her physical and nutritional condition prior to the birth. Though some breeds may regularly produce larger litters of lambs (records stand around nine lambs at once), most produce either single or twin lambs. At some point, usually at the beginning of labour or soon after the births have occurred, ewes and lambs may be confined to small lambing jugs. These pens, which are generally two to eight feet in length and width, are designed to aid both careful observation of ewes and to cement the bond between them and their lambs.

Ovine obstetrics can be problematic. By selectively breeding ewes that produce multiple offspring with higher birth weights for generations, sheep producers have inadvertently caused some domestic sheep to have difficulty lambing. However, it is a myth that sheep cannot lamb without human assistance; many ewes give birth directly in pasture without aid. Balancing ease of lambing with high productivity is one of the dilemmas of sheep breeding. While the majority of births are relatively normal and do not require intervention, there are still a large number of possible complications that may arise. A lamb may present in the normal fashion (with both legs and head forward), but may simply be too large to slide out of the birth canal. This often happens when large rams are crossed with diminutive ewes (this is related to breed, rams are naturally larger than ewes by comparison). Lambs may also present themselves with one shoulder to the side, completely backward, or with only some of their limbs protruding. Lambs may also be spontaneously aborted or stillborn. Reproductive failure is a common consequence of infections such as toxoplasmosis and foot-and-mouth disease. Some types of abortion in sheep are preventable by vaccinations against these infections.

In the case of any such problems, those present at lambing (who may or may not include a veterinarian, most shepherds become accomplished at lambing to some degree) may assist the ewe in extracting or repositioning lambs. After the birth, ewes ideally break the amniotic sac (if it is not broken during labour), and begin licking clean the lamb. The licking clears the nose and mouth, dries the lamb, and stimulates it. Lambs that are breathing and healthy at this point begin trying to stand, and ideally do so between a half and full hour, with help from the mother. Generally after lambs stand, the umbilical cord is trimmed to about an inch (2.54 centimetres). Once trimmed, a small container (such as a film canister) of iodine is held against the lamb's belly over the remainder of the cord to prevent infection.

In normal situations, lambs nurse after standing, receiving vital colostrum milk. Lambs that either fail to nurse or are prevented from doing so by the ewe require aid in order to live. If coaxing the pair to accept nursing does not work, one of several steps may then be taken. Ewes may be held or tied to force them to accept a nursing lamb. If a lamb is not eating, a stomach tube may also be used to force feed the lamb in order to save its life. In the case of a permanently rejected lamb, a shepherd may then attempt to foster an orphaned lamb onto another ewe. Lambs are also sometimes fostered after the death of their mother, either from the birth or other event.

Scent plays a large factor in ewes recognizing their lambs, so disrupting the scent of a newborn lamb with washing or over-handling may cause a ewe to reject it. Conversely, various methods of imparting the scent of a ewe's own lamb to an orphaned one may be useful in fostering. If an orphaned lamb cannot be fostered, then it usually becomes what is known as a bottle lamb—a lamb raised by people and fed via bottle.

After lambs are stabilized, lamb marking is carried out–this includes ear tagging, docking, castration and usually vaccination. Ear tags with numbers are the primary mode of identification when sheep are not named; it is also the legal manner of animal identification in the European Union: the number may identify the individual sheep or only its flock. When performed at an early age, ear tagging seems to cause little or no discomfort to lambs.

However, using tags improperly or using tags not designed for sheep may cause discomfort, largely due to excess weight of tags for other animals.

Ram lambs not intended for breeding are castrated, though some shepherds choose to avoid the procedure for ethical, economic or practical reasons. Ram lambs that will be slaughtered or separated from ewes before sexual maturity are not usually castrated. In most breeds, lambs' tails are docked for health reasons. The tail may be removed just below the lamb's caudal tail flaps (docking shorter than this may cause health problems such as rectal prolapse), but in some breeds the tail is left longer, or is not docked at all. Docking is not necessary in short-tailed breeds, and it is not usually done in breeds in which a long tail is valued, such as Zwartbles. Though docking is often considered cruel and unnatural by animal rights activists, it is considered by sheep producers large and small alike to be a critical step in maintaining the health of sheep. Long, wooly tails make shearing more difficult, interfere with mating, and make sheep extremely susceptible to parasites, especially those that cause flystrike. Both castration and docking can be performed with several different instruments. An elastrator places a tight band of rubber around an area, causing it to atrophy and fall off in a number of weeks. This process is bloodless and does not seem to cause extended suffering to lambs, who tend to ignore it after several hours. In addition to the elastrator, a Burdizzo, emasculator, heated chisel or knife are sometimes used. After one to three days in the lambing jugs, ewes and lambs are usually sufficiently stabilized to allow reintroduction to the rest of the flock.

In the large sheep producing nations of South America, Australia and New Zealand sheep are usually bred on large tracts of land with much less intervention from the graziers or breeders. Merinos, and much of the land in these countries does not lend itself to the mob intervention that is found in smaller flock breeding countries. In these countries there is little need, and no option but for ewes to lamb outdoors as there are insufficient structures to handle the large flocks of ewes there. New Zealand ewes produce 36 million lambs each spring time, which is an average of 2250 lambs per farm. Australian graziers, too, do not receive the financial support that governments in other countries provide to sheep breeders. Low-cost sheep breeding is based on large numbers of sheep per labour unit and having ewes that are capable of unsupervised lambing to produce hardy, active lambs.

Managerial Aspects

For breeders intent on strict improvements to their flocks, ewes are classed and inferior sheep are removed prior to mating in order to maintain or improve the quality of the flock. Muffled faces have long been associated with lower fertility rates. Stud or specially selected rams are chosen with aid of objective measurements, genetic information and evaluation services that are now available in Australia and New Zealand. The choice of mating time is governed by many factors including climate, market requirements and feed availability. Rams are typically mated at about 2.5 per cent depending on the age of the sheep, plus consideration as to the size and type of mating paddocks. The mating period ranges from about 6 to 8 weeks in commercial flocks. Longer mating times result in management problems with lamb marking and shearing etc.

After mating, in areas where foxes are a problem, a Coordinated Fox Control Project is held in conjunction with the local Rural Lands Protection Board (RLPB) and National Parks and Wildlife Service (NPWS) to facilitate a neighbourhood baiting campaign.

Good nutrition is vital to ewes during the last 6 weeks of pregnancy in order to prevent pregnancy toxaemia, especially in twin bearing ewes. Overfeeding, however, may result in over large single lambs and dystocia. Shearing ewes before lambing reduces the number of ewes that are cast (i.e. unable to rise unassisted), and the number of lambs and ewes that are lost. Lambs, too, are aided in finding the udder and suckling a shorn ewe.

After shearing ewes are typically placed in well sheltered paddocks that have good feed and water. Attention to ewes that are lambing varies according to the breed, size and locations of properties. Unless they are stud ewes it unlikely that they will receive intensive care. On stations with large paddocks there is a policy of non-interference. On other properties the mobs are inspected by stockmen at varying intervals to stand cast ewes and deal with dystocia. Producers also sometimes quietly drift pregnant ewes away from ewes that have already lambed, in order to prevent mis-mothering.

Lambs are usually marked at 3 to 6 weeks of age, but a protracted lambing season may necessitate two markings.

In the major sheep countries of Argentina, Uruguay, Brazil, Perú and Chile, breeders are also utilizing fleece testing and performance recording schemes as a means of improving their flocks. New research.

For the first time in history, researchers at Chiswick CSIRO research station, between Uralla and Armidale, New South Wales have used stem cells to develop surrogate rams and bulls. These males then produce the viable semen of another male.

The approach in these sheep experiments involves irradiating a ram's testes while placing stem cells from a second ram into the testes of the first, ram A. In the following weeks ram A produces semen the usual way, but is using the stem cells of ram B and therefore producing semen carrying the genetics of ram B rather than those of his own. Ram A therefore has effectively become a surrogate ram.

The viable semen is then implanted in the ewe and the many lambs born through this process are proving to be normal and healthy. DNA tests have proved that up to 10 per cent of the lambs are sired by the surrogate ram and carry the genetics of the donor ram.

Sheep Shearing

Sheep shearing, shearing or clipping is the process by which the woollen fleece of a sheep is cut off. The person who removes the sheep's wool is called a *shearer*. Typically each adult sheep is shorn once each year (a sheep may be said to have been "shorn" or "sheared", depending upon dialect). The annual shearing most often occurs in a shearing shed, a facility especially designed to process often hundreds and sometimes more than 3,000 sheep per day.

Up until the 1870s squatters washed their sheep in nearby creeks prior to shearing. Later some expensive hot water installations were constructed on some of the larger stations for the washing. Sheep washing in Australia was influenced by the Saxony sheep breeders in Germany who washed their sheep and by the Spanish practice of washing the wool after shearing. There were three main reasons for the custom in Australia:

The English manufacturers demanded that Australian woolgrowers provide their fleeces free from vegetable matter, burrs, soil, etc.

The dirty fleeces were hard to shear and demanded that the metal blade shears be sharpened more often.

Wool in Australia was carted by bullock team or horse teams and charged by weight. Washed wool was lighter and did not cost as much to transport.

The practice of washing the wool rather than the sheep evolved from the fact that hotter water could be used to wash the wool, than that used to wash the sheep. When the practice of selling wool in the grease occurred in the 1890s, wool washing became obsolete.

Australia and New Zealand had to discard the old methods of wool harvesting and evolve more efficient systems to cope with the huge numbers of sheep involved. After 1888 machine shearing was introduced, reducing second cuts and shearing time. By 1915 most large sheep station sheds in Australia had installed machines, driven by steam or later by internal combustion engines.

Shearing tables were invented in the 1950s and have not proved popular, although some are still used for crutching.

Today, large flocks of sheep are shorn by professional shearing teams working eight hour days, most often in spring, by machine shearing. These contractor teams will consist of shearers, shed hands and a cook (in the more isolated areas). The shed staff working hours and wages are regulated by industry awards. A working day starts at 7:30 AM and the day is divided into four "runs" of two hours each. "Smoko" breaks of a half hour each are at 9:30 AM and again at 3:00 PM. The lunch break is taken at 12:00 PM for one hour. Most shearers are paid on a piece rate, i.e., per sheep. Shearers who "tally" more than 200 sheep per day are known as "gun shearers". Typical mass shearing of sheep today follows a well-defined workflow: remove the wool, throw the fleece onto the wool table, skirt, roll and class the fleece, place it in the appropriate wool bin, press and store the wool until it is transported. In 1984 Australia became the last country in the world to permit the use of wide combs, due to previous Australian Workers Union rules. Although they were rare in sheds, women now take a large part in the shearing industry by working as pressers, wool rollers, rouseabouts, wool classers and also shearing, too.

A sheep is caught by the shearer from the catching pen and taken to his "stand" on the shearing board. It is then shorn using mechanical handpiece (see *Shearing devices* below). The wool is removed by following an efficient set of movements, devised by Godfrey Bowen in c. 1950, (the *Bowen Technique*) or the *Tally-Hi* method. In 1963 the Tally-hi shearing system was developed by the Australian Wool Corporation and promoted using synchronised shearing demonstrations. Sheep struggle less using the Tally-Hi method, reducing strain on the shearer and there is a saving of about 30 seconds shearing each sheep. The shearer begins by removing the sheep's belly wool, which is separated from the main fleece by a rouseabout, while the sheep is still being shorn. A professional or "gun" shearer typically removes a fleece without badly marking or cutting the sheep in two to three minutes, depending on the size and condition of the sheep, or less than two in elite competitive shearing. The shorn sheep is moved from the board via a chute in the floor, or wall, to a counting out pen, efficiently removing it from the shed.

The CSIRO in Australia has developed a non-mechanical method of shearing sheep using an injected protein that creates a natural break in the wool fibres. After fitting a retaining net to enclose the wool, sheep are injected with the protein. When the net is removed after a week, the fleece has separated and is removed by hand. In some breeds a similar process occurs naturally.

Skirting the Fleece

Once the entire fleece has been removed from the sheep, the fleece is *thrown*, clean side down, on to a wool table by a shed hand (commonly known in New Zealand and Australian sheds as a *rouseabout* or *roustie*). The wool table top consists of slats spaced approximately 12 cm apart. This enables short pieces of wool, the *locks* and other debris, to gather beneath the table separately from the fleece. The fleece is then *skirted* by one or more wool rollers to remove the sweat fribs and other less desirable parts of the fleece. The removed pieces largely consist of shorter, seeded, burry or dusty wool etc. which is still useful in the industry. As such they are placed in separate containers and sold along with fleece wool. Other items removed from the fleece on the table, such as faeces, skin fragments or twigs and leaves, are discarded a short distance from the wool table so as not to contaminate the wool and fleece.

Wool Classing

Following the skirting of the fleece, it is folded, rolled and examined for its quality in a process known as wool classing, which is performed by a registered and qualified wool classer. Based on its type, the fleece is placed into the relevant wool bin ready to be pressed (mechanically compressed) when there is sufficient wool to make a wool bale.

Blade Shears

Blade shears consist of two blades arranged similarly to scissors except that the hinge is at the end farthest from the point (not in the middle). The cutting edges pass each other as the shearer squeezes them together and shear the wool close to the animal's skin. Blade shears are still used today but in a more limited way. Blade shears leave some wool on a sheep and this is more suitable for cold climates where the sheep needs some protection from the elements. For those areas where no powered-machinery is available blade shears are the only option. Blades are more commonly used to shear stud rams.

Machine Shears

Machine shears, known as handpieces, operate in a similar manner to human hair clippers in that a power-driven toothed blade, known as a cutter, is driven back and forth over the surface of a comb and the wool is cut from the animal. The original machine shears were powered by a fixed hand-crank linked to the handpiece by a shaft with only two universal joints, which afforded a very limited range of motion. Later models have more joints to allow easier positioning of the handpiece on the animal. Electric motors on each stand have generally replaced overhead gear for driving the handpieces. The jointed arm is replaced in many instances with a flexible shaft. Smaller motors allowed the production of shears in which the motor is in the handpiece; these are generally not used by professional shearers as the weight and heat of the motor becomes bothersome with long use.

A culture has evolved out of the practice of sheep shearing, especially in post-colonial Australia and New Zealand. *Shearing the Rams,* a painting by

Australian impressionist painter Tom Roberts is considered to be iconic of the livestock-growing culture or "life on the land" in Australia.

For an inversion, Michael Leunig's *Ramming the Shears* can be seen as a sign of the shifts in Australian culture, and the extent to which the dominant rural culture is being eroded by an increasingly urban population.

The expression that Australia's wealth rode on *the sheep's back* in parts of the twentieth century no longer has the currency it once had.

In 2001, Mandy Francis of Hardy's Bay, NSW constructed a blackbutt seat for the Street Furniture Project at Walcha, New South Wales. This seat was inspired by the combs, cutters, wool tables and grating associated with the craft and industry of shearing.

During the long weekend in June 2010, 111 machine shearers and 78 blade shearers shore 6,000 Merino ewes and 178 rams at the historic 72 stand North Tuppal station. Along with the shearers there were 107 wool handlers and penners-up and more than 10,000 visitors to witness this event in the restored shed. Over this weekend the scene in Tom Robert's *Shearing of the Rams* was twice re-enacted for the visitors.

Many stations across Australia no longer carry sheep due to lower wool prices, drought and other disasters, but their shearing sheds remain, in a wide variety of materials and styles, and have been the subject of books and documentation for heritage authorities. Some farmers are reluctant to remove either the equipment or the sheds, and many unused sheds remain intact.

Sheep shearing and wool handling competitions are held regularly in parts of the world, particularly Ireland, the UK, South Africa, New Zealand and Australia. As sheep shearing is an arduous task, speed shearers, for all types of equipment and sheep, are usually very fit and well trained. In Wales a sheep shearing contest is one of the events of the Royal Welsh Show, the country's premier agricultural show held near Builth Wells.

The world's largest sheep shearing and wool handling contest, the Golden Shears, is held in the Wairarapa district, New Zealand.

World Championships

World Championships are hosted by different countries every 2–3 years and eight different countries have hosted the event. The first World Championships were held at the Bath & West showground, England, in 1977, and the first Machine-Shearing winner was Roger Cox from New Zealand. Other countries that have hosted the sheep shearing World Championships have been New Zealand (3 times), England (3 times), Australia (2 times), Wales, Ireland, Scotland, South Africa & Norway. Out of 13 World Championships, New Zealand have won the team Machine contest 10 times, and famous New Zealand sheep-shearer David Fagan has been World Champion a record 5 times.

In October, 2008 the event was hosted in Norway. It was the first time ever that the event was hosted by a non-English speaking country. The newly crowned World Machine Shearing champion is Paul Avery from New Zealand. New Zealand also won the team event, and the traditional blade-shears World Champion is Ziewilelle Hans from South Africa. A record 29 countries competed at the 2008 event. The next World Championship will be held at the Royal Welsh Show, Llanelwedd, Wales in July, 2010.

Rooing

In some primitive sheep (for example in many Shetlands), there is a natural break in the growth of the wool in spring. By late spring this causes the fleece to begin to peel away from the body, and it may then be plucked by hand without cutting – this is known as *rooing*. Individual sheep may reach this stage at slightly different times.

The raising of domestic sheep has occurred in nearly every inhabited part of the globe, and the variations in cultures and languages which have kept sheep has produced a vast lexicon of unique terminology used to describe sheep husbandry. A few of the more major terms include:

Backliner — An externally applied medicine, applied along the backline of a freshly shorn sheep to control lice or other parasites. In the British Isles called pour-on.

Bale — A wool pack containing a specified weight of pressed wool as regulated by industry authorities.

Bell sheep — A sheep (usually a rough, wrinkly one) caught by a shearer, just before the end of a shearing run.

Bellwether — Originally an experienced wether given a bell to lead a flock; now mainly used figuratively for a person acting as a lead and guide.

Black wool — Any wool that is not white, but not necessarily black.

Board — The floor where the shearing stands are in a wool shed.

Bolus — An object placed in the reticulum of the rumen, remaining there for some time or permanently. Used for long-term administration of medicines, or as a secure location for an electronic marking chip.

Bottle lamb — An orphan lamb reared on a bottle. Also *poddy lamb* or *pet lamb*.

Boxed — When different mobs of sheep are mixed.

Break — A marked thinning of the fleece, producing distinct weakness in one part of the staple.

Broken-mouth — A sheep which has lost or broken some of its incisor teeth, usually after the age of about six years.

Broad — Wool which is on the strong side for its quality number, or for its type.

Broomie — A rouseabout in a shearing shed.

Butt — An underweight bale of greasy wool in a standard wool pack.

Callipyge — (pronounced a natural genetic mutation that produces extremely muscled hindquarters in sheep. These lambs are found in the US and lack tenderness.

Cast — Unable to regain footing, possibly due to lying in a hollow with legs facing uphill and/or having a heavy fleece. Also see *riggwelter*.

CFA or cast for age — Sheep culled because of their age. Also see *cull ewe, killer.*

Clip — All the wool from a flock (in Australian Wool Classing).

Clipping — Cutting off the wool: see *shearing* and *rooing*.

Comeback — The progeny of a mating of a Merino with a British longwool sheep.

Crimp — The natural wave formation seen in wool. Usually the closer the crimps, the finer the wool.

Cull ewe — a ewe no longer suitable for breeding, and sold for meat. Also see *killer*.

Crutching — Shearing parts of a sheep (especially the hind end of some woollier breeds such as Merino), to prevent fly-strike. Also see *dagging*.

Cut-out — The completion of shearing a flock.

Dags — Clumps of dried dung stuck to the wool of a sheep, which may lead to fly-strike. (Hence "rattle your dags!", meaning "hurry up!", especially used in New Zealand.

Dagging — Clipping off dags. Also see *crutching*.

Devil's Grip — A serious conformation defect, appearing as a depression behind the withers.

Dewlap — The upper fold under the neck of a Merino sheep.

Dipping — Immersing sheep in a plunge or shower dip to kill external parasites. Backliners are now replacing dipping.

Downs — Breeds of sheep belonging to the short wool group.

Draft ewe — A ewe too old for rough grazing (such as moorland), *drafted* (selected) out of the flock to move to better grazing, usually on another farm. Generally spelt "draft", but in the British Isles either as "draft" or "draught".

Folding — Confining sheep (or other livestock) onto a restricted area for feeding, such as a temporarily fenced part of a root crop field, especially when done repeatedly onto a sequence of areas.

Foot rot — Infectious pododermatitis, a painful hoof disease commonly found in sheep (also goats and cattle), especially when pastured on damp ground. Gimmer (pronounced , not – a young female sheep, usually before her first lamb (especially used in the north of England and Scotland). Also *theave.*

Graziers' alert — A cold-weather warning issued by the weather bureau to sheep graziers. Greasy – a sheep shearer.

Greasy wool — Wool as it has been shorn from the sheep and therefore not yet washed or cleaned. Also see *lanolin.*

Guard llama — A llama (usually a castrated male) kept with sheep as a guard. The llama will defend the flock from predators such as foxes and dogs.

Hefting — The instinct in some breeds of keeping to a certain *heft* (a small local area) throughout their lives. Allows different farmers in an extensive landscape such as moorland to graze different areas without the need for fences, each ewe remaining on her particular area. Lambs usually learn their heft from their mothers.

Hogget or — A young sheep of either sex from about 9 to 18 months of age (until it cuts two teeth). Also the meat of a hogget. Also *teg, old-season lamb, shearling*.

Hoof-shears — Implement similar to secateurs, used to trim the hoofs of sheep.

In lamb — Pregnant.

Joining — The placing of rams with ewes for mating.

Ked — *or sheep ked – Melophagus ovinus*, a species of louse-fly, a nearly flightless biting fly infesting sheep.

Kemp — A short, white, hollow, hairy fibre usually found about the head and legs of sheep.

Killer — A sheep that has been selected for slaughter on an Australian property. Also see *cull ewe.*

Lamb — A young sheep in its first year. In many eastern countries there is a looser use of the term which may include hoggets. Also the meat of younger sheep.

Lambing — The process of giving birth in sheep. Also the work of tending lambing ewes (shepherds are said to *lamb* their flocks).

Lambing jug — A small pen to confine ewes and newly born lambs.

Lamb marking — The work of earmarking, docking and castration of lambs.

Lambing — The number of lambs successfully reared in a flock compared with the number of ewes that have been mated – effectively a measure of the success of lambing and the number of multiple births. May vary from around 100 per cent in a hardy mountain flock (where a ewe may not be able to rear more than one lamb safely), to 150 per cent or more in a well-fed lowland flock (whose ewes can more easily support twins or even triplets).

Lamb's fry — Lamb's liver (as food).

Lamb fries — Lamb testicles when served as food.

Lanolin — A thick yellow greasy substance in wool, secreted by the sheep's skin. Also called *wool fat, wool wax, wool grease, adeps lanae* or *yolk*. Extracted from raw wool and used for various purposes.

Livestock — A dog bred and trained to guard sheep from predators such as bears, wolves, people or other dogs. Usually a large type of dog, often white and woolly, apparently to allow them to blend in with the sheep. Sometimes given a spiked collar to prevent attack by wolves or dogs. Does not usually muster the sheep. Sometimes called a *sheepdog* – but also see separate entry for this.

Lug mark — Local term in Cumbria for *earmark*.

Marking knife — A knife with a clamp or hook made for lamb marking.

Micron — One millionth of a metre, a measure of fibre diameter of wool in wool measurement. Term used in preference to "micrometre", the SI name for the same unit.

Mob — A group or cohort of sheep of the same breed that have run together under similar environmental conditions since the previous shearing (in Australian Wool Classing).

Monorchid — A male mammal with only one descended testicle, the other being retained internally. Monorchid sheep are less fertile than full rams, but have leaner meat than wethers.

Mule — A type of cross-bred sheep, both hardy and suitable for meat (especially in northern England). Usually bred from a Bluefaced Leicester ram on hardy mountain ewes such as Swaledales. May be qualified according to *guardian.*

The female parent — For example a Welsh Mule is from a Blue-faced Leicester ram and a Welsh Mountain ewe.

Mulesing — A practice in Australia of cutting off wrinkles from the crutch area of Merinos, to prevent fly strike. Controversial, and illegal in some parts of the world. Named after a Mr Mules.

Mustering — The round up of livestock for inspection or other purposes.

Mutton — The meat of an older ewe or wether. May also refer to goat meat in eastern countries. Derived from the Anglo-Norman French word *mouton* ("sheep").

NSM — Not station mated. A term used in sale advertisements indicating that those ewes have not been mated.

Off shears — Sheep have been recently shorn.

Old-season — A lamb a year old or more. Also *hogget, shearling, teg.*

Orf, scabby — A highly contagious viral disease of sheep (and goats) attacking damaged skin areas around the mouth and causing sores, usually affecting lambs in their first year of life.

Plain bodied — A sheep that has relatively few body wrinkles.

Poddy lamb — An orphan lamb reared on a bottle. Also *cade lamb,* or *placer.*

Raddle — Coloured pigment used to mark sheep for various reasons, such as to show ownership, or to show which lambs belong to which ewe. May be strapped to the chest of a ram, to mark the backs of ewes he mates (different rams may be given different colours). Also a verb ("that ewe's been raddled"). Also *ruddy.*

Ram — An un castrated adult male sheep. Also *tup.*

Riggwelter — A sheep that has fallen onto its back and is unable to get up (usually because of the weight of its fleece).

Ring — A mob of sheep moving around in a circle.

Ringing — The removal of a circle of wool from around the pizzle of a male sheep.

Rooing — Removing the fleece by hand-plucking. Done once a year in late spring, when the fleece begins to moult naturally, especially in some breeds, such as Shetlands.

Rouseabout — (often abbreviated to 'rousie'), shedhands who pick up fleeces after they have been removed during shearing.

Ruddy — Local Cumbrian term for *raddle*.

These sheep have been "raddled" (marked).

Scab or sheep — A type of mange in sheep, a skin disease caused by attack by the sheep scab mite *Psoroptes ovis*, a psoroptid mite.

Scrapie — A wasting disease of sheep and goats, a transmissible spongiform encephalopathy (TSE, like BSE of cattle) and believed to be caused by a prion. Efforts have been made in some countries to breed for sheep genotypes resistant to scrapie.

Shearing — Cutting off the fleece, normally done in two pieces by skilled shearers. A sheep may be said to have been either *sheared* or *shorn*, depending on dialect. Also *clipping*.

Shearling — A yearling sheep before its first shearing. Also *hogget, old-season lamb, teg*.

Sheepdog or — A dog used to move and control sheep, often very highly trained. Other types of dog may be used just to guard sheep (see *livestock guarding dog*), and these are sometimes also called *sheepdogs*.

Sheep — The species, or members of it. The plural is the same as the singular, and it can also be used as a mass noun. Normally used of individuals of any age, but in some areas only for those of breeding age.

Sheepwalk — An area of rough grazing occupied by a particular flock or forming part of a particular farm.

Shepherd — A stockperson or farmer who looks after sheep while they are in the pasture.

Shepherding — The act of shepherding sheep, or sheep husbandry more generally.

Shornie — A freshly shorn sheep

Shepherd's — A staff with a hook at one end, used to catch sheep by the neck or leg (depending on type).

Slink — A very young lamb.

Rollover sheep handler for crutching, foot inspection and paring, general husbandry, udder inspection etc.

Stag	— A ram castrated after about 6 months of age.
Staple	— A group of wool fibres that formed a cluster or lock.
Store	— A sheep (or other meat animal) in good average condition, but not fat. Usually bought by dealers to fatten for resale.
Sucker	— An unweaned lamb.
Teg	— A sheep in its second year. Also *hogget, old-season lamb, shearling*.
Theave or	— A young female sheep, usually before her first lamb (used especially in lowland England). Also *gimmer*.
Top knot	— Wool from the forehead or poll of a sheep.
Tup	— An alternative term for *ram*.
Tupping	— Mating in sheep, or the mating season (autumn, for a spring-lambing flock).
Weaner	— A young animal that has been weaned, from its mother, until it is about a year old.
Wether	— A castrated male sheep (or goat).
Wigging	— the removal of wool from around a sheep's eyes to prevent wool-blindness.
Wool-	— When excessive wool growth interferes with the normal sight of a sheep.
Wool-grease	— See *lanolin*.
Wool pack	— A standard-sized woven nylon container manufactured to industry specifications for the transportation of wool.
Woolsack	— A ceremonial cushion used by the Lord Speaker of the UK House of Lords, filled with wool to symbolise the importance of the wool trade for the prosperity of the country.
Yoke	— Two crossed pieces of timber or a forked branch fixed to the neck of a habitually straying sheep in an attempt to prevent it breaking through hedges and fences.

CHAPTER 4

The Importance of Livestock in India

Growing human population, rising per capita income, and increasing urbanization are fuelling rapid growth in the demand for food of animal origin in the developing countries. However, current per capita consumption is low. For instance, in India in 1993-94, per capita annual consumption of milk was 51 kg and meat 1.7 kg, much less than the world average of 75 kg milk and 34 kg meat. By 2020 the per capita consumption of milk is likely to more than double and that of meat more than triple.

On the supply side, production of both milk and meat has increased at a rate of about five per cent annum-1. If these trends continue, increases in demand would be met adequately from domestic supplies. The sustainability of these trends, however, is uncertain. In the past, expanding livestock populations mainly contributed to the observed increases in production. India has a huge livestock population comprising different species, and further increase in the livestock population would be constrained severely by the declining land availability. Productivity of Indian livestock is low compared to many developed and developing countries. Cattle milk yield in India is about 12-15 per cent that in the USA, Canada, and Israel. Meat yield of sheep and goats is about 60 per cent less. Feed and fodder scarcity has been the main constraint in raising livestock productivity. Most of the feed requirement is met from crop by-products and grazing on common lands. The latter, however, have been dwindling quantitatively as well as qualitatively. The levels of adoption of breeding-, feed and nutrition-, and health-related technologies are low. It is imperative to raise these since future growth in the livestock subsector has tocome from technological changes.

The importance of livestock in India goes beyond the function of food production. It is an important source of draught power, manure for crop production and fuel for domestic use. Thus, by minimizing use of nonrenewable energy, livestock make a positive contribution to the environment. Although crops and livestock are interdependent to a large extent, the latter constitute an important mechanism for coping with the risks of crop failure. In land-scarce economies livestock provide livelihood support in terms of income and employment generation to the millions of landless and small landholders. In India, livestock wealth is mainly concentrated among the majority of marginal and small landholders. Technology-induced growth in the livestock subsector would thus improve food and nutritional security, alleviate poverty, and reduce interregional and interpersonal economic inequities. India spends only about 0.5 per cent of the agricultural gross domestic product on agricultural research. This is low compared to the average of developing countries (0.7 %) and developed countries (2.5%). Livestock research receives about 20 per cent of the total agricultural research resources. This corresponds to the contribution of livestock to the agricultural gross domestic product.

Despite the low intensity of investment in research, animal ience research over the last few decades has generated a umber of technologies in the areas of animal genetics and breeding, feed and nutrition, health, and management.

The technical feasibility of many of these has been proven under experimental conditions. Examples include crossbreeding in cattle, sheep, pigs, and poultry; chemical and biological treatment of cereal straws; and vaccines against rinderpest, influenza, and foot and mouth disease.

Studies on returns to investment in livestock research are limited.

However, sporadic evidences indicate a very high payoff to investment in livestock research and development. Despite this, the application of many technologies in the field remains limited. Except for crossbreeding, not much information is available regarding adoption and impact of other technologies. There is, thus, considerable scope to raise the productivity of livestock through application of the existing technologies.

It is against this background that the National Centre for Agricultural Economics and Policy Research (NCAP), New Delhi – an offshoot of the Indian Council of Agricultural Research (ICAR) – and the International Crops Research Institute for the Semi-Arid Tropics (ICRISAT), Patancheru, jointly organized a workshop entitled *Documentation, Adoption and Impacts of Livestock Technologies in Mixed Crop-livestock Farming Systems in India* on January 18-19, 2001 at ICRISAT. The overall goal of the workshop was toassess the technological changes taking place in India's livestock subsector and their potential in sustaining the production of livestock in particular and agricultural economy in general.

The specific objectives were to:

- Document livestock technologies related to breeding, health, nutrition, and processing.
- Identify potential technologies whose adoption and impact assessment could be tracked.
- Identify constraints in large-scale dissemination of these technologies.

Adoption and Impact of Livestock Technologies

The workshop was multidisciplinary in nature and was attended by 30–35 experts from animal, crop, and social sciences. The deliberations, apart from documentation and identification of potential technologies for their adoption and impact, also brought out some technical, socioeconomic, infrastructure, and policy issues that could help accelerate the pace of adoption of existing technologies. A synthesis of the major conclusions is presented below:

Adoption of Technologies

Over the past few decades, animal science research has offered a number of technological options that could raise the productivity of different livestock species if adopted area-wide. These include genetic enhancement of indigenous breeds through crossbreeding with exotic breeds, improvement of nutritive quality of feed and fodder through biological and chemical treatments, development of vaccines against animal diseases, improved livestock management practices, and post harvest management. Additionally, processing technologies have been developed to strengthen the vertical linkages between the farm and dairy industry. The adoption pattern of these technologies varies widely across species, farm typologies and regions.

Breeding Technologies

Genetics and breeding research have evolved many new breeds of cattle, pig, sheep, and poultry using crossbreeding techniques. These breeds have better production coefficients compared to indigenous ones. However, their adoption in the field is limited and sporadic; only about 8 per cent of cattle, 5 per cent of 4 sheep, 15 per cent of pigs, and 33 per cent of poultry populations belong to the crossbred/ improved category. The adoption level is higher in urban areas compared to rural areas. In general wide scale adoption of crossbreeds is restricted due to their non-acclimatization to the tropical climates prevailing in most parts of the country. Besides, their higher maintenance cost, lower disease resistance, and the poor success of artificial insemination (AI) are other barriers to adoption of crossbreeding. There are also species-specific constraints. The crossbred cow has to be replaced frequently to maintain the flow of benefits.

Thus, frequent and higher acquisition costs, lack of disposal facilities (cattle slaughter is banned in most Indian states), and poor draught characteristics of male cattle are important impediments to wide-scale adoption of crossbreeding technology in cattle. Nonetheless, under certain ecological and economic conditions, adoption of crossbreeding technology in cattle has been quite encouraging. The States of Kerala and Punjab, for instance, have a considerably higher proportion of crossbred cattle.

Sheep husbandry in India is practiced largely by the poor and is dependent on availability of grazing lands, which have been deteriorating in terms of both quantity and quality. In contrast to the indigenous sheep breeds that are capable of surviving even on sparse vegetation, the crossbred sheep require better nutrition. This also applies to pigs, which are often managed in scavenger systems.

In the dairy subsector the buffalo could emerge as a promising alternative to crossbred cattle because of its adaptability to varied ecological conditions, higher milk yield and higher fat content, realizing a premium price. Unlike cattle, buffalo slaughter is not banned and animals have a disposal value. These factors have favored a higher growth in buffalo population even without improved breeding interventions. However, in certain regions, nondescript low-yielding species have been upgraded using high-yielding breeds such as the Murrah.

The poultry subsector has responded well to technological changes and has grown faster than the dairy and ruminant meat sector. Enhancement of genetic potential has been the most important factor in the growth of this sector. However, this has been complemented by health and nutrition technologies. The growth trends are more prominent in specialized periurban/ urban poultry systems, because of higher demand for poultry meat and eggs in urban areas. Here, the entry of the private sector has boosted the adoption of technology and growth in poultry outputs. Backyard poultry production, however, continues to languish technologically.

Feed and Nutrition Technologies

A large number of India's livestock, particularly in the arid and semi-arid environments, suffer from inadequate feeding. The feed and fodder shortages, in fact, have been the main limiting factors in raising livestock productivity.

Cereal crop residues comprise the main feed for livestock. However, these are deficient in crude protein and several other nutrients. Concentrate feeding is restricted to lactating, high-yielding bovines and work animals. Small ruminants derive their feed requirements mainly from grazing on common lands.

Animal nutrition and crop breeding (straw/stover) research has yielded many new technologies that could augment production and improve the nutritional quality of feeds and fodder. Research on breeding for higher yield and superior quality crop residues (such as in rice, wheat, sorghum, and millets) is in progress. Studies have indicated that a 1 per cent increase in digestibility of sorghum/millet straw increases bovine milk yield by 5-6 per cent. Apart from traditional techniques of fodder chopping and conservation, technologies such as urea treatment of fodder, strategic supplementation, urea molasses mineral blocks, and bypass protein use have the potential to alleviate feed and fodder scarcity. These technologies improve digestibility and palatability of feed, reduce feed requirements, avoid feed wastage, and contribute towards improving animal productivity.

Some of these techniques, such as fodder chopping and bypass protein use, have long been in practice in many parts of the country, but are not practiced widely. The main constraint to large-scale adoption of nutrition technologies in general has been the lack of information to users.

The area under green fodder crops is also low; constituting no more than five per cent of the gross cropped area. The growth in area under fodder crops has been sluggish in most parts of the country, except in the irrigated regions. This is a reflection of the rising competition between food and fodder crops for limited land and other resources. Crop breeding research has evolved high-yielding varieties of a number of forage crops. However, these have not been adopted widely due to lack of awareness about new cultivars, nonavailability of irrigation water throughout the year, and problems of insect pests/diseases.

Common grazing lands comprise an important source of grasses, and there exists considerable scope to raise the production of grasses/shrubs from these lands through technological and management interventions.

Technological interventions such as reseeding with high-yielding grasses and watershed development, complemented with appropriate management
6 interventions such as preventing encroachment, promotion of rotational grazing practices, and charging grazing fees have helped raise the productivity of common grazing resources and thereby improved animal performance.

Disease Control Technologies

Diseases reduce the production potential of livestock. In India many deadly diseases such as rinderpest, foot and mouth disease, hemorrhagic septicemia, and black quarter are major threats to profitable livestock production.

Livestock disease control has undergone a paradigm shift in recent years. A number of biological products (vaccines) have been developed for preventive and curative disease management. The infrastructure for disease control has also expanded considerably. The main limitations to effective livestock health management are an inadequate focus on preventive measures, lack of medicines and equipment in the veterinary clinics, and ignorance among the farmers about the diseases and preventive measures. This is reflected in the frequent occurrence of many of these diseases in most parts of the country.

Processing Technologies

Postharvest technologies help producers to realize better gains from technological changes in the primary production sector. But the postharvest processing facilities are lacking in the country. Only about 20 per cent of the total milk production is processed into value-added products. The bulk of it, however, is processed into *ghee* and curds by the producers, and a large proportion of this is consumed at source. Although considerable efforts have gone into developing infrastructure for milk processing in the cooperative sector, only about 5 per cent of the total milk output is processed into table butter, cheese, milk powder, and baby foods. Information on the proportion of other livestock products entering into the value-added chain is not available. There is a considerable demand for processed meat products, but it remains constricted due to inadequate processing facilities. The same applies to export of these products. Furthermore, not enough attention has been paid towardssanitary and phytosanitary measures. Slaughterhouses are often ill equipped and unhygienic.

Low-cost processing technologies have been developed for both cottage and large industries. The rising demand for processed milk products in urban and rural areas is expected to boost future adoption of processing technologies.

Impact of Technological Change

Technological change improves the production potential of livestock and is reflected in productivity growth. The improvements in production lead to increased welfare of the producers as well as consumers of livestock products. In India, although the intensity of adoption of different technologies is low, the technological changes as discussed above, together with improved management practices have contributed to the increased output of many livestock products.

Productivity and Production

In the last three decades milk production has increased at an annual rate of about 4.5 per cent, and meat and egg production at about 5.5 per cent each. The Total Factor Productivity (TFP) index, which is a joint measure of contribution of technology and technical efficiency, has grown at a rate of 1.4 per cent a year since 1970, while the pre-1970 growth in TFP index was marginally negative. The growth in TFP is largely a result of yield-augmenting technological changes that have taken place in the dairy and poultry subsectors. The milk yield of cattle and buffalo has grown at a rate of 3.2 per cent and 1.9 per cent, respectively. In the case of poultry the egg yield has almost doubled and the feed conversion efficiency in broiler production has improved tremendously. The growth in productivity of species such as sheep and goats has been negligible.

Consumption, Prices, and Trade

Per capita consumption of livestock products has increased in the last three decades. The share of livestock products in food expenditure has almost doubled to 21 per cent since 1972–73. This is due partly to increases in the availability of livestock products and a decline in prices of major products such as milk and eggs. The real prices of milk, eggs, and pork have declined, partly due to technology-driven growth in outputs. The real prices of products of sheep and goat, where technology uptake had been lacking, witnessed an upward movement.

Improvements in productivity of dairy animals have also helped achieve self-sufficiency in milk production. The imports of milk and milk products have declined to almost zero. Also, exports of certain livestock products are increasing.Livestock are an important source of income for the rural poor. The growth in the livestock subsector is expected to contribute to poverty alleviation, as the livestock wealth is largely concentrated among the marginal and small landholders. These categories of farmers, however, face the problem of feed and fodder scarcity. Technologies, particularly those related to nutrition and health, are not capital intensive and could easily be adopted by them.

Nevertheless, the intensity of adoption of capital-intensive technologies such as crossbreeding cattle has been observed to be higher on the landless and marginal farms; in 1991–92 there were about 10 per cent crossbreeds in the adult female cattle herds of large landholders, while the landless and marginal landholders maintained 20 per cent of the crossbreeds in their herds. It is thus conjectured that technological change in the livestock subsector would generate more income and employment opportunities for the resource-poor households and contribute towards alleviation of poverty and improvements in interpersonal income distribution.

Rural-Urban Disparities

Peri-urban/urban livestock systems have long existed to cater to the urban demand for foods of animal origin. Rising urbanization and a higher growth in per capita income of the urban population is causing rapid growth in demand for food of animal origin. Developments in processing and packaging technologies have also contributed considerably to this. Thus, to meet the rapidly growing demand for milk, meat, and eggs, peri-urban livestock systems have developed much faster than the rural systems. Technology adoption and production coefficients are better in peri-urban systems. Thus this type of technological dualism is likely to strengthen with further increase in the urban demand for animal foods.

Looking Ahead

Several important points emerged from the deliberations in the workshop that need to be taken into consideration in future research and development programmes for the livestock subsector. These are:

- The success or failure of crossbreeding technologies in certain species and in certain ecologically- and economically-different environments calls for a critical review of the crossbreeding programme, particularly from the point of view of adaptability of the crossbreeds to different agroecological conditions and socioeconomic environments. The future research and development strategies should be devised accordingly, but with due consideration to animal biodiversity. In view of frequent and higher acquisition cost of crossbred cattle and a lack of outlets for surplus animals due to the ban on cattle slaughtering, the crossbreeding programme should emphasize species with a short generation interval and high social demand.
- The success rate of AI is currently low (about 20%). AI services are largely in the public sector and are heavily subsidized. The low success rate seems to act as a deterrent to adoption. It is, therefore, imperative to improve quality of breeding material, techniques, and delivery services so as to instill and reclaim the confidence of livestock owners in AI.
- Buffalo should receive increased attention in research and development programmes in view of their better adaptability to varied climates, higher milk yields, higher fat content, and disposal value.
- India is considered a storehouse of animal biodiversity in terms of species and breeds. Although India has a rich database on numbers of different species, their genetic characterization has been limited. This makes it difficult to assess the genetic diversity and evolve conservation strategies.
- Enumeration of breeds is a difficult task that needs considerable resources and the establishment of interdepartmental linkages, especially between those dealing with field surveys and animal husbandry.

- The huge livestock populations of different species are still growing (although at a slower rate) putting pressure on the feed and fodder resources. The numbers of different species thus need to be optimized considering the demand for their products and the availability of feed and fodder resources.
- Technological alternatives to improve quantity and quality of feed require greater emphasis. There are a number of traditional and new feed and fodder production and management technologies that are cost-effective and have sufficient potential to mitigate feed and fodder scarcity. The best way to promote these technologies is to generate wide awareness among the farmers and to publicize their improved benefit-cost ratios.
- Cereal crop residues form the bulk of the feed dry matter. Therefore, cropbreeding programmes should emphasize breeding of superior quality straw/stover of dual-purpose crops without sacrificing grain yield. Straw quality should also be improved through better management of diseases.
- In view of the small proportion of total cropped area under fodder crops and sluggish growth therein, crop breeding should focus on high-yielding and high-quality fodder and forage varieties. Economic incentives (input subsidies for growing forage crops) and vertical integration of the livestock subsector, by developing marketing and processing infrastructure and institutions, would result in farmers bringing more land into fodder crop production.
- Deterioration of common grazing lands is a matter of concern, particularly for sustainability of small ruminant production in ecologically-fragile regions. It is therefore imperative to check quantitative and qualitative deterioration of common grazing lands through technological (watershed management, reseeding with improved grasses), social (participatory management), and policy interventions (legal action against encroachment).
- Disease monitoring should be accorded a high priority, considering the frequent occurrence of many potentially lethal animal diseases. The policy emphasis should shift from curative to preventive disease management. There is sufficient manpower available for this in the public sector that can be utilized gainfully without much additional overhead costs. Marginal investments in medicines and supplies would yield considerable economic and social benefits.
- Linkages between research and extension need to be strengthened for effective transfer of technologies. The huge numbers of field veterinarians and auxiliaries should shoulder the responsibility of technology transfer.

- Social scientists should play a proactive role in evaluation of technologies for their social acceptability, constraints, and impact. This kind of integration of biological and social sciences would help improve the social and economic efficiency of research.
- Developments in biotechnology are expected to provide solutions to many problems constraining livestock production. The biotechnology research however needs to be prioritized considering the importance of the production constraints. The largest impact of biotechnology in the shortterm can be realized in the field of animal nutrition and health.

CHAPTER 5
Livestock Sub-sector in India

Livestock are an integral component of agriculture in India and make multifaceted contributions to the growth and development of the agricultural sector. Livestock help improve food and nutritional security by providing nutrient-rich food products, generate income and employment and act as a cushion against crop failure, provide draught power and manure inputs to the crop subsector, and contribute to foreign exchange through exports. Also, by using crop residues as feed, livestock save land for food production that would otherwise be used for fodder production. Additionally, livestock makesubstantial contributions to environmental conservation, supplying draught power and manure for fertilizer and domestic fuel that save on the use of petro-products. This paper assesses the contribution of livestock subsector to the growth of agriculture and socioeconomic development.

India possesses one of the largest livestock populations in the world. In 1992 the country had 205 million cattle, 84 million buffalo, 115 million goats, 51 million sheep, 13 million pigs, one million horses and 307 million poultry. The livestock sector is both expanding and adapting in response to economic, technological, and environmental factors. In general, the numbers of different species are increasing; populations of poultry, pigs, goats, and buffalo have grown faster compared to other species. The populations of draught animals have witnessed negative and decelerating trend.

Broadly the Trends Indicate:

- Deceleration in growth of populations of almost all species except poultry. The decelerating trend is, however, stronger in the case of small ruminants. Thus there is a tendency towards stabilization of the livestock population in the long run.

- A gradual shift in favour of animals that are less capital intensive, have short generation intervals, and better feed conversion and economic efficiency.

In terms of output flow, milk continues to dominate the production structure with meat and meat products coming next. However, the economic structure of livestock production is undergoing a gradual transformation. The shares of mutton and pork, beef, poultry meat, and eggs have been increasing, while that of milk is declining. The share of buffalo milk in total milk production is increasing. The structure of meat production is shifting from small to large ruminants, poultry, and pigs.

Livestock are linked closely with crop production. The linkages arestronger on smaller land holdings. Households having less than 2 ha of land possess a larger share of livestock. The average size of livestock holding is small. The average number of animals per 100 households is 198 bovines and 85 ovines. The number of animals owned, however, has a direct relationship with size of land-holding.

Livestock production involves few cash expenses; animals are often fed on homegrown crop residues and grasses from common grazing lands. Crop residues account for more than 50 per cent of the total dry matter intake in several regions. Use of concentrate feed is low and is limited only to more productive bovines. Small ruminants are maintained mainly by grazing. This results in low productivity. Mean milk yield of lactating indigenous cattle is 620 kg annum, cross-bred cattle 2130 kg annum and buffalo 1340 kg annum^{-1}. Cattle milk yield is about half of the world average and about 12 per cent to 15 per cent of that in the USA, Canada, and Israel. Average meat yield of goats, sheep, and pigs in India is 10, 12, and 55 kg annum respectively; about 60 per cent less than those of the above countries. Offtake rate of cattle and buffalo is low. About 6 per cent cattle, 11 per cent buffalo, 38 per cent goats, and 33 per cent sheep are slaughtered every year. These figures suggest considerablescope for raising livestock productivity and production.

Economic Contributions

Even at low productivity and off-take rates, livestock contribute significantly to economic development. Their developmental role in the mixed farming systems transcends direct economic benefits. Use of manure contributes to agricultural sustainability and conservation of the environment. Using draught animal power helps save nonrenewable energy such as petroleum. Livestock provide raw material for industry. Additionally, livestock act as a storehouse of capital and an insurance against crop failure. With production concentrated among small landholders, livestock help improve income distribution.

Contribution to National Income

In 1997-98 the livestock subsector accounted for about 23 per cent of the agricultural gross domestic product (AgDP). This has increased gradually from 14 per cent in 1980-81. On the other hand the contribution of the agricultural sector to gross domestic product (GDP) decreased from 35 per cent in 1980-81 to 26 per cent in 1997-98. In other words the livestock subsector has grown at a faster rate than the crop sector. The respective annual rates of growth in GDP from livestock and agriculture are about 7.3 per cent and 3.1 per cent respectively.

Agricultural Input

Livestock provide draught power and dung manure to the crop subsector. In 1996–97, draught animals accounted for 14 per cent of the total power available to the agricultural sector. Share of livestock in the total power availability declined sharply from 69 per cent in 1961-62 to 25 per cent in 1981-82. However, its absolute contribution has remained almost unchanged at about 20 million kilo Watt.

Dung manure is an important contribution. About half of the total dung produced is used as manure and the rest as domestic fuel. In 1970-71 dung manure accounted for about 43 per cent of the total value of manure and fertilizers used in agriculture. This declined drastically to 23 per cent in 1980-81 and to about 13 per cent during the 1990s. However the absolute value of manure has been increasing steadily.

Employment and Poverty

Livestock provide livelihood support to millions of people having little access to land. About one-third of the population lives below the poverty line, mainly comprising of landless, marginal, and small farmers. Since the distribution of livestock is more equitable compared to land, growth in the livestock sector is considered to be anti-poverty and equity-oriented. Though the contribution of livestock to AgGDP has been rising continuously, contribution to rural employment is not so encouraging. In terms of principal activity status livestock employs about five per cent of the rural work force. Its share however has declined to three per cent in 1990s. Low share in rural employment is because livestock rearing in India is taken up as a subsidiary to crop production.

Food and Nutrition

The diet of an average Indian is cereal-based and lacks nutrient-rich foods such as pulses, fruits, vegetables, and animal products. Low intake of these products results in nutritional deficiencies. About 30 per cent of the population suffers from malnutrition. The problem is severe in populations having little access to cultivated land. Diversification of diet towards animal products can help improve nutrition. Intake of livestock products, however, is low compared to that in many developing and developed countries. The food basket, though, is gradually diversifying towards livestock products. In 1972-73 livestock products accounted for about 14 per cent of the food expenditure, which gradually increased to about 20 per cent in 1993-94. Consumption of livestock products is expected to increase faster with sustained economic growth and attendant increases in per capita incomes.

Trade in Livestock

India has a negligible share in world trade in livestock products. During the triennium ending 1998, the average value of livestock product exports was Rs. 13500 million annum^{-1}, which was only one per cent of the total export earnings and 6.2 per cent of the agricultural export earnings. Meat and meat products are the main livestock products exported, accounting for over 90 per cent of the total export earnings from the livestock subsector. In recent years the export performance of livestock products has improved due to trade liberalization.

In 1998 India imported livestock products worth Rs. 1877 million comprising 0.1 per cent of total imports and 1.5 per cent of agricultural imports. Hides and skins account for 95 per cent of the total value of livestock product imports. India's import of milk, hides, and skins has declined sharply in the past few years. At present almost the entire demand for milk is met through domestic supplies.

Livestock also contribute towards environmental conservation, although in the past years this has been criticized by environmentalists due to certain negative externalities caused by overgrazing and greenhouse gas emissions. Despite these criticisms, the livestock subsector will remain an important economic activity benefiting millions of landless, marginal, and small farmers in the country.

The contribution of science and technology to the growth and development of India's agricultural sector since the mid-1960s is self-evident. Developments in research and production infrastructure and encouraging government policies acted as catalysts for the technology-driven growth in agriculture, helping the country achieve self-sufficiency in foodgrains and many other commodities. In other areas such as horticulture, fisheries, and livestock considerable technical progress has taken place, but impacts have been slow and sporadic, and its analysis in an economic framework has largely remained undocumented. The contribution of livestock to income and employment generation is second only to that of crops. However, its productivity is low compared to the world average. Cattle milk yield is about half the world average of 2072 kg annum^{-1}, and the same applies to beef and pork production. The situation becomes more depressing when compared with the developed countries. Average milk yield of cattle is 13 per cent that of the USA and 16 per cent that of Canada.

Sheep and pork yields are about 60 per cent less. These figures suggest considerable scope for improvement of India's livestock productivity. Nonetheless, in recent years certain outputs of livestock such as milk, meat, and eggs have been growing at an annual rate of 5 per cent or more. The sustainability of these trends in the long run is unclear, as the current production environment has several constraints. Feed has been a limiting constraint to ruminant livestock production and this problem is likely to continue in the near future, considering the huge dimensions of livestock populations. Common grazing lands have been deteriorating quantitatively as well qualitatively. Animals are fed on crop by-products and grasses from roadsides and other marginal lands. Feeding of grains and other concentrates is inadequate, and the competition for grains will intensify with increasing human and livestock populations. Thus technology will be a key factor in improving the productivity of India's livestock subsector.

Status of Technological Change

Significant research advances have been made in the areas of animal breeding, nutrition, and health. Many research products have been found to be technically and economically viable under controlled experimental conditions, but the extent of their on-farm application has been rather low. Examples of such technologies include improved animal breeds, and chemical/biological treatment of straw and fodder. A brief review of the existing, as well as potential, technologies that could influence the growth of the livestock subsector is presented below.

Breed Improvement

Cross-breeding of low-yielding indigenous breeds with high-yielding exotic breeds has been widely acknowledged as a valuable strategy to improve animal productivity. Sporadic attempts to improve the genetic potential of different livestock species (poultry, sheep, and cattle) in India were initiated during the latter half of the nineteenth century, but no significant achievements were reported. In the 1950s, systematic crossbreeding research and development programmes were initiated. Cross-breeding research has focused mainly on cattle because of their dual role of milk production and use as draught animals in the crop subsector. A number of cross-breeds with improved production potentials have evolved, which include Haryana × Friesian, Haryana × Jersey, Haryana × Brown Swiss, Rathi × Jersey, Gir × Jersey, Gir × Friesian, and Sahiwal × Jersey.

Adoption of crossbreeding technology has been slow. Only 7.5 per cent of the cattle population consists of crossbreeds. In other animal species too the status of crossbreeding is similar. About 5 per cent of the sheep and 15 per cent of pigs are crossbreeds.

The reasons are nonacclimatization of crossbreeds to the Indian climate and lack of resistance to disease. The poultry subsector, however, has achieved notable success. Improved poultry constitute about 34 per cent of the total population. Cross-breeding is also practised in other species. Statistical information regarding these, however, is lacking. Between 1982 and 1992, the population of cross-bred cattle increased at an annual rate of 5.6 per cent. On the other hand, indigenous stock seemed to be approaching stabilization. The annual growth rate of indigenous cattle was 0.5 per cent although the female population witnessed a slightly higher growth. Low milk yield and decreasing demand for draught animals are the main factors for slow growth in indigenous stock. These trends indicate a gradual substitution of indigenous cattle by cross-breds.

Despite being an important milch species, the buffalo has not received much attention in breed improvement. Development efforts have focused on upgrading low-yielding breeds through artificial insemination. The buffalo population increased at a rate of 1.9 per cent per year between 1982 and 1992. The female population witnessed faster growth than the male population. Its adaptability to a wide range of climatic conditions, higher milk yield compared to indigenous cattle, and price premium on milk due to its higher fat content have favoured faster growth in the buffalo population. Furthermore, the disposal value of buffalo is higher; unlike cattle there are fewer restrictions on buffalo slaughter.

The population of improved poultry grew at an annual rate of about nine per cent, more than double that of indigenous poultry. Technological transformation of the poultry subsector seems to be market-driven as the demand for poultry meat and eggs is income-elastic and has been rising continuously. The populations of cross-bred sheep and pigs also grew faster than their indigenous counterparts.

Despite this, cross-breeding technology has not gained a foothold. One of the possible reasons is nonacclimatization of cross-bred animals to varying climatic conditions in the country, causing a number of health- and physiology-related problems. In this context, researcher mentions that 'in using exotic breeds as a strategy forimprovement it seems to have been assumed that genotype-environmental interactions do not exist or the optimal economic and sustainable crossing structure would automatically be developed. Indeed in much of Asia, there appears to be a history of introducing breeds without proper evaluation andwith little or no thought given to the breeding structure which will best use the available material'. Higher initial investment and maintenance costs also limit widespread adoption of cross-breds. The first cross animals perform very well, but the performance of animals from subsequent crosses declines significantly.

Therefore, cross-bred animals need to be replaced frequently in order to sustain the flow of benefits. Frequent acquisition of first cross-breds, without realizing appropriate disposal value of the subsequently crossed animals, renders cross-breeding technology capital intensive. In this context more than 50 per cent of the farmers in Karnataka maintaining crossbreeds depend on the market for replacement of first cross animals. This is to avoid the risk of getting unwanted male calves and the associated problems of breeding and feeding the calf.

As indigenous cattle are sources of both milk and draught power for agriculture, their replacement by cross-bred cattle has been slow. Cross-bred males are considered inefficient for draught purposes compared to indigenous males, although animal physiology research has shown that the difference is marginal. Furthermore, machines have emerged as a major source of power in Indian agriculture, although mechanization does not appear to have affected the population of working animals significantly. The number of tractors per thousand ha increased from 0.6 in 1972 to 10.9 in 1992, while the working bovines declined marginally. Mechanization has affected working bovines mainly on medium and large farms. The number of working bovines declined from 410 in 1972 to 180 per 1000 ha in 1992 on medium farms and from 210 to 50 on large farms. On small and marginal farms, most of which did not have tractors, working animals provided most of the draught power requirement in 1972. In 1992, the number of tractors on these farms had increased to 4.1 and 7.8 per thousand ha without a concomitant decline in the number of working animals.

Nonetheless, crossbreeding strategies have been successful under certain environments and economic conditions as in Kerala and Punjab. In Kerala the milk production system is cattle-based. Indigenous breeds are poor as milk producers and for draught power. Cropping pattern is largely plantation-oriented, requiring less draught power. Furthermore, unlike in many other states, cattle slaughter is not prohibited by law in Kerala, thus making it easier to cull out the low-yielding and unwanted animals. In Punjab, on the other hand, increasing intensification of agriculture required more power to perform agricultural operations on time, which indigenous cattle were not capable of providing. Moreover, feed resources have never been a problem in Punjab.

Feed and Nutrition

Adequate provision of feed is essential to livestock production, and its scarcity has been one of the major limiting factors in improving productivity in India. Crop residues and by-products comprise the main feeds, accounting for 40 per cent of the total consumption. Green fodder contributes 26 per cent, while concentrates contribute only three per cent. The rest comes from grazing. Stall-feeding is largely confined to buffalo, cross-bred cattle, and draught animals. Small ruminants mainly feed on grasses from village common property resources, roadsides, and harvested fields, and supplementary feeding is lacking except in large commercial herds.

There is a large gap between requirement and availability of feed at the national level. Recent estimates indicate that in India the dry fodder deficit is 31 per cent, green fodder 23 per cent and concentrates 47 per cent. Regional deficits are however, more important than the national deficit. Of 55 microagroecoregions, 43 are deficient in feed. Most of the deficient regions lie in the arid and semi-arid agroecological zones. The feed deficiency is due to heavy population pressure, the quantitative and qualitative deterioration in common grazing lands resulting in low biomass production, and the lack of adoption of fodder production technologies. The problem of underfeeding can be overcome partly throughtechnological interventions such as the biological/chemical treatment of feed.

Techniques such as urea treatment of straws, urea-molasses mineral blocks, and bypass protein improve nutritional value of feed and its palatability. Urea treatment has been reported to reduce green fodder requirements by about 20-40 per cent and increase cattle milk yield by 10-20 per cent. Under experimental conditions, bypass protein technology has been found to reduce concentrate requirements by 40 per cent and dry matter requirements by 24 per cent. Despite such benefits, its application is limited because of supply constraints and a lack of concerted efforts to transfer the technologies and demonstrate their cost-benefit ratios.

The area under fodder crops in the country has hardly ever exceeded five per cent of the gross cropped area and it is uncertain whether this will increase in the future. Increasing demand for livestock products calls for more allocation of land to fodder crops, but current priorities for food grains, pulses, and oilseeds seem to constrain the fodder area expansion. Availability of by-products of food crops as animal feed is expected to increase with an increase in area under these crops.

Plant breeding research has also focused more on increasing grain yield than vegetative yield, both in terms of quantity and quality. In an ex-ante framework have estimated that one per cent improvement in digestibility of coarse cereal fodder through genetic manipulation would enhance production of different livestock outputs by 3-10 per cent.

Animal Health

Diseases reduce the production potential of livestock. There are a number of diseases such as rinderpest (RP), foot and mouth disease (FMD), hemorrhagic septicemia (HS), mastitis, brucellosis, tuberculosis, and black quarter (BQ) that affect livestock production and cause enormous economic losses. An estimated livestock output worth Rs 50 billion is lost annually due to disease. In view of this, the National Commission on Agriculture (1976) observed that 'livestock development programmes cannot possibly succeed unless a well organized animal health service is built up and protection of livestock against diseases and pests, particularly the deadly infectious ones, is assured'. To this end, animal health infrastructure has been strengthened. Between 1984-85 and 1997-98 the number of veterinary polyclinics, hospitals, and dispensaries has increased considerably. There are 27,543 first aid centres and mobile dispensaries. Apart from these, there are 250 diagnostic laboratories and 26 veterinary vaccine production units. Twenty-one viral vaccines, bacterial vaccines and 13 diagnostic reagents are now produced in the country.

Impact of Technological Change

Contribution of Technology

The contribution of the livestock subsector to agricultural gross domestic product has increased from 14 per cent in 1980-81 to 23 per cent in 1998-99 at 1980-81 prices. Since 1970-71 the livestock subsector has been growing at a rate of about 3.6 per cent a year. The growth is a result of technological change, better feeding and management The Total Factor Productivity (TFP) index, a joint measure of contribution of technology and technical efficiency, has been growing at an annual rate of 1.4 per cent since 1970, while in the pre-1970s growth in the TFP index was marginally negative. This implies that technology along with management is gradually becoming a driving force in the growth of the livestock subsector.

Production and Productivity

From the point of research and development priorities, it is more important to assess the contribution of technology at the commodity or species level. However the data limitations, particularly on the input side, make it difficult to generate commodity-specific estimates of TFP. Still, productivity trends provide a fair assessment of the impact of technological change.

Milk

Between 1972 and 1997 cattle and buffalo milk production grew at rates of 5.2 per cent and 4.4 per cent a year, respectively. The productivity of cattle andbuffalo increased at a rate of 3.2 per cent and 1.9 per cent, respectively, and thus contributed about 61 per cent (cattle) and 44 per cent (buffalo) to their output growths.

Over time the growth in production, as well as in productivity, has accelerated, although productivity has increased faster than production. This indicates that milk production growth is gradually becoming productivity-centered. In cattle, acceleration in productivity growth is partly due to an increase in the population of crossbreeds with high milk yielding capacity.

Average milk yield of a cross-bred lactating cow in 1993-94 was 5.8 kg day^{-1} about 3.5 times more than that of a lactating indigenous cow. Lactating cross-bred cows comprised 14.2 per cent of the total lactating cows and contributed 36.3 per cent to total cattle milk production. Buffalo accounted for 45 per cent of total lactating bovines and contributed 57 per cent to total milk production.

Despite substantial growth in productivity, a large gap remains between obtainable and realized yield. In 1993-94 mean annual yield of indigenous cattle was 618 kg, while the lactation yield on research farms for some of the important milch breeds varied from 1137 kg to 1931 kg. In cross-bred cows and buffalo the yield gap, however, is not as large as for indigenous cows. Average milk yield of cross-bred cows was 2127 kg a year, as against the obtainable lactation yield range of 2326 kg to 3196 kg. Similarly in buffalo, the annual milk yield was 1333 kg, while the obtainable yield varied between 1111 kg to 1855 kg per lactation depending on the breed. In the eastern and northeastern states milk yield is abysmally low.

In Orissa, Nagaland, Mizoram, Meghalaya, and Assam the average milk yield of indigenous cattle ranges between one-fourth to one half of the national average. Buffalo milk yield in these states is also much less than the national average. These figures indicate both the severity of constraints and opportunities in raising milk production in such areas.

Meat

Total meat production in the country grew at a rate of 4.2 per cent annually between 1972 and 1997. The growth in contributions from different species, however, varied widely. Maximum growth occurred in beef and veal output (7.1%), followed by pork (6.3%), poultry meat (5.6%), buffalo meat (4.1%), goat meat (2.4%), and mutton and lamb (2.2%). Growth in total meat production has improved slightly in recent years, mainly due to accelerated growth in contributions from buffalo, sheep, and poultry.

Growth in meat production is due largely to increases in the number of animals slaughtered, as the increase in yield is negligible in almost all species. Recent trends, however, indicate improvement in meat yield of cattle, buffalo, and sheep, and a decline in meat yield of goats and pigs. A number of factors are responsible for poor meat productivity and growth. Cattle and buffalo are raised mainly for milk and provide meat as an adjunct. Poor quality animals are slaughtered. Only surplus buffalo males and unproductive cattle and buffalo stock, often old, infertile, and malnourished are sent to slaughterhouses. Among the reasons for stagnation in yields of small ruminants are a deterioration of common grazing lands, and lack of supplementary feeding. Improved nutrition and veterinary care would help raise meat yields. However, in the long run, genetic improvement would be a key factor in sustaining the output growth of these animals.

Eggs

During 1972–97, egg and poultry meat production increased at the rate of 5.6 per cent a year. However, in recent years, growth in poultry meat production accelerated while egg production growth decreased substantially. Genetic improvement efforts contributed substantially to fast growth of the poultry subsector. About two-thirds of the total egg production in the country in 1993-94 came from improved layers that comprised 48 per cent of the total egg laying population. Average egg yield of an improved layer is 232 eggs annum^{-1} more than double the yield of an indigenous layer. There is clearly considerable scope for increasing egg production by substituting indigenous layers with improved breeds.

Incidence of Disease

Many diseases such as FMD, BQ, HS, and anthrax still prevail in varying intensities despite the substantial growth in animal health infrastructure. However concerted efforts under the rinderpest eradication programme have achieved notable success in alleviating the incidence of the disease. On the other hand, the incidence of FMD, BQ, and HS has increased in recent years. This implies a lack of focus on preventive disease management.

Livestock Products and Their Prices

Technological change influences commodity prices via a shift in supply. A downward shift in supply of a commodity is expected to bring down its price, *ceteris paribus*. The price of milk did not exhibit any definite trends during the 1970s. It showed some stability during the 1980s and thereafter started declining. A similar trend is observed in the case of butter, except during the late 1980s when its price showed an upward trend. There has been significant growth in milk production in the country since the initiation of the Operation Flood programme under which concerted efforts have been made to create a production and marketing infrastructure. Besides raising domestic production it also helped reduce dependence on imports, so that about 99 per cent of the milk demand in the country is met through domestic production.

The real wholesale price of mutton has shown a rising trend with slight year to year fluctuations. This is because of slow growth in mutton production. On the other hand, beef prices showed a declining trend between. 1974-75 and 1985-86, and began increasing thereafter due to a rise in export demand. The general trend in the price of pork is declining but with wide fluctuations. The real price of eggs has been declining steadily.

Putting together price and productivity trends gives an idea of the impact of technological change in the livestock subsector. In general a negative relationship exists between productivity and real price trends in the case of milk, egg, and pork, supplies of which have partially increased due to adoption of improved technology.

Equity

Improving efficiency of livestock production through technological interventions is considered equity-oriented on the premise that the livestock wealth is more equitably distributed than land. The relationship between rate of adoption of cross-bred cattle and size of land holding shows higher proportions of crossbreeds in total cattle stock in the landless and marginal farm categories, although the size of cattle holding there is smaller. It is thus conjectured that technological change would create more income-generating opportunities for landless and marginal farmers. But larger farmers would benefit more from it by virtue of having larger number of crossbreeds and better access to feed resources. This is however a contentious issue and needs to be examined further.

Rural-Urban Disparities

The rising urban populations are causing a rapid increase in the demand for animal foods. This has resulted in the rapid growth of peri-urban livestock systems. Higher growth in urban livestock populations is an indicator of this. Unlike rural livestock systems, peri-urban systems are commercially oriented and intensive in nature, depending mainly on purchased inputs.

Technical coefficients of cross-bred animals are better under peri-urban systems and adoption of technology is therefore also expected to be higher. For instance, in 1992 about 20 per cent of the cattle and 45 per cent of the poultry population in urban areas were that of cross-bred/improved species. Corresponding figures for rural areas stood at seven per cent and 32 per cent. Adoption of technologies related to health, nutrition, and management is also expected to be higher in peri-urban areas. Thus there might be increasing technological dualism between rural and urban areas with the rising demand for livestock products.

Future Scenario

India's livestock subsector is at the crossroads. On the one hand India has an enormous and diverse livestock population, the production potential of which remains untapped due to feed and fodder scarcity and poor application of technologies. On the other hand sustained economic growth, market-oriented policies, and trade liberalization are opening up opportunities for the growth and development of this subsector. The demand for livestock products is income elastic and is expected to grow further. India can also derive substantial benefits from the emerging international economic order under WTO through export of livestock products. At present, export of livestock products is constrained by low livestock productivity, lack of value addition, and inadequate phytosanitary standards. The pace of development and diffusion of yield-improving technologies and the development of processing infrastructure would determine largely how best the emerging opportunities could be used for the benefit of producers and consumers.

- Cross-breeding programmes should be reviewed at regional levels for their success as well as failure. The strategy of introducing exotic breeds to improve the local breeds also requires rethinking.
- The buffalo, which holds the promise of increasing milk production considering its adaptability to a wide range of climatic conditions and better feed conversion efficiency, should be studied intensively. Unlike cattle,there are few restrictions on buffalo slaughter and a breakthrough in buffalo crossbreeding would provide a big impetus to the livestock economy.
- Optimization of the livestock population and qualitative improvements in feed resources are the main ways to improve productivity. This involves culling of unproductive and unwanted surplus population, which is often not feasible because of restrictions on cattle slaughter and sociocultural and religious taboos on meat consumption. The export of live cattle to countries where demand for beef is high is a possibility that should be explored. Besides earning foreign exchange, this would also relieve pressure on feed resources and improve productivity of the remaining stock. Improving quality of available feed resources is technology dependent and should be accorded high priority in the research agenda of both crop and animal science research.
- Disease prevention and control must complement these efforts. Veterinary institutions often lack the essential medicines and equipment, and the quality of veterinary services is poor. The emphasis should shift from curative to preventive disease management and to improvement of infrastructure.

- Developments in biotechnology are expected to provide solutions to many problems currently constraining the livestock production potential. The role of biotechnology in improving fodder quality is well established.
- Similarly, research in the areas of animal breeding, embryo transfer, and gene cloning could help improve animal productivity. Research strategies must be prioritized on the basis of their urgency, gestation period, probability of success and adoption, availability of research resources, and economic outcomes. Research strategies that are less capital intensive, with a low gestation period, a higher probability of success and acceptability by clientele, and that yield a good rate of return should be emphasized. Animal nutrition and health fall in this category. In the long run however, genetic research would be a key factor in growth and development of the livestock subsector.
- Current livestock economics research is inadequate for a proper understanding of the livestock subsector as it has focused mainly on assessment of microlevel production efficiency of cross-bred cattle vis-à-vis other dairy animals. Aspects related to nutrition, health, and processing technologies have remained largely unexplored. There is a similar lack of socioeconomic studies on ovine, caprine, equine, and poultry production systems. Social sciences, particularly economics, should therefore be integrated into biological research in a significant way from the initiation of technology generation to its diffusion and impact assessment.
- Other issues of economic importance that should be addressed are estimation of feed consumption, and economic losses due to disease. The former are currently based on feeding norms and few efforts have been made to estimate actual feed fodder consumption or the contributions from grazing lands and forests. Similarly, information available on economic losses due to disease is based on guesses rather than on sound economic principles. These issues need to be addressed in a multidisciplinary mode for proper planning of development of the livestock subsector. Issues of sustainability of livestock production systems, their environmentaleffects, and the role of technology in addressing these issues also merit attention for an in-depth empiricism in a resource economics perspective.

CHAPTER 6
Indigenous Dairy Breeds

Planned development of the livestock subsector in India began with the launch of the First Five-year Plan in 1951. This sought to break the centuries-old vicious cycle of large numbers, acute shortage of feeds, recurrent animal epidemics, and low productivity. The First Plan goals in cattle development were primarily to:

- Increase milk production.
- Improve milk supply to the large urban demand centers; and
- Improve the quality and supply of draught animals for agriculture.

The policies laid down for achieving these goals were selective breeding of indigenous cows belonging to the descript dairy breeds, upgrading of non-descript cows with indigenous dairy breeds, and selective breeding of draught breeds.

The launch of the Key Village Scheme (KVS) in 1951 was the action programme to increase milk production and, to an extent, alleviate the shortages in fodder supply. The Livestock Improvement Act enabling compulsory castration of scrub bulls was an attempt to regulate the cattle population growth as well as to enforce a degree of selectivity in breeding. Artificial insemination (AI) was introduced around the same period, as a tool for rapid improvement in the genetic make-up of the stock. Cross-breeding of Indiancattle with European dairy breeds was introduced as an experiment in the hill areas during this period.

The country's milk production continued to be stagnant over the first two decades postindependence. The increase in milk production during the first three plan periods was a mere three million tonnes. By the end of the third plan the inadequacies of the KVS were apparent, and serious policy reorientation was required to engineer sustained increases in milk production.

The interval between the third and fourth plans during 1966–69 witnessed some of the most momentous policy initiatives by the government in the livestock subsector, particularly for cattle. Development of rural milk sheds and movement of processed milk from the rural areas to urban demand centers became the cornerstone of government policy. This single, epochmaking policy of the government in the late 1960s – to develop dairying in rural milk sheds through milk producers' cooperatives – galvanized the Indian dairy industry to erupt into unprecedented growth.

This policy found institutionalization in the National Dairy Development Board (NDDB), its translation into action in the "Operation Flood Project" and the nationwide cooperative movement launched under the project for marketing the rurally produced milk during the early 1970s. The sluggishness in milk production gave way to rapid growth – from 22 million tonnes in 1970 to nearly 69 million tonnes in 1996. The KVS matured into the Intensive Cattle Development Project, which later became the Government's flagship programme for cattle development. Cross-breeding of nondescript cattle became the National Policy for increasing milk production and gained momentum and economic relevance, as the cooperative network under Operation Flood provided the much needed market stimulus and price support for milk. Under the different Five Year Plans, the central policy for cattledevelopment was direct action through state departments. All breeding support activities such as production of bulls, evaluation of bulls, andproduction of semen are part of the direct action of the various state governments. Infrastructure for generating these inputs, such as breeding farms, semen production stations, and training institutions, is exclusively in the government sector. Over the 60 years of planned development, this has saddled the state governments with a vast infrastructure and an army of professionals.

Breeding Policy for Cattle

Breeding policies for cattle were formally attempted and finalized by the state and central governments based on the recommendations of the working group appointed by the Ministry of Agriculture in 1962. The breeding policy recommended:

- Selective breeding of the pure Indian dairy breeds of cattle for milk production.Selective breeding of pure Indian draught breeds of cattle for better draught animals.
- Selective breeding of dual-purpose breeds for improving both their milk and work output.

- Upgrading of the nondescript Indian cattle with selected Indian donor breeds for improving body size and milk/work output.

Cross-breeding of Indigenous Cattle

Cross-breeding of Indian cattle with exotic dairy breeds was a practice encouraged by the British in the late 19th century and there were many pockets of high-yielding cross-bred cows, particularly the plantation areas in the hills. With the advent of AI and the limited introduction of cross-breeding in the hill areas, official policy started recognizing cross-breeding of cattle with European donor breeds as a major option for improving milk production. Several bilateral cross-breeding projects in collaboration with external age ncies (UNDP in Haringhatta, West Bengal; Indo-Danish Project in Hasserghatta, Bangalore, Karnataka; and the Indo-Swiss Project in Mattupatty, Kerala) were established during 1962–64, to study the potential of the policy and to evaluate its impact on milk production and sustainability under Indian conditions.

Cross-breeding of non-descript Indian cattle on field scale started only in 1964 with the launch of the Intensive Cattle Development Project (ICDP) by the Government of India. By 1969 it had become the official policy. The pioneering work on large-scale cross-breeding in different parts of India by the Bharathiya Agro-Industries Foundation (BAIF) and the strong recommendations of the National Commission on Agriculture (NCA) in 1974, laid all adverse criticism to rest and legitimised cross-breeding as a powerful tool to rapidly enhance milk production in India.

The technical programme for cross-breeding approved by the governments was to use nondescript cattle as the foundation stock and to breed them using semen from exotic donor breeds. This would produce half-breeds with equal inheritance from the two widely different parents, one contributing endurance and the other the much-needed higher productivity. The policy thereafter was to breed the half-breeds among themselves inter se in subsequent generations, to create large intermating populations of half-breeds, perpetually maintaining the share of inheritance halfway between the Indian and the exotic parents.

Genetic progress in the intermating populations would be maintained andpromoted through use of genetically evaluated half-bred sires for the *inter se* mating. The exotic donor breeds initially used were Jersey, Brown Swiss, Red Dane, and Holstein-Friesian. The choice of the exotic donor has now narrowed down to Jersey and Holstein – with Holstein predominating by popular choice.

The government did not plan to cross-breed pure Indian breeds of cattle, but the spectacular increase in milk yield in the cross-bred progenies generated overwhelming demand for such cattle all over India. This necessitated the expansion of the cross-breeding programme nationwide; even to the home tracts of the pure Indian breeds. The policy for selectively breeding indigenous breeds of cattle did not take off for various reasons:

- Improvement in production and productivity were not spectacular enough to encourage farmers to progressively support it.
- Proven sires among these breeds were not available.
- There were no breeders' organisations for these breeds in their respective home tracts to provide technical and advisory services to breeders.

Technologies Involved in Cross-breeding of Cattle

Cross-breeding of cattle is based on the following techniques from two major branches of biological sciences, reproductive biology, and quantitative genetics:

- Genetic evaluation of sires and dams as aids for selection.
- Artificial insemination for moving massive genetic payloads into animal populations.
- Multiple ovulation and embryo transfer to improve the intensity and accuracy of selection and to reduce the period of evaluation.

The rapid growth of molecular biology and biotechnology found application in the field of animal reproduction not only to develop and exploit domesticated animals, but also as models for epoch-making research in embryo biotechnology such as cloning, gene therapy, gene transfers, and transgenic animals. This explosion of knowledge has influenced breeding technology, particularly in bovine species, and presented the professionals in this field with powerful technologies and precision techniques.

For *inter se* mating of half-breeds, genetically evaluated half-breed bulls are a basic requirement that India does not have in adequate numbers. Bulls to be used for AI are evaluated for their ability to transmit economic traadvantageous to the breeders and the industry, i.e. milk yield, fat and protein percentage, fertility, and a number of allied factors. None of these factors can be measured on the bull itself. The bulls are evaluated on the basis of actual measurement of the desired traits in their daughters (progeny tests) or siblings, both full and half (sibling tests in open nucleus breeding systems or ONBS).

Genetic Evaluation of Cross-bred Sires

Sire Evaluation through Progeny Tests

A progeny-testing programme requires:

1. a large ongoing AI service; and
2. a well-structured Field Performance Recording Programme.

The duration of the test under Indian conditions would be about 60 months for the provisional evaluation based on past records of daughters, and 65 months for evaluation based on full first lactation records. By the time the test is completed the bull is 5 to 6 years old. Only a few select institutions have succeeded in producing proven cross-bred sires through progeny tests. The Kerala Livestock Development Board (KLDB) has been successfully testing several batches of cross-bred bulls for the past 20 years. The BAIF, Pune and the Sabarmati Ashram Gaushala, Bidaj, Gujarat, have ongoing programmes for progeny testing of cross-bred bulls.

The test involves complex statistical models for analysis of the data once collected, but the data themselves and the data collection procedures are simple enough, even though they need organisation and accuracy. The statistical design involves testing of provisionally selected bulls, at least 20 to a batch, testing mating (a minimum of some 2000 randomly identified mates per bull spread over several districts or even states), and collection of the first lactation records of at least 200 randomly chosen daughters per bull.

The principle of the test is to analyze the variance among the records, partition the genetic variance from the total variance, and work out the breeding value of the bulls. The actual procedure practiced is to compare the standardized records of the daughters of each bull with the daughters of all other bulls in the batch and estimating the breeding values of the bulls using best linear unbiased prediction (BLUP) or similar procedures.

The bulls are then ranked according to their breeding value for milk yield as well as fat and protein yield and percentage (Sire Index). The top two or three bulls in each batch are used to produce the breeding stock for the next generation. This process is continued generation after generation and brings in steady genetic improvement in the population with each successive generation. Data on thecross-bred bull progeny-testing programme from the KLDB are given in, an example of the sire-evaluation programmes for cross-bred bulls in the country. The steadily increasing milk yield of the test daughters is a measure of the genetic progress in the population. The data on standard first lactation milk yield are presented in. Milk yield is an additive genetic trait with thousands of gene pairs interacting in its inheritance and manifestation.

Therefore, heterosis has very little role to play in these hybrids and their *inter se* mating populations. The behaviour of the *inter se* mated populations of cross-breds in Kerala with regard to nonadditively inherited traits such as age at first calving, calving interval, and service period show higher variance over several generations ofinter se mating, but no decline in the mean values. These traits show not only some heterosis, but also the mitigating impact of selection on heterosis.

Sire Evaluation Through Sibling Tests

With the advent of Multiple Ovulation and Embryo Transfer (MOET), it is now possible to produce genetically evaluated crossbred bulls for the AI system in about half the time required under the conventional progeny test route. MOET enables the product ion of several embryos per cow per year and therefore many offspring per bull mother per year. It is thus possible to evaluate young bulls while they are growing up, using what is called a Sibling Test, based on the records of the number of contemporary full sisters (full - sibs) and half sisters (half-sibs). Using the Sibling Test it is possible to prove a bull in less than 40 months while traditional progeny tests take up to 65 months.

Other things being equal, the accuracy of the selection under Sibling Test in ONBS could be lower than that achieved under the progeny test, but this is more than compensated for by the greatly reduced generation interval and therefore the greater genetic gain per generation. The Sibling Test is a newtechnique and the accuracy of genetic evaluation in this test has yet to be correlated with that under the progeny test. For this reason, bulls produced through Sibling Tests in ONBS must be put through conventional progeny test procedures for at least the first ten batches.

This is possible while the young bulls are already in use for AI. Selection of AI bulls through Sibling Tests in ONBS are of immense importance to the national cross-breeding programme as it gives the programme a head start even in the absence of sires proven through progeny performance.

This technique will provide genetically evaluated bulls in large numbers for the inter se breeding programmes within four years of its inception. The Sibling Test needs an open nucleus herd of donors (dams) of some 100 elite breeding females from a selected Indian dairy breed (Sahiwal/Red Sindhi/ Gir), of which 20 per cent move out and 20 per cent move in each year. This herd can be in a farm or preferably in a compact area of some 20 selected villages. Each year 32 dams from these are selected and divided into 8 sire families (4 cows to each sire; exotic frozen semen from top proven Holstein/ Jersey bulls from the world market). The dams are superovulated and inseminated to produce about 16 embryos per cow. These are transferred to recipients in the farm or the villages, resulting in 8 offspring per cow, 4 male, and 4 female. Each male under this arrangement will have 4 full sisters and 12 half sisters (probability).

Evaluation of the bull is based on the first records of the full and half sisters, the available records of the dam, and breeding value of the sire.

Sibling Tests in ONBS are currently in operation only in the Sabarmati Ashram Goshala, managed by the NDDB in Bidaj, Gujarat. So far three sets of bulls have been produced, of which the first set of siblings have completed their first lactation. The first set comprises 4 exotic bulls, and 4 sire families, and yielded 143 offspring. Of these 11 bulls were selected and are now in semen production.

Artificial Insemination

Artificial insemination is the most significant scientific invention for increasing animal productivity in the 20th century. This is still the only tool available to mankind for moving massive genetic payloads into populations and for rapidly re-engineering the desired changes in their genetic architecture. Planned and systematic use of AI, combined with the principles of quantitative genetics, has aided genetic improvement programmes in bovines the world over with spectacular productivity gains. Although developed in the early part of the 20 century, application of AI for breeding cattle began only in the late 1940s in developed countries. Large-scale use of AI in India started with the First Five-year Plan in 1951.

AI made a quantum leap when the technique of cryopreservation of bovine semen was developed for commercial application in the late 1950s.The next major development occurred in the early 1980s, when MOET and the many allied applications of embryo bio-technology such as cryopreservation, splitting, cloning, and sexing of embryos became routinely available. The infrastructure for the development and application of these techniques is available in India. India established its first large scale Frozen Bovine Semen Production Station in Mattupatty, Kerala in 1965. Extensive use of frozen bovine serum for AI began here. Today virtually all AI carried out in India uses frozen semen.

In 1999 about 19 million AIs were carried out in the country by the state departments (5% of them in buffalo), five million AI by the milk cooperative system (3.3 million in cattle, 1.7 million in buffalo) and 0.5 million jointly by NGOs and other private AI practitioners.

Institutions for Technology Development and Delivery of Services

The State Departments of Animal Husbandry and Dairy Development and the Milk Producers' Cooperative Unions are the institutions responsible for development and dissemination of AI technologies, and for training and human resources development. The Animal Sciences Research Institutes under the ICAR and the State Agricultural Universities (SAUs) provide support to the AI system.

India has perhaps the world's largest AI network – over 40 thousand AI outlets altogether – of which 28 thousand are owned by the government,

10 thousand by the milk cooperatives, and the rest by NGOs and others. The 28 thousand AI centers directly operated by the government departments are stationary centers where the farmer has to bring the animal for service. This limits their reach, covering approximately 500 adult females per centre. The cooperative sector AI centers are located in the village dairy cooperative societies and deliver AI at those premises within the village. The nongovernmental, voluntary, and private sectors deliver AI to the farmer's doorstep.

In spite of such a vast spread of institutions the reach of the system is limited to less than 20 per cent of adult females among cattle and less than 10 per cent in buffalo. The service is of poor quality and the conception rate is less than 20 per cent. The bulls are not genetically evaluated and therefore, AI does not result in superior progeny generation after generation.

The Central and State governments have recently reviewed the AI system and initiated a major restructuring of the entire cattle and buffalo breeding programme, infrastructure,institutions and breeding operations in the country. The aim is to maximise the returns on existing investments, to ensure that the system covers much larger populations of breeding animals, and creates genetically superior progeny generation after generation. To this end, the Government of India has now launched a National Project for Cattle and Buffalo Breeding.

Adoption of Cross-breeding

After the initial slow start, cross-breeding spread throughout the country and in its wake brought problems of overzealous application and issues related to sustainability. The breeding policy prescribed by the government was scientifically and environmentally appropriate, but the application of the policy was mismanaged by almost all states except Kerala, parts of Gujarat, and Andhra Pradesh. The adoption of cross-breeding across the country, andthe speed with which it spread, is clearly established in the successive rounds of the Livestock Census. Separate enumeration of cross-breds started only with the 1982 Census round. The growth rate of the cross-breeds would have been much higher if the AI service in India was of higher quality.

Eighty-five per cent of the total 24.5 million AIs are conducted to generate cross-breeds, but less than 20 per cent of these result in pregnancies and even fewer calves are born. The demand for cross-breeding of cattle is high in all states except Rajasthan and Gujarat, where the agroclimatic conditions are extremely unsuitable for cross-bred cattle to thrive. Also the indigenous breeds of cattle in Rajasthan and Gujarat are some of the best dairy and draught breeds in India and there is immense scope for their development through selective breeding.

In States such as Kerala and Punjab cross-bred cattle have virtually replaced the indigenous cattle and now account for 70 per cent of the cattle population in Kerala and 80 per cent in Punjab. The other states with large cross-bred cattle populations are Uttar Pradesh, Tamil Nadu, Maharashtra, and West Bengal.

Impact of Cross-breeding

The impact of cross-breeding on the Indian economy and at the farm level is impressive. However the enormous increase in milk production in the country is more due to market pull, improved though discriminatory feeding practices, and increase in the number of animals. Milk production in India increased from 19 million tonnes in 1951 to 74.7 million tonnes by 1999. Of this, 55 per cent comes from buffalo, cattle accounting for only 41 per cent. The projected population of cross-bred cows in 2001 is about 9.35 million and their estimated contribution to total milk production is 10 million tonnes or 33 per cent of the total cattle output. The contribution of the milk group to the total output value of the livestock subsector in 1998-99 was Rs. 826.24 billion, with cross-bred cattle contributing about Rs 110.61 billion.

At the farm level the impact is more dramatic as the milk yield increase in cross-bred cows is three- to five-fold. The farmers profit from themuch higher output of milk and comparatively lower cost per unit of milk output. Yield increases and better breeding parameters in the cross-bred cows are universally accepted facts even under farm conditions.

While most states were indifferent to the prescribed breeding policyKerala had been following it strictly with commendable results. Punjab completely deviated from the central prescription and followed a policy of itsown, for progressive upgrading of the local cattle with Holsteins, taking into account the quality of farmers in Punjab, and the resources available in the state. Several years of this policy implementation endowed Punjab with a highly productive population of cattle closer to the Holstein both in production traits and appearance.

There are many micro-studies establishing the advantages of cross-bred cows in household herds. One of the most documented schemes in India on this front is the *Intensive Mini Dairy Project* (IMDP) of the Uttar Pradesh Dairy Development Department. This is primarily a rural employment scheme enabling eligible milk producers in dairy cooperative society areas access to commercial credit for replacing their local milch animals with two to four cross-bred cows or improved milch buffalo. A comprehensive review ofthe project (impact study involving over 10 thousand project units) carried outby the ICCMRT, Lucknow in 1994 shows that income from dairying increases dramatically without altering the quantum of income from other sources, if two cross-bred cows are added to the farm.

Social Dimensions and Farming Systems

In India milk is produced in over 70 million small, marginal, and landless holdings scattered across the length and breadth of the country. The vast majority of these holdings are comprised of mixed crop-livestock systems and farmers keep livestock depending on the crop residues available. The stock holdings are tiny – two to three animals, cows, and/or buffalo per holding is the modal holding size. Large holdings are seen only among the nomadic herders in Gujarat and Rajasthan; and in stables in cities such as Mumbai and Kolkata. There are some specialized dairy farms among the smallholders, but the numbers are very few and they are mostly in the peri-urban areas, dairy cooperative society villages, or close to processing plants. Organized modern dairy farms also exist, but their numbers are far too small to express as a percentage of total holdings. Larger landowners tend to hold larger herds and the stock holding size is larger as a rule in Punjab, Haryana, and Western UP.

Livestock holdings seem to be less skewed compared to land holdings and therefore, gains from livestock production are more equitably distributed. In1977, the bottom 60 per cent of the households in rural areas owned only 41 per cent of the total milch animals. This inequity in the distribution of livestock appears to bedeclining over time. All-India Input Surveys in 1981-82 and 1986-87 indicate that the share of the bottom 60 per cent households in the ownership of bovines increased from 59 to 66 per cent during this period . By 1992, the small and marginal farmers accounted for 62 per cent of all rural households. They constituted the core of the milk production subsector and owned two-thirds of all milk in animals. The more productive cross-bred cows too seem to fit this distribution pattern. Many among the landless, who account for some 20 per cent of rural households, also own milch animals and participate in milk production. Among all livestock in India, cattle are the most critical threat to sustainability as they account for the bulk of the livestock load on land.

Production of work animals for the crop system was all along the excuse for the relentless increase in overall cattle population size. With draught animals becoming increasingly redundant, this excuse is no longer valid. Even though there is a decreasing trend in the cattle population over the last two decades, an increase in mechanization of farm operations and growing numbers of higher-yielding cross-bred cows have not yet produced a matching reduction incattle numbers. Progressive replacement of the indigenous cattle population by cross-breeds and cows of developed Indian dairy breeds would reduce overall cattle numbers and improve sustainability. Cross-breeding of non-descript indigenous cattle is thus a major solution to India's oversized cattle population.

Constraints in Adoption of Cross-breeding

- The millions of tiny stock holdings across the country comprising two or three animals per holding are a major constraint in the spread of newer technologies. Fragmentation of these smallholdings year after year, reducing their size and viability, relentlessly pushes the smallholders below the poverty line. This compels the state to invest increasingly larger resources on poverty alleviation and livelihood protection measures. Often the bottom end of the smallholder spectrum is therefore unable to adopt newer technologies without subsidy/credit support.
- There are huge and progressively widening gaps between supply and demand of feed for livestock as shown by estimates over the last fifty years. These estimates are mostly inaccurate (population numbers grew two- to three fold and output of all species grew four times between 1951 and 1991). However it is a fact that feed resources in the country are scarce and inadequate. A reduction in bovine numbers, therefore, assumes high priority in the policy framework. The common property resources have shrunk by 30 per cent between 1950 and 1990. What little is left can no longer support any meaningful livestock production, as it is in an advanced state of degradation, with scanty biomass cover and little or no maintenance.
- Almost all diseases of livestock, many of them already eradicated or under control in the more developed countries, are still rampant in India. Livestock production is seriously hampered by the regular recurrence of devastating epidemics in all species throughout the country, leading to annual losses of over Rs. 50 billion, thus denying India access to lucrative global markets for animal products. Development of high-yielding milchanimals without adequate protection against disease is a very high-risk investment.
- All services in the livestock subsector such as veterinary services, AI, and production support are offered exclusively by the state departments of animal husbandry and are usually absolutely free. This overwhelming government monopoly in delivery of free services has compromised quality and accountability, and crowded out the emergence of free markets for these services.
- The need to take the animals to the center for AI services limits its reach and coverage and also causes severe stress to the animal. Stress being inconducive to pregnancy, is one of the major causes for low conception rates due to AI in India.
- Breeding of cattle is almost random, as 80 per cent of the breeding females receiveno scientific or organised human intervention. The vast

state government AInetwork currently covers less than 20 per cent of the breeding female cattle and only 10 per cent of the buffalo.

- Use of unselected bulls for AI leads to progeny with virtually no genetic progress from generation to generation.
- The apparent fertility problems in cross-bred bulls seriously hamper their selection. The rejection rate among cross-bred bulls is as high as 40 per cent andthere is no research support to mitigate the problem.
- Extension support to agricultural production was recognized as essential when planned increases in agricultural production were initiated in the early 1950s. Despite a promising start, by the end of the Third Five-year Plan, extension services degenerated into mere delivery of services by animal husbandry departments. While a reasonably effective extension network evolved in the crop production subsector nationwide, no such effort was made in the livestock subsector. Absence of a well-conceived extension support system seriously undermined the pace of development under the different plans.
- Socio-cultural factors are a negative influence on dairy enterprise in the country. Culling of unproductive cattle is seldom undertaken, leading to large numbers in the population. Over 30 per cent of the adult female cattle are not fit for breeding. Lack of reforms in the alternate use of animals saps the Indian dairy industry of almost 40 per cent of its supplementary revenue, greatly compromising the interests of the dairy farmer.
- Accelerating livestock subsector development in India has to be balanced with conservation of ecology, as livestock - particularly cattle - are a major cause of environmental degradation. The relentless growth of the cattle population far beyond the land's capacity to support it is a threat that needs well-focused policy attention while exploiting livestock potential forlivelihood generation and alleviation of poverty.

CHAPTER 7

The Draught Animals

Before the introduction of new technologies (modern seeds, chemical fertilizers, and pesticides) in the mid-1960s, draught animals (particularly male cattle) were the major source of motive power (tractive and rotary) for Indian agriculture. Increasing use of new technologies led to expansion of area under crops and intensive use of land. This demanded more draught power to ensure timeliness in field operations. The draught animals were not capable of meeting the increased demand and thus machines were introduced/used to fill the gap. Machines subsequently replaced the draught animals for various farm operations such as irrigation and threshing. Further, with increasing subdivision of land holdings, maintaining draught animals became an uneconomical proposition for small landholders. These farmers therefore prefer custom hiring of tractors, threshers, and power tillers to maintaining draught animals. Custom hiring of tractor-drawn tillage equipment is now an accepted practice in many parts of the country. This paper investigates the trends in use of draught animal power *vis-à-vis* mechanical power in Indian agriculture.

During the last 63 years the net cultivated area has remained more or lessstagnant (138-142 million ha), while the gross cropped area has increased to 189 million ha. The average size of holdings is 1.6 ha, with 79 per cent of holdings below 1.3 ha. Indian farmers have been dependent on draught animal power for irrigation, threshing, transport, tillage, sowing, and cultivation. As croppingintensity has increased, animate power has been found inadequate to maintain schedules, and has been supplemented by mechanical power sources (tractors,engines, and electric motors). Tillage, irrigation, and threshing operations, which require higher energy and are arduous to perform, are gradually being performed using mechanical power. Small farmers in agriculturally backward regions are still using the traditional animal-operated country plow.

Trends in the numbers of bullock-operated implements such as steel plow, puddler, disc harrow, sprayer and duster, spring tine harrow, and sowing devices since the early 1970s. The numbers of traditional implements such as wooden plows, cane crushers, Olpad thresher, Persian wheels, and bullock carts have either remained almost unchanged or decreased marginally, while those of improved implements such as the steel plow and puddler have increased.

Human Power

Human power is predominantly used for sowing, transplanting, fertilizerapplication, harvesting, and digging. Use of human power is likely to continue in hilly regions, *diara* lands, smallholdings, and in areas where mechanization has not been adopted. The population of agricultural workers has grown from 97.2 million in 1951 to 186.5 million in 1991, so human power in agriculture is available in plenty.

Draught Animal Power

Draught animal power (DAP) is used for crop production and transportation. Bullock and male buffalo over three years of age are the main draught animals for field operations. India possesses famous draught breeds of cattle such as Nagori, Khilari, Helikar, Amrit Mahal, Kangayam, Malvi, Hariana, Gir, Angol, Tharparkar, and Gaulao. Adult male and female camels are used for field operations and for transport, but their population is estimated at less than 1 per centof total draught animals. The population of draught animals declined from 80.8 million in 1971-72 to about 77.7 million in 1991-92. Thepower availability too declined from 20.2 mkW to 19.4 mkW during this period.

Tractors

There were only 8635 tractors in use in 1951. Local tractor production began in 1961–62 with 880 tractors. Today, India manufactures more than 265 000 tractors per year. Different sizes of tractors are manufactured in India, ranging from less than 15 kW to more than 37.5 kW, but the most popular range is 15–30 kW.

Power Tillers

Power tillers were introduced in the country in the 1960s, but did not become as popular as the tractor due to limitations in the field and on the road, and ergonomic weaknesses. Power tillers are presently used more in rice and sugarcane-producing areas of Tamil Nadu, Andhra Pradesh, Kerala, Karnataka, West Bengal, Orissa, Bihar, and Maharashtra. The annual production was about 14,000 units in 1999-2000. The potential power availability is estimated to be 0.66 mkW.

Diesel Engines and Electric Motors

These are used for stationary operations, especially the lifting of water for irrigation and operating grain mills, oil *ghanis*, sugarcane crushers, power threshers, and chaff cutters. The number of irrigation pumps has increased from 0.11 million in 1951-52 to about 15.3 million in 1996-97. As a result, the gross irrigated area increased from 22.6 to 70.6 million ha. Governmentsupport through financial incentives for irrigation hardware has played an important role in this growth. The electric pumps are preferred in electrified areas due to lower recurring cost.

In 1996-97 the number of electric motors used for irrigation was 9.7 million with potential power availability of 36.3 mkW, and that of diesel engines was 5.6 million with potential power availability of 30.2 mkW. Farm power per unit area is one of the parameters used for expressing the mechanization status. The total farm power availability in 1951-52 was 0.20 kW ha^{-1}, which increased to one kW ha^{-1} in 1996-97. Human and animal power contributed 60 per cent of the total farm power in 1971-72 and mechanical and electrical together contributed only 40 per cent. In 1996-97 the contribution from human and animal power was reduced to 21 per cent, and the contribution of mechanical and electrical power increased to 79 per cent.

However, in terms of area coverage, draught animals continue to dominate. About 55 per cent of the area is dependent on draught animals. One-fifth of the area uses mechanical power. The remainder, especially shifting cultivation, hilly land, and waterlogged areas is cultivated by human power.

Changes in DAP

Zebu cattle (*Bos indicus*) and buffalo (*Bubalus bubalis*) are the main draught animals in India. In most parts of the country only male bovines are used for draught purposes. Cows are generally not used due to social and religious considerations. From 1961-62 to 1991-92, the population of working bovines has remained constant. The ratio of males to females hasdeclined from 1.2 in 1961-62 to 1.0 in 1992. A similar decline occurred in thecase of buffalo. This shows a shift away from draught animals, which has been facilitated by rising mechanization of agriculture.

Camels are used primarily for transport and as pack animals, and are also used for tractive power in states such as Rajasthan, Gujarat, Haryana, and Punjab for field operations and for lifting of water from open wells. The total camel population has increased marginally from 0.9 to 1.0 million. About 60 per cent of the adults are used for tillage as well as transport.

Pack Animals

Camels, donkeys, mules, horses, ponies, yaks, and mithuns are used mainly as pack animals and to pull carts. The population of horses and donkeys decreased between 1961-62 and 1991-92. Camel and mule populations showed positive growth. The total population of adult pack animals for work in 1961 was 3 million, but this declined to 2.5 million in 1992. The farmers' preference for faster modes of mechanical transport such as tractor, *Maruta* (local improvised four-wheel transport), and the mini-truck for haulage is one of the reasons for a decrease in the population of pack animals.

Draught Animals and Size of Land Holdings

Although all groups of farmers possess draught animals, the areacommanded by a pair of animals on semi-medium, medium, and large farm holdings is very large, indicating that owners of these holdings may not be in a position to perform farm operations on schedule. Marginal and small farmers have a lower area per animal pair, but the ownership of draught animals is limited.

Animal Energy Use in Crop Production

The animal energy used in crop production, computed from the information in the Cost of Cultivation of Principal Crops in India operated by the Ministry of Agriculture, Government of India. There has been a decrease in use of animal energy for all crops since 1971-72. A maximum decrease of 5 per cent per annum was recorded in wheat, 3 per cent in sugarcane, and 2.8 per cent in pulses. On average, there has been a gradual reduction in use of animal energy. It has been reduced from 159 pair hours ha- n 1971-72 to 109 pair hours ha n 1991-92. This indicates that although the population of draught animals has not changed much over time, their utilization has declined considerably. Male cattle and buffalo are the chief sources of DAP for field operations.

Although use of mechanical and electrical power has increased, draughtanimals continue to be a major farm power source in India for small and marginal farmers, In 1991-92, the total DAP population for field operations was about 35.8 million pairs. As a result of the introduction of mechanical power in agriculture, use of DAP declined gradually. There has been a gradual increase in adoption of the improved bullock-drawn steel plow, cultivator, puddler, seed-cum-fertilizer drill and bullock cart in India, but most small and marginal farmers still use traditional implements for tillage and sowing.

CHAPTER 8
Dairy Farming

Dairy farming is a class of agricultural, or an animal husbandry, enterprise, for long-term production of milk, usually from dairy cows but also from goats and sheep, which may be either processed on-site or transported to a dairy factory for processing and eventual retail sale.

Most dairy farms sell the male calves born by their cows, usually for veal production, or breeding depending on quality of the bull calf, rather than raising non-milk-producing stock. Many dairy farms also grow their own feed, typically including corn, alfalfa, and hay. This is fed directly to the cows, or is stored as silage for use during the winter season.

Dairy farming has been part of agriculture for thousands of years. Historically it has been one part of small, diverse farms. In the last century or so larger farms doing only dairy production have emerged. Large scale dairy farming is only viable where either a large amount of milk is required for production of more durable dairy products such as cheese, butter, etc or there is a substantial market of people with cash to buy milk, but no cows of their own.

Hand Milking

Centralized dairy farming as we understand it primarily developed around villages and cities, where residents were unable to have cows of their own due to a lack of grazing land. Near the town, farmers could make some extra money on the side by having additional animals and selling the milk in town. The dairy farmers would fill barrels with milk in the morning and bring it to market on a wagon. Until the late 19th century, the milking of the cow was done by hand. In the United States, several large dairy operations existed in some northeastern states and in the west, that involved as many as several hundred cows, but an individual milker could not be expected to milk more than a dozen cows a day. Smaller operations predominated.

For most herds, milking took place indoors twice a day, in a barn with the cattle tied by the neck with ropes or held in place by stanchions. Feeding could occur simultaneously with milking in the barn, although most dairy cattle were pastured during the day between milkings. Such examples of this method of dairy farming are difficult to locate, but some are preserved as a historic site for a glimpse into the days gone by. One such instance that is open for this is at Point Reyes National Seashore.

Vacuum Bucket Milking

The first milking machines were an extension of the traditional milking pail. The early milker device fit on top of a regular milk pail and sat on the floor under the cow. Following each cow being milked, the bucket would be dumped into a holding tank. This developed into the Surge hanging milker. Prior to milking a cow, a large wide leather strap called a surcingle was put around the cow, across the cow's lower back. The milker device and collection tank hung underneath the cow from the strap. This innovation allowed the cow to move around naturally during the milking process rather than having to stand perfectly still over a bucket on the floor.

With the availability of electric power and suction milking machines, the production levels that were possible in stanchion barns increased but the scale of the operations continued to be limited by the labor intensive nature of the milking process. Attaching and removing milking machines involved repeated heavy lifting of the machinery and its contents several times per cow and the pouring of the milk into milk cans. As a result, it was rare to find single-farmer operations of more than 50 head of cattle.

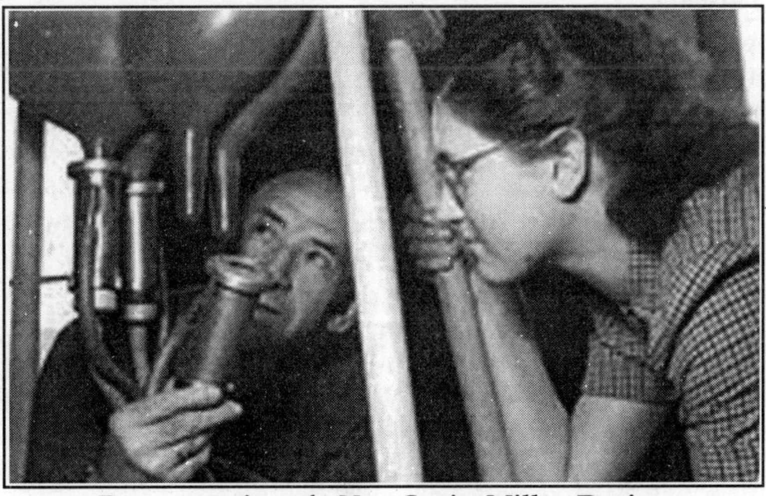

Demonstration of a New Soviet Milker Device

Step-Saver Milk Transport

As herd size began to increase, the bucket milker system became laborious. A vacuum milk-transport system known as the Step-Saver was developed to transport milk to the storage tank. The system used a long vacuum hose coiled around a receiver cart, and connected to a vacuum-breaker device in the milkhouse, allowing farmers to milk many cows without the necessity of walking increasingly longer distances carrying heavy buckets of milk.

Milking Pipeline

The next innovation in automatic milking was the milk pipeline. This uses a permanent milk-return pipe and a second vacuum pipe that encircles the barn or milking parlour above the rows of cows, with quick-seal entry ports above each cow. By eliminating the need for the milk container, the milking device shrank in size and weight to the point where it could hang under the cow, held up only by the sucking force of the milker nipples on the cow's udder. The milk is pulled up into the milk-return pipe by the vacuum system, and then flows by gravity to the milkhouse vacuum-breaker that puts the milk in the storage tank. The pipeline system greatly reduced the physical labor of milking since the farmer no longer needed to carry around huge heavy buckets of milk from each cow.

The pipeline allowed barn length to keep increasing and expanding, but after a point farmers started to milk the cows in large groups, filling the barn with one-half to one-third of the herd, milking the animals, and then emptying and refilling the barn. As herd sizes continued to increase, this evolved into the more efficient milking parlour.

Milking Parlours

Innovation in milking focused on mechanizing the milking parlour to maximize throughput of cows per operator which streamlined the milking process to permit cows to be milked as if on an assembly line, and to reduce physical stresses on the farmer by putting the cows on a platform slightly above the person milking the cows to eliminate having to constantly bend over. Many older and smaller farms still have tie-stall or stanchion barns, but worldwide a majority of commercial farms have parlours.

The milking parlour allowed a concentration of money into a small area, so that more technical monitoring and measuring equipment could be devoted to each milking station in the parlour. Rather than simply milking into a common pipeline for example, the parlour can be equipped with fixed measurement systems that monitor milk volume and record milking statistics for each animal. Tags on the animals allow the parlour system to automatically identify each animal as it enters the parlour.

Recessed Parlours

More modern farms use recessed parlours, where the milker stands in a recess such that his arms are at the level of the cow's udder. Recessed parlours can be herringbone, where the cows stand in two angled rows either side of the recess and the milker accesses the udder from the side, parallel, where the cows stand side-by-side and the milker accesses the udder from the rear or, more recently, rotary (or carousel), where the cows are on a raised circular platform, facing the centre of the circle, and the platform rotates while the milker stands in one place and accesses the udder from the rear. There are many other styles of milking parlours which are less common.

Herringbone and Parallel Parlours

In herringbone and parallel parlours, the milker generally milks one row at a time. The milker will move a row of cows from the holding yard into the milking parlour, and milk each cow in that row. Once all or most of the milking machines have been removed from the milked row, the milker releases the cows to their feed. A new group of cows is then loaded into the now vacant side and the process repeats until all cows are milked. Depending on the size of the milking parlour, which normally is the bottleneck, these rows of cows can range from four to sixty at a time.

Rotary Parlours

In rotary parlours, the cows are loaded one at a time onto the platform as it slowly rotates. The milker stands near the entry to the parlour and puts the cups on the cows as they move past. By the time the platform has completed almost a full rotation, another milker or a machine removes the cups and the cow steps backwards off the platform and then walks to its feed. Rotary cowsheds, as they are called in New Zealand, started in the 1980s but are expensive compared to Herringbone cowshed - the older New Zealand norm. To justify the costs herds have got bigger with 1 person milking 500-600 cows. A rotary is about 25 per cent faster than a herringbone shed for the same number of cows.

Automatic Milker Take-Off

It can be harmful to an animal for it to be over-milked past the point where the udder has stopped releasing milk. Consequently, the milking process involves not just applying the milker, but also monitoring the process to determine when the animal has been *milked out* and the milker should be removed. While parlour operations allowed a farmer to milk many more animals much more quickly, it also increased the number of animals to be monitored simultaneously by the farmer. The automatic take-off system was developed to remove the milker from the cow when the milk flow reaches a preset level, relieving the farmer of the duties of carefully watching over 20 or more animals being milked at the same time.This is a standard procedure in New Zealand.

Fully Automated Robotic Milking

In the 1980s and 1990s, robotic milking systems were developed and introduced (principally in the EU). Thousands of these systems are now in routine operation. In these systems the cow has a high degree of autonomy to choose her time of milking within pre-defined windows. These systems are generally limited to intensively managed systems although research continues to match them to the requirements of grazing cattle and to develop sensors to detect animal health and fertility automatically.

History of Milk Preservation Methods

Cool temperature has been the main method by which milk freshness has been extended. When windmills and well pumps were invented, one of its first uses on the farm besides providing water for animals was for cooling milk, to extend the storage life before being transported to the town market.

The naturally cold underground water would be continuously pumped into a tub or other containers of milk set in the tub to cool after milking. This method of milk cooling was extremely popular before the arrival of electricity and refrigeration.

Refrigeration

When refrigeration first arrived (the 19th century) the equipment was initially used to cool cans of milk, which were filled by hand milking. These cans were placed into a cooled water bath to remove heat and keep them cool until they were able to be transported to a collection facility. As more automated methods were developed for harvesting milk, hand milking was replaced and, as a result, the milk can was replaced by a bulk milk cooler. 'Ice banks' were the first type of bulk milk cooler. This was a double wall vessel with evaporator coils and water located between the walls at the bottom and sides of the tank. A small refrigeration compressor was used to remove heat from the evaporator coils. Ice eventually builds up around the coils, until it reaches a thickness of about three inches surrounding each pipe, and the cooling system shuts off. When the milking operation starts, only the milk agitator and the water circulation pump, which flows water across the ice and the steel walls of the tank, are needed to reduce the incoming milk to a temperature below 40 degrees.

This cooling method worked well for smaller dairies, however was fairly inefficient and was unable to meet the increasingly higher cooling demand of larger milking parlours. In the mid 1950s direct expansion refrigeration was first applied directly to the bulk milk cooler. This type of cooling utilizes an evaporator built directly into the inner wall of the storage tank to remove heat from the milk. Direct expansion is able to cool milk at a much faster rate than early ice bank type coolers and is still the primary method for bulk tank cooling today on small to medium sized operations.

Another device which has contributed significantly to milk quality is the plate heat exchanger (PHE). This device utilizes a number of specially designed stainless steel plates with small spaces between them. Milk is passed between every other set of plates with water being passed between the balance of the plates to remove heat from the milk. This method of cooling can remove large amounts of heat from the milk in a very short time, thus drastically slowing bacteria growth and thereby improving milk quality. Groundwater is the most common source of cooling medium for this device. Dairy cows consume approximately 3 gallons of water for every gallon of milk production and prefer to drink slightly warm water as opposed to cold ground water. For this reason, PHE's can result in drastically improved milk quality, reduced operating costs for the dairymen by reducing the refrigeration load on his bulk milk cooler, and increased milk production by supplying the cows with a source of fresh warm water.

Plate heat exchangers have also evolved as a result of the increase of dairy farm herd sizes in the U.S. As a dairyman increases the size of his herd, he must also increase the capacity of his milking parlour in order to harvest the additional milk. This increase in parlour sizes has resulted in tremendous increases in milk throughput and cooling demand. Today's larger farms produce milk at a rate which direct expansion refrigeration systems on bulk milk coolers cannot cool in a timely manner. PHE's are typically utilized in this instance to rapidly cool the milk to the desired temperature (or close to it) before it reaches the bulk milk tank. Typically, ground water is still utilized to provide some initial cooling to bring the milk to between 55 and 70°F (21°C). A second (and sometimes third) section of the PHE is added to remove the remaining heat with a mixture of chilled pure water and propylene glycol. These chiller systems can be made to incorporate large evaporator surface areas and high chilled water flow rates to cool high flow rates of milk.

Milking machines are held in place automatically by a vacuum system that draws the ambient air pressure down from 15 to 21 pounds per square inch (100 to 140 kPa) of vacuum. The vacuum is also used to lift milk vertically through small diameter hoses, into the receiving can. A milk lift pump draws the milk from the receiving can through large diameter stainless steel piping, through the plate cooler, then into a refrigerated bulk tank.

Milk is extracted from the cow's udder by flexible rubber sheaths known as liners or inflations that are surrounded by a rigid air chamber. A pulsating flow of ambient air and vacuum is applied to the inflation's air chamber during the milking process. When ambient air is allowed to enter the chamber, the vacuum inside the inflation causes the inflation to collapse around the cow's teat, squeezing the milk out of teat in a similar fashion as a baby calf's mouth massaging the teat. When the vacuum is reapplied in the chamber the flexible rubber inflation relaxes and opens up, preparing for the next squeezing cycle.

It takes the average cow three to five minutes to give her milk. Some cows are faster or slower. Slow-milking cows may take up to fifteen minutes to let down all their milk. Milking speed is only minorly related to the quantity of milk the cow produces-milking speed is a separate factor from milk quantity; milk quantity is not determinative of milking speed. Because most milkers milk cattle in groups, the milker can only process a group of cows at the speed of the slowest-milking cow. For this reason, many farmers will cull slow-milking cows.

The extracted milk passes through a strainer and plate heat exchangers before entering the tank, where it can be stored safely for a few days at approximately 42ºF (6ºC). At pre-arranged times, a milk truck arrives and pumps the milk from the tank for transport to a dairy factory where it will be pasteurized and processed into many products.

As measured in phosphorus, the waste output of 5,000 cows roughly equals a municipality of 70,000 people. In the U.S., dairy operations with more than 1,000 cows meet the EPA definition of a CAFO (Concentrated Animal Feeding Operation), and are subject to EPA regulations. For example, in the San Joaquin Valley of California a number of dairies have been established on a very large scale. Each dairy consists of several modern milking parlour set-ups operated as a single enterprise. Each milking parlour is surrounded by a set of 3 or 4 loafing barns housing 1,500 or 2,000 cattle. Some of the larger dairies have planned 10 or more series of loafing barns and milking parlours in this arrangement, so that the total operation may include as many as 15,000 or 20,000 cows. The milking process for these dairies is similar to a smaller dairy with a single milking parlour but repeated several times. The size and concentration of cattle creates major environmental issues associated with manure handling and disposal, which requires substantial areas of cropland (a ratio of 5 or 6 cows to the acre, or several thousand acres for dairies of this size) for manure spreading and dispersion, or several-acre methane digesters. Air pollution from methane gas associated with manure management also is a major concern. As a result, proposals to develop dairies of this size can be controversial and provoke substantial opposition from environmentalists including the Sierra Club and local activists.

The potential impact of large dairies was demonstrated when a massive manure spill occurred on a 5,000-cow dairy in Upstate New York, contaminating a 20-mile (32 km) stretch of the Black River, and killing 375,000 fish. On Aug. 10, 2005, a manure storage lagoon collapsed releasing 3,000,000 US gallons (11,000,000 l; 2,500,000 imp gal) of manure into the Black River. Subsequently the New York Department of Environmental Conservation mandated a settlement package of $2.2 million against the dairy.

When properly managed, dairy and other livestock waste, due to its nutrient content (N, P, K), makes an excellent fertilizer promoting crop growth, increasing soil organic matter, and improving overall soil fertility and tilth characteristics. Most dairy farms in the United States are required to develop nutrient management plans for their farms, to help balancc the flow of nutrients and reduce the risks of environmental pollution. These plans encourage producers to monitor all nutrients coming onto the farm as feed, forage, animals, fertilizer, etc. and all nutrients exiting the farm as product, crop, animals, manure, etc. For example, a precision approach to animal feeding results in less overfeeding of nutrients and a subsequent decrease in environmental excretion of nutrients, such as phosphorus. In recent years, nutritionists have realized that requirements for phosphorus are much lower than previously thought. These changes have allowed dairy producers to reduce the amount of phosphorus being fed to their cows with a reduction in environmental pollution.

In New Zealand the average dairy farmer has 500 cows which are milked twice per day taking about two hours per milking. All cows are grazed on grass pasture. Dung and urine from the milking shed is flushed into drains by large high pressure hoses, which lead to open pits. Over time the solid matter settles to the bottom and is removed by truck about once per year. The relatively clean water is allowed to percolate through natural swamp and creeks back to major rivers. Local authorities check that water entering rivers meets minimum standards. Farmers are fined and forced to change their systems to meet the standards. Repeated infringement means the farm is closed down. Local councils often supply large numbers of native swamp plants grown in their own nurseries to farmer at a low cost. Planting is also done by environmental groups, and schools as part of their science program and groups of unemployed on relief work.

Use of Hormones

It is possible to maintain higher milk production by injecting cows with growth hormones known as recombinant BST or rBST, but this is controversial due to its effects on animal and possibly human health. The European Union, Japan, Australia, New Zealand and Canada have banned its use due to these concerns.

In the US however, no such prohibition exists, and approximately 17.2 per cent of dairy cows are treated in this way. The U.S. Food and Drug Administration states that no "significant difference" has been found between milk from treated and non-treated cows but based on consumer concerns several milk purchasers and resellers have elected not to purchase milk produced with rBST.

Management of the Herd

Modern dairy farmers use milking machines and sophisticated plumbing systems to harvest and store the milk from the cows, which are usually milked two or three times daily. In New Zealand some farmers seeking a better life style, are milking only once per day, trading a slight reduction in production of milk for increased leisure time. During the summer months, cows may be turned out to graze in pastures, both day and night, and are brought into the barn to be milked.

Barns may also incorporate tunnel ventilation into the architecture of the barn structure. This ventilation system is highly efficient and involves opening both ends of the structure allowing cool air to blow through the building. Farmers with this type of structure keep cows inside during the summer months to prevent sunburn and damage to udders. During the winter months the cows may be kept in the barn, which is warmed by their collective body heat. Even in winter, the heat produced by the cattle requires the barns to be ventilated for cooling purposes. Many modern facilities, and particularly those in tropical areas, keep all animals inside at all times to facilitate herd management.

Housing can be either loose in stalls (called cow cubicles in UK). There is little research available on dimensions required for cow stalls, and much housing can be out of date, however increasingly companies are making farmers aware of the benefits, in terms of animal welfare, health and milk production.

In the southern hemisphere such as in Australia and New Zealand, cows spend most of their lives outside on pasture, although they may receive supplementation during periods of low pasture availabliity. Typical supplementary feeds in Australasia are hay, silage or ground maize. The trend in New Zealand is towards feeding cows on a concrete pad to prevent loss of feed by trampling. In New Zealand slower growing winter pasture is rationed. It is carefully controlled by light weight portable electric break feeding fences run on mains power that can be easily repositioned.

The production of milk requires that the cow be in lactation, which is a result of the cow having given birth to a calf. The cycle of insemination, pregnancy, parturition, and lactation, followed by a "dry" period of about two months before calving which allows udder tissue to regenerate. Dairy operations therefore include both the production of milk and the production of calves. Bull calves are either castrated and raised as steers for beef production or veal.

Health and well-being

Common ailments affecting dairy cows include infectious disease (e.g. mastitis, endometritis and digital dermatitis), metabolic disease (e.g. milk fever and ketosis) and injuries caused by their environment (e.g. hoof and hock lesions).

Lameness is commonly considered one of the most significant animal welfare issues for dairy cattle. It can be caused by a number of sources, including infections of the hoof tissue (e.g. fungal infections that cause dermatitis) and physical damage causing bruising or lesions (e.g. ulcers or hemorrhage of the hoof). While housing and management features common in modern conventional dairy farms (such as concrete barn floors, limited access to pasture and suboptimal bed-stall design) have been identified as contributing risk factors, small farms in developing countries can also demonstrate high rates.

There is a great deal of variation in the pattern of dairy production world wide. Many countries which are large producers consume most of this internally, while others (in particular New Zealand), export a large percentage of their production. Internal consumption is often in the form of liquid milk, while the bulk of international trade is in processed dairy products such as milk powder.

Worldwide, the largest producer is India, the largest exporter is New Zealand, and the largest importer is Japan.

The European Union is the largest milk producer in the world, with 143.7 million tonnes in 2003. This data, encompassing the present 25 member countries, can be further broken down into the production of the original 15 member countries, with 122 million tonnes, and the new 10 mainly former Eastern European countries with 21.7 million tonnes.

Dairy production is heavily distorted due to the Common Agricultural Policy—being subsidized in some areas, and subject to production quotas in other.

United States

In the United States, the top five dairy states are, in order by total milk production; California, Wisconsin, Idaho, New York and Pennsylvania. Dairy farming is also an important industry in Florida, Minnesota, Ohio and Vermont. There are 65,000 dairy farms in the United States.

Pennsylvania, however, is the state with the heaviest dependence on dairy farming — there it is the number one industry. Pennsylvania is home to 8,500 farms and 555,000 dairy cows. Milk produced in Pennsylvania yields about US$1.5 billion in farm revenue every year, and is sold to various states up and down the east coast.

Milk prices collapsed in 2009. Senator Bernie Sanders accused Dean Foods of controlling 40 per cent of the country's milk market. He has requested the United States Department of Justice to pursue 'an anti-trust investigation. Dean Foods says it buys 15 per cent of the country's raw milk.

Competition

Most milk-consuming countries have a local dairy farming industry, and most producing countries maintain significant subsidies and trade barriers to protect domestic producers from foreign competition , but New Zealand, the largest dairy exporting country, does not apply any subsidies to dairy production.

The milking of cows was traditionally a labor-intensive operation and still is in less developed countries. Small farms need several people to milk and care for only a few dozen cows, though for many farms these employees have traditionally been the children of the farm family, giving rise to the term "family farm".

Advances in technology have mostly led to the radical redefinition of "family farms" in industrialized countries such as the United States. With farms of hundreds of cows producing large volumes of milk, the larger and more efficient dairy farms are more able to weather severe changes in milk price and operate profitably, while "traditional" very small farms generally do not have the equity or cash flow to do so. The common public perception of large corporate farms supplanting smaller ones is generally a misconception, as many small family farms expand to take advantage of economies of scale, and incorporate the business to limit the legal liabilities of the owners and simplify such things as tax management.

Before large scale mechanization arrived in the 1950s, keeping a dozen milk cows for the sale of milk was profitable. Now most dairies must have more than one hundred cows being milked at a time in order to be profitable, with other cows and heifers waiting to be "freshened" to join the milking herd . In New Zealand the average herd size, depending on the region, is about 350 cows.

Herd size in the US varies between 1,200 on the West Coast and Southwest, where large farms are commonplace, to roughly 50 in the Northeast, where land-base is a significant limiting factor to herd size. The average herd size in the U.S. is about one hundred cows per farm.

Currently, concerns regarding monopolies created by Dean Foods, Kraft, and other major buyers of bulk dairy products on the Chicago Mercantile Exchange have been raised, as American dairy farms have suffered extreme price depression and chaotic fluctuations while processors and retailers report record profits. Many theorize that unregulated imports of milk protein concentrate used by processors to boost cheese yield has artificially and unfairly influenced the markets in an effort to force consolidation and vertical integration in what has historically been a highly diversified industry.

Dairy Cattle

Dairy cattle (dairy cows) are cattle cows (adult females) bred for the ability to produce large quantities of milk, from which dairy products are made. Dairy cows generally are of the species *Bos taurus*.

Historically, there was little distinction between dairy cattle and beef cattle, with the same stock often being used for both meat and milk production. Today, the bovine industry is more specialized and most dairy cattle have been bred to produce large volumes of milk. The United States dairy herd produced 185 billion pounds of milk in 2007, up from 116 billion pounds in 1950. Yet there are more than 9 million cows on U.S. dairy farms—about 13 million fewer than there were in 1950.

Dairy cows may be found either in herds on dairy farms where dairy farmers own, manage, care for, and collect milk from them, or on commercial farms. Herd sizes vary around the world depending on landholding culture and social structure. Dairy cow herds in the United States range in size from small farms of a dozen animals to large herds of more than 15,000. The United Kingdom dairy herd overall has nearly 2 million cows, with about 100 head reported on an average farm. In New Zealand, the average herd has more than 375 cows, while in Australia, there are approximately 220 cows in the average herd.

To maintain high milk production, a dairy cow must be bred and produce calves. Depending on market conditions, the cow may be bred with a "dairy bull" or a "beef bull." Female calves (heifers) with dairy breeding may be kept as replacement cows for the dairy herd. If a replacement cow turns out to be a substandard producer of milk, she then goes to market and can be killed for beef. Male calves can either be used later as a breeding bull or sold and used for veal or beef. Dairy farmers usually begin breeding or artificially inseminating heifers around 13 months of age. A cow's gestation period is approximately nine months. Newborn calves are removed from their mothers quickly, usually within three days, as the mother/calf bond intensifies over time and delayed separation can cause extreme stress on the calf.

Domestic cows can live to 20 years, however those raised for dairy rarely live that long, as the average cow is removed from the dairy herd around age four and marketed for beef. In 2009, approximately 19 per cent of the US beef supply came from cull dairy cows: cows that can no longer be seen as an economic asset to the dairy farm. These animals may be sold due to reproductive problems or common diseases of milk cows such as mastitis and lameness.

In India, the Hindu majority holds the cow as sacred and a motherly figure due to her capacity to give milk. Cow slaughter is banned in parts of India and remains a contentious issue in states where it is legal. Spent dairy cows don't go to slaughter, but are often seen as roaming on the city streets, and they die of old age or disease. Some pious Hindu organizations manage "old age homes" (Hindi: *Gaushala*) for aged dairy cows.

Market calves are generally sold at two weeks of age and bull calves may fetch a premium over heifers due to their size, either current or potential. Calves may be sold for veal, or for one of several types of beef production, depending on available local crops and markets. Such bull calves may be castrated if turnout onto pastures is envisaged, in order to render the animals less aggressive. Purebred bulls from elite cows may be put into progeny testing schemes to find out whether they might become superior sires for breeding. Such animals may become extremely valuable.

Most dairy farms separate calves from their mothers within a day of birth to reduce transmission of disease and simplify management of milking cows. Studies have been done allowing calves to remain with their mothers for 1, 4, 7 or 14 days after birth. Cows whose calves were removed longer than one day after birth showed increased searching, sniffing and vocalizations. However, calves allowed to remain with their mothers for longer periods showed weight gains at three times the rate of early removals as well as more searching behavior and better social relationships with other calves.

After separation, most young dairy calves subsist on commercial milk replacer, a feed based on dried milk powder. Milk replacer is an economical alternative to feeding whole milk because it is cheaper, can be bought at varying fat and protein percentages. A day old calf consumes around five litres of milk per day.

A bull calf with high genetic potential may be reared for breeding purposes. It may be kept by a dairy farm as a herd bull, to provide natural breeding for the herd cows. A bull may service up to 50 or 60 cows during a breeding season. Any more and the sperm count will decline, leading to cows "returning to service" (to be bred again). A herd bull may only stay for one season since over two years old their temperament becomes too unpredictable.

Bull calves intended for breeding commonly are bred on specialized dairy breeding farms, not production farms. These farms are the major source of stocks for artificial insemination

Milk Production Levels

A cow will produce large amounts of milk over her lifetime. Certain breeds produce more milk than others; however, different breeds produce within a range of around 15,000 to 25,000 lbs of milk per lactation. The average for a single dairy cow in the US in 2007 was 20,204 pounds per year, excluding milk consumed by her calves.

Production levels peak at around 40 to 60 days after calving. The cow is then bred. Production declines steadily afterwards, until, at about 305 days after calving, the cow is 'dried off', and milking ceases. About sixty days later, one year after the birth of her previous calf, a cow will calve again. High production cows are more difficult to breed at a one year interval. Many farms take the view that 13 or even 14 month cycles are more appropriate for this type of cow.

Dairy cows may continue to be economically productive for many lactations. Ten or more lactations are possible. The chances of problems arising which may lead to a cow being culled are high, however; the average herd life of US Holsteins is today fewer than three lactations. This requires more herd replacements to be reared or purchased. Over 90 per cent of all cows are culled for 4 main reasons:

Infertility — failure to conceive and reduced milk production.

Cows are at their most fertile between 60 and 80 days after calving. Cows remaining "open" (not with calf) after this period become increasingly difficult to breed, which may be due to poor health. Failure to expel the afterbirth from a previous pregnancy, luteal cysts, or metritis, an infection of the uterus, are common causes of infertility.

Mastitis — persistent and potentially fatal mammary gland infection, leading to high somatic cell counts and loss of production.

Mastitis is recognized by a reddening and swelling of the infected quarter of the udder and the presence of whitish clots or pus in the milk. Treatment is possible with long-acting antibiotics but milk from such cows is not marketable until drug residues have left the cow's system.

Lameness — persistent foot infection or leg problems causing infertility and loss of production.

High feed levels of highly digestible carbohydrate cause acidic conditions in the cow's rumen. This leads to laminitis and subsequent lameness, leaving the cow vulnerable to other foot infections and problems which may be exacerbated by standing in feces or water soaked areas.

Production — some animals fail to produce economic levels of milk to justify their feed costs.

Production below 12 to 15 liters of milk per day are not economically viable.

Herd life is strongly correlated with production levels. Lower production cows live longer than high production cows, but may be less profitable. Cows no longer wanted for milk production are sent to slaughter. Their meat is of relatively low value and is generally used for processed meat.

Reproduction

Since the 1950s, artificial insemination (AI) is used at most dairy farms; these farms may keep no bull. Advantages of using AI include its low cost and ease compared to maintaining a bull, ability to select from a large number of bulls to match the anticipated market for the resulting calves, and predictable results.

More recently, embryo transfer has been used to enable the multiplication of progeny from elite cows. Such cows are given hormone treatments to produce multiple embryos. These are then 'flushed' from the cow's uterus. 7-12 embryos are consequently removed from these donor cows and transferred into other cows who serve as surrogate mothers. The result will be between 3 and 6 calves instead of the normal single, or rarely, twins.

Hormone Use

Hormone treatments are given to dairy cows to increase reproduction and to increase milk production.

The hormones are used to produce multiple embryos have to be administered at specific times to dairy cattle to induce ovulation. Frequently, for economic considerations, these drugs are also used to synchronize a group of cows to ovulate simultaneously. The hormones Prostaglandin, Gonadotropin Releasing Hormone, and Progesterone are used for this purpose and sold under the brand names Lutalyse, Cystorelin, Estrumate, Factrel, Prostamate, Fertagyl. Insynch, and Ovacyst. They may be administered by injection, insertion or mixed with feed.

About 17 per cent of dairy cows in the United States are injected with Bovine somatotropin, also called recombinant bovine somatotropin (rBST), recombinant bovine growth hormone (rBGH), or artificial growth hormone. The use of this hormone increases milk production from 11 per cent - 25 per cent, but also increases the likelihood of cattle developing mastitis, reduction in fertility and lameness. The U.S. Food and Drug Administration (FDA) has ruled that rBST is harmless to people, although critics point out increased levels of insulin-like growth factor 1 (IGF-1) in milk produced using this hormone. The use of rBST is banned in Canada, parts of the European Union, Australia and New Zealand.

Nutrition plays an important role in keeping cattle healthy and strong. Implementing an adequate nutrition program can also improve milk production and reproductive performance. Nutrient requirements may not be the same depending on the animal's age and stage of production.

Forages, which refer especially to hay or straw, are the most common type of feed used. Cereal grains, as the main contributors of starch to diets, are important in meeting the energy needs of dairy cattle. Barley is one example of grain that is extensively used around the world. Barley is grown in temperate to sub-artic climates, and it is transported to those areas lacking the necessary amounts of grain. Although variations may occur, in general, barley is an excellent source of balanced amounts of protein, energy, and fiber.

Ensuring adequate body fat reserves is essential for cattle to produce milk and also to keep reproductive efficiency. However, if cattle get excessively fat or too thin, they run the risk of developing metabolic problems. Scientists have found that a variety of fat supplements can benefit conception rates of lactating dairy cows. Some of these different fats include oleic acids, found in canola oil, animal tallow, and yellow grease; palmitic acid found in granular fats and dry fats; and linolenic acids which are found in cottonseed, safflower, sunflower, and soybean. It is also important to note that proper levels of fat also improve cattle longevity.

Using by-products is one way of reducing the normally high feed costs. However, lack of knowledge of their nutritional and economic value limits their use. Although the reduction of costs may be significant, they have to be used carefully because animal may have negative reactions to radical changes in feeds, *e.g.* fog fever. Such a change must then be made slowly and with the proper follow up.

A survey of the primary dairy producing areas in the US indicated that 13 per cent of lactating animals were treated with insecticides permethrin, pyrethrin, coumaphos, and dichlorvos primarily by daily or every-other-day coat sprays. Workers, particularly in stanchion barns, may be exposed to higher than recommended amounts of these pesticides.

Breeds

In the United States, dairy cattle are divided into six major breeds. These are the: Holstein-Friesian, Brown Swiss, Guernsey, Ayrshire, Jersey, and Milking Shorthorn.

In Rajasthan, an indigenous breed called *Tharparkar* exists, named from the Tharparkar District, now in Sindh Pakistan. Another type of dairy cow known as *Nagauri* from Nagaur District, the bull of which is renowned for its ability to plow fields and run. Traditionally, they used to pull covered wagons, known as *rath*, and in marriages to transport the newlywed couple. They are now a crutch for thriving agricultural and livestock rearing societies of the Thar Desert.

Many other breeds are used nearly exclusively for beef, or for both dairy and beef purposes.

CHAPTER 9
Livestock and Small Farm Systems

India is endowed with huge livestock populations of various species. It has about 300 million bovines, which are used to produce milk, draught power, and dung manure. There are about 180 million small ruminants that provide meat and fibre. The animal productivity is, however, far below the world average. Malnutrition and poor health are the two most important constraints to raising animal productivity. Animals primarily feed on crop residues and common grazing lands. Supplementation with green fodder and concentrate feed is inadequate. Public sector animal health and breeding infrastructure has seen unrestrained growth, but the delivery of these services is poor.

The emphasis in health services is on curative treatment rather than on preventive management. As a result, many fatal diseases that have been eradicated elsewhere in the world are rampant among Indian livestock. This indicates that there is considerable scope to raise productivity of Indian livestock through technological and policy interventions. Accordingly, the aim of this paper is to document the livestock technologies available for field applications.

Livestock Production Under Small Farm Systems

India is predominantly a country of small farms, which account for nearly three-fourths of the total milk and meat production. More than 70 per cent of rural households possess one or two large animals or 2 to 5 small animals such as the goat, pigs, and poultry. Animals are largely maintained on crop residues. Large animals are partially stallfed and partly grazed on community land. Small animals are maintained solely on grazing. Their movements are not controlled and they are free to mix with other animals.

Most small livestock holders do not have proper housing facilities for animals. The animals are either kept outdoors or indoors with the humans. Some farmers maintain thatched or *pucca* sheds for large animals.

Small holders rarely apply scientific technology for breeding, feeding, health care, or management. They are unable to isolate or suitably care for sick animals. Nor can the farmers control the feeding or movements of their animals. Thus, the animals are exposed to diseases and environmental stress.

Potential Livestock Technologies to Augment Productivity

Researchers have long been striving to produce technologies in the fields of animal health, feeding, breeding, and management relevant to small farm systems. Various institutes such as the Indian Veterinary Research Institute (IVRI), National Dairy Research Institute (NDRI), Central Sheep and Wool Research Institute (CSWRI), Central Avian Research Institute (CARI), Central Institute for Research on Goats (CIRG), Central Institute for Research on Buffaloes (CIRB), Indian Grassland and Fodder Research Institute (IGFRI), and State Agricultural Universities are engaged in developing technologies relevant to smallholders.

The Indian Council of Agricultural Research (ICAR) has sanctioned several coordinated research projects and specific problem-oriented research projects on various aspects of animal husbandry. The All-India Coordinated Research Projects (AICRPs) on Breeding of Cattle, Buffalo, Pigs, Sheep, Goats, and Poultry.

Coordinated Projects on Economic Ration and Agro-Industrial By-products Utilization; and a number of other research projects/schemes have successfully evolved useful and adaptable technologies. These can be grouped into two broad categories: *(a)* technologies that can be used only by veterinarians (e.g. those related to disease diagnostic tests, preservation of semen and vaccines, and surgical treatment); and *(b)* those that can be adopted and used by farmers either on their own or with the help and guidance of field veterinarians (e.g. those related to cross breeding, vaccination, balanced ration, animal feed, improved management practices, and prophylactic measure against animal diseases).

Adoption of Livestock Technologies

Unlike agriculture, studies relating to adoption and impact of technologies in animal husbandry are limited and sporadic. Most of these are micro-level studies focusing on only a few technologies. This section reviews such studies.

Studies reveal varying levels of different livestock technologies. Researcher observed a very high adoption of improved breeding and disease control practices, while the adoption of feeding and management practices was low.

Several studies have reported that protective vaccination against contagious diseases, fodder feeding, clean watering, and proper shelter for animals are the technologies having the highest adoption percentages. AI has been partially adopted at some places and not at others. Practices such as dehorning calves, castrating young calves, use of improved fodder seeds, crossbreeding, balanced feeding, and scientific milking have had very low adoption levels.

Furthermore, some technologies are suitable for smallholders, while others are more suited to the large farmers. Researcher reported that spacious housing and year-round fodder production are more likely to be adopted by resourceful dairy farmers. Practices like taking special care of the calves and feeding of good quality grass during periods of scarcity have a better chance of adoption by smaller farmers. Some other technologies, such as AI and pregnancy diagnosis, are almost uniformly applicable to all categories of farmers. A study conducted in the Karnal district of Haryana found that "feeding rations for milk production" by landless agricultural labourers, marginal farmers, small farmers, and medium farmers was a highly suitable innovation. On the other hand, vaccination against hemorrhagic septicemia (HS), rinder pest (RP), foot and mouth disease (FMD), black quarter (BQ) and anthrax was found to be most suitable for adoption by large farmers. Scientists identified a number of constraints related to the adoption of various livestock technologies. He reported that the presence of unimproved bulls, males of crossbreeds, poor conception rates, and unavailability of AI facilities on farm are all constraints to adoption of breeding technologies. Unavailability of fodder seed, mineral mixture, and compound cattle feeds at convenient places, and their high costs, are the constraints inadoption of feeding technologies. The unavailability and high cost of medicine and absence of precise advice on cheap and comfortable housing are the main constraints to animal health and improved management practices.

Livestock Technologies and Small Production Systems

A number of technologies that are technically feasible under experimental conditions do not find wide acceptance among the final users because a majority of the users is either unaware of the technologies or unable to meet the requirements to make the technologies a success. Technologists attribute non-adoption or poor adoption to the inability of the extension systems to transfer such technologies, while extension personnel argue that farmers do not adopt technologies because of the mismatch between resource requirements of the technologies and their availability to the farmers. This is particularly the case with small and marginal farmers.

Livestock Technology Generation and Adoption

Animal science research has generated a number of useful technologies that can be gainfully adopted by farmers. The adoption level of most of the technologies is very low. The major reasons for the low level of adoption are:

- High cost of available technologies.
- Lack of awareness among the users (farmers).
- Lack of training in the proper use of technology.
- Technology is not situation-or farmer-specific.
- Inadequacy of veterinary facility for livestock in rural areas.
- Lack of adequate, organized processing and marketing facilities for animal products.
- Side effects of technology.
- Absence of field-testing and refinement of technology.

This analysis has questioned the appropriateness of livestock technologies under small farming systems prevailing in India. The alternatives are either to change the conditions as per the requirement of technology, which of course is impossible, or to generate technology appropriate to the resource-poor, risk-prone, diversified, and scattered small production units.

Generation of technology appropriate to such conditions is possible only through two approaches:

- Generation of technology through on-farm experimentation at the site and on the animals under small farming system unit – which is difficult and not always possible.
- Generation of technology at the research stations and its subsequent assessment and refinement through experimentation in collaboration with the farmers. The lack of established and standardized methodology for assessment and refinement of livestock technology and for conducting experimentation at the unorganized scattered small farm units needs to be viewed seriously. Research needs to be diverted to the design and development of such methodologies and approaches under participatory modes. Proper recognition and necessary incentives to the scientists, as well as farmers, would encourage participatory research.

CHAPTER 10
The Modern Poultry Industry

The emergence of the modern poultry industry in India has its roots in backyard poultry farming. It began with the introduction of scientific poultry farming by a few Christian missionary organisations towards the end of the nineteenth century with imports of some improved poultry breeds from their countries. However, systematic efforts to develop the poultry industry on scientific lines began postindependence. In the last five decades (1950 to 2000), egg production increased from 2.8 million to 30,000 million. Similarly, broiler production too witnessed considerable growth.

The tremendous growth in the poultry subsector is a result of application of modern technologies and growth of commercial poultry farming. There are now 60 thousand poultry farms under modern intensive systems of management. The indigenous fowl, however continues to play the key role in backyard poultry, and more than 100,000 families have flocks ranging from 5-250 birds.

The per capita availability of poultry products is considerably low; eggs and 500g meat per annum as against the requirement of 160 eggs and 10 kg meat per annum. The growing human population and sustained growth in per capita income will fuel higher growth in demand for eggs and poultry meat. There is thus a considerable potential for development of the poultry subsector in the country.

Extensive research has been carried out in various areas of poultry production such as breeding, nutrition, health care, and management. The paper briefly discusses the research achievements in the poultry subsector, and identifies future research thrusts to accelerate its growth.

Development of the Poultry Industry

Commercial poultry farming began under the first Five Year Plan (1951-55) with the establishment of 33 extension centres for providing improved breeds to interested farmers. The Second Five-year Plan gave further impetus to backyard poultry farming in rural areas and commercial farming in urban areas. In subsequent Five-year Plans poultry developments efforts were further strengthened with aid from foreign agencies such as United States Agency for International Development (USAID) and United Nations Development Programme (UNDP), and collaborations with foreign hatcheries.

Poultry research is conducted in both the public and private sectors. In the public sector, ICAR, the apex organisation for agricultural research in the country plays the key role in poultry research and development (R&D) activities. Research is carried out through its institutes such as the Central Avian Research Institute (CARI) and Indian Veterinary Research Institute (IVRI), Izatnagar project directorate, and also through 26 State Agricultural Universities (SAUs), and two veterinary universities. Other public sector institutions that contribute are Central Poultry Breeding Farms (CPBF), Central Food Technology Research Institute (CFTRI), and Animal Husbandry Departments of state governments. In the private sector the research focus is on pure-line breeding of layers and broilers, development of compounded feed, vaccines, and biologicals. Various poultry equipment such as incubators, hatchers, and farm equipment are also manufactured by private sector agencies.

Development of Superior Germplasm Commercial Layers and Broilers

Production of superior germplasm was the main focus of poultry development. Since the indigenous fowl was central to backyard farming, initial efforts aimed at genetically improving the indigenous stock. Later, the large-scale import of elite poultry stock as grand parents by the private sector, and as pure lines by the public sector, opened the way for commercial poultry farming. The incorporation of elite stock provided poultry breeders with a choice and resulted in a substantial increase in poultry meat and egg production. Initially, White Leghorn was imported for egg production, and thebreed was further improved through the family-selection method.

Subsequently, Rhode Island Red (RIR) populations were imported and other criteria for selection such as part-period production and egg mass were used for improvement. Rock and Cornish breeds were imported for crossing and selection to improve broiler production. Multi-trait selection index procedures were also used for selecting the better genotype in layers and broilers. The specialized selection and breeding programmes such as

Reciprocal Recurrent Selection (RRS), modified RRS and diallele were employed for selecting parent lines suitable for hybrid production.

The Central Avian Research Institute (CARI) explored possibilities for bringing an overall improvement in poultry productivity. A number of pure breeding programmes were established at CARI, at different centres of the All India Coordinated Research Project (AICRP) on poultry and at SAUs for development of superior germplasm of layers and broilers. The pure lines were then used for production of high-yielding hybrids. High performing syntheticbroiler stocks were also developed at the Punjab Agricultural University, Ludhiana (PAU), and CARI. As a result different superior layer and broiler stocks evolved and were released for use by the commercial poultry industry.

Backyard Poultry Farming

The indigenous poultry population is approximately 70 million, with annual egg production of 55-60 eggs per hen and egg weight of 40 g. Early efforts for improvement of the indigenous fowl failed due to the introduction of high-yielding commercial stocks. There is now a new concept of "Phenotypic replica of indigenous fowl" in backyard poultry farming for improving productivity. A number of crossbred stocks resembling indigenous fowls have been developed. Also, CARI has contributed significantly to the conservation and improvement of indigenous germplasm.

Testing and Evaluation of Germplasm

The superior stocks developed have undergone intensive testing by poultry breeders, large private hatcheries, non-governmental organisations (NGOs), and different centres using random sample poultry performance tests (RSPPT). Most of the layer and broiler stocks developed at CARI and different centres of the AICRP on poultry have repeatedly given excellent performances at RSPPT and were found comparable to those of private sector hatcheries. The commercial broilers developed at CARI attained a body weight of 1700 g at six weeks and 2100 g at seven weeks of age in RSPPT. The CARI stocks also had maximum survival rate and ranked higher in competition. The superior layer stock developed at different institutions showed encouraging performance. CARI-golden stock topped the brown egger entries with an egg production (HH) of 281 and 283 (HD) at random sample layer test (RSLT).

Required Inputs

To increase and sustain productivity of superior stocks, inputs such as quality feed, better health care, and a package of management practices need to be strengthened. The research and technological advancement in these areas are summarized below.

Nutrition and Feed Technology

Feed accounts for 70-75 per cent of the total operational cost of poultry production. Therefore, improving feed efficiency is important in maximizing profitability.

Poultry feed formulations were developed/revised for tropical climatic conditions and alternative and nonconventional feed resources were identified. Research proved the acceptability of de-oiled rice polish, sorghum, finger millet, pearl millet, and rice polish in poultry mashes and de-oiled sunflower cake, and ramtill cake as protein sources. The fishmeal was reduced and replaced by synthetic amino acids (lysine and methionine) and vitamins. The nutrient requirement of different classes and age groups of birds were determined to optimize production. Methods for improving nutrient values (enzyme utilization) were evolved, nonconventional poultry feeds were identified, and procedures for detoxification and improving the quality of feedstuff were standardized.

Health Care and Biosecurity

High mortality and morbidity caused by various diseases have been the major handicap in poultry production in the past. The facilities for disease diagnosis and production of phamaceuticals and vaccines were inadequate. However in the last three decades there has been a significant break through in poultry disease control. At present there are about 250 diagnostic laboratories, 28 veterinary colleges, three major vaccine producing projects in the private sector and 14 in the public sector. The advances in technologies such as.

Specific Pathogen Free (SPF) egg, monoclonal antibodies, rDNA and membrane antigen system are used for vaccine production. Research has generated effective diagnostic measures and vaccines against several killer diseases such as Newcastle Disease (ND), fowl pox (FP), Marek's disease;

(MD), and Infectious Bursal disease (IBD). There is still, however, a lack of facilities for testing vaccine efficacy, spot diagnosis, and farmer-oriented health care in rural areas.

Uncontrolled movement of poultry and its products has further complicated the situation. The changing management practices have enabled pathogens to modify themselves and appear as new pathogens causing new diseases. There has been a re emergence of old diseases such as ND, Avian Influenza (AI) and FP, and new disease problems such as leechi disease, Inclusion Body Hepatitis (IBH) and Egg Drop Syndrome (EDS) have also emerged. Variation of recognized diseases such as IBD, Infectious Bronchitis (IB), and MD and syndromes, resulting from the interaction of more than one pathogen, such as Swollen Head Syndrome (SHS), Blue Wing disease, and infectious enteropathies have also been observed. Biotechnological tools such as diagnostic probes and PCR-based DNA amplification have proved useful in proper diagnosis. Use of endogenous and thermostable microorganisms for vaccine development have proved efficient in controlling diseases in rural areas. The development of immunomodulators and pharmaceuticals has also contributed significantly.

Poultry Reproduction

Poultry reproduction technologies have contributed considerably towards increasing the use of superior germplasm. Advances in semen evaluation, semen diluents, and artificial insemination of poultry germplasm have all helped augment the production. A simple semen diluent has been developed that successfully preserves the fertilizing ability of chicken spermatozoa for 24 hours at low temperature. A technique for evaluating the fertilizing ability of male quail has also been developed.

Poultry Equipment

India has made considerable progress in manufacturing a wide range of housing, incubation, watering, and vaccination equipment. The automation and innovation in poultry-shed ventilation and environmentally controlled houses have been demonstrated widely. There has been a rise in the use of automated feeding and drinking systems, nipple and cup drinkers, mediators and dosers, electric time switches, manure drying and disposal machines, and beak trimming and mass vaccination equipment. The hatchery equipment segments are manufacturing large incubators.

Automatic small, broiler processing plants that meet local demand and export norms are the need of the new millennium. The quality of factorydressed chicken, cut-up parts, and deboned chicken needs to be improved.

Potential Benefits

The superior stocks of broilers and layers have altogether revolutionized the poultry industry. In the 1950s a layer used to produce 200-220 eggs with an efficiency of 3.4-3.5 kg feed kg^{-1} egg., which has now increased to 290-300 eggs with efficiency of 2.5-2.6 kg feed kg^{-1} egg. Similarly, 30-40 years ago, broilers used to attain a body weight of 0.8 kg in eight weeks and approximately 3.2 kg feed was required per kg body weight. Now, average body weight reaches 1.7-1.8 kg, with feed efficiency of 1.8-2.0 kg feed kg^{-1} live weight at six weeks.

Adoption of Technologies

The level of adoption of technologies in the organized sector has been adequate. A large number of farmers and commercial poultry breeders have dopted many technologies related to poultry breeding, nutrition, health and management. However, in the unorganized sector, the adoption is slow due to several constraints. On average, more than one-third of the total poultry population in the country belongs to the improved category.

The dissemination and adoption of technologies take place via different pathways. In the public sector, the ICAR institutes such as CARI, Izatnagar and Project Directorate on Poultry (PDP), Hyderabad are the main centres that develop technologies and disseminate them among farmers, large private hatcheries and NGOs. The large commercial breeders and hatcheries in the private sector procure and develop the superior grandparent stock. The parent stocks are sold to the franchisees, which ultimately produce the commercial hybrids that are sold to end-users. Thus, there is a network of functionaries engaged in poultry farming. The superior stocks require better feed, proper vaccination, medication, and a package of improved management practices. The main constraint in the adoption of technologies is higher cost of inputs resulting in low profitability.

Fluctuating market trends in terms of seasonality in consumption of poultry products and their prices also restrict adoption. Various myths prevalent in Indian society were also responsible for the non-adoption of new techniques during the early years of introduction of improved poultry. These included the idea that the egg from the indigenous fowl is more nutritious than that of commercial hybrids, and that the same holds good for the meat. Illiteracy, lack of awareness, and religious taboos have also been major causes for slow adoption of poultry technologies. The myths are however on the wane and increasing literacy and easily available credit facilities are encouraging poultry farmers to adopt new technologies.

Other Poultry Germplasm

The chicken has been in the forefront of research because it accounts for more than 90 per cent of the poultry population. Ducks come next and are popular in states such as Assam, West Bengal, Orissa, Andhra Pradesh, Tamil Nadu, Kerala and Tripura. However, the research efforts on ducks are severely lacking.

Quail has enormous potential as a producer of meat of excellent quality, taste and delicacy. Quails were primarily imported as pilot animals in 1974 at the Poultry Research Division (now the CARI) of IVRI. The good qualities of quail include smaller gestation interval, small space requirement, and high productivity, making this species suitable for commercial exploitation. The research at CARI has led to production of superior stock , as well as development of a package of practices for quail farming. Quail meat and eggs are now becoming popular in several parts of the country. Nevertheless, more research efforts are required to expand quail farming.

Research on guinea fowl was initiated about a decade ago. Selective breeding for juvenile weight and high immuno-competence has resulted in increased body weights and improved lifespan. Guinea fowl is popular for its excellent meat, foraging habits, inherent hardiness, and resistance to common poultry diseases. Recently, research on turkeys has also been initiated at CARI with the objective of developing an adaptable small turkey.

Emerging Technologies

Ex Vivo Embryo Culture, Chimera Production and Transgenesis

The advances in the areas of molecular biology and embryo manipulation have made it possible to transfer the gene of choice from a donor to a heterologous recipient to augment its production or to produce the pharmaceuticals/protein of choice. The chick has become a classical model system in developmental biology, providing a vast amount of detailed morphological and descriptive data of the processes of growth and differentiation. Traditional work in chickens has also led to significant advances in the understanding ofvertebrate immunology and physiology.

There has been excellent progress in the background techniques required specifically for poultry such as the double window ex vivo embryo culture system, single stage embryo-culture system, and ex vivo culture system for guinea fowl and quail. The first millennium chick and the world's first guinea fowl keet using *ex vivo* embryo culture system were produced at CARI. These new techniques and modifications have improved embryo survival rate andenabled faster and easier application of microinjection, and blastodermal celland primordial germ cell (PGC) transfer procedures for production of transgenic poultry.

The stage × blastoderm cells collected from freshly laid eggs contain PGC and start to differentiate at around stage × from the pluripotent blastodermal cells. For transgenic chicken to be produced using blastodermal cell chimeras, techniques for in vitro genetic modification of blastodermal cells are required. Since chicken embryonic stem cell lines are currently unavailable and blastodermal cells capable of forming germline chimeras can only be maintained in culture for up to seven days, research to date hasfocused on the transfection of freshly isolated blastodermal cells.

Breeding for Tolerance to Climatic Stresses

Certain major genes, such as those for the naked neck and frizzle, contribute significantly to heat stress tolerance. These genes reduce the total feather cover and the feather structure of the bird to enable more efficient heat dissipation. Research has resulted in the production of a naked neck population (CARI-MRITUNJAI) that is better adapted to tropical climates.

Naked neck stocks developed at CARI performed excellently when tested at different centres of RSPPT and in the field.

Molecular and Immuno Competence Investigations

Variability is one of the important tools for improving stocks. The variability investigated at genome level, through RAPD-PCR and DNA fingerprinting, enables selection of suitable parents for production of commercial hybrids. Research on these lines has generated a lot of data in layers and broilers. Molecular investigations may thus prove of immense value in augmenting production through production of further superior germplasm. Genetic resistance to diseases has always been an important issue for poultry research. Several investigations have shown that indirect selection byincorporating immunocompetence traits into selection procedure is the best method for enhancing the bird's overall resistance to diseases. Investigations have shown that commercial broilers have high immunocompetence levels. Further investigations through marking lines for immunological traits and studying the differences at major histocompatibility complex (MHC) region are under way in order to find suitable marker(s)/ immunological trait(s) thatcan be used as selection criteria.

Future Perspectives

Although the poultry industry has grown tremendously on all fronts there is still scope for improving productivity. The explosion of knowledge in molecular biology will have profound impact on all branches of poultry science.

Molecular Genetic Mapping and Transgenesis

- Good progress has been made at integrating poultry maps, representing some 1400 loci so far. The average spacing between markers on the combined linkage maps is approaching 2 centi Morgans (cM), which is adequate for knowing the location of functional genes. Such a minimal genome map is normally a prerequisite for locating useful Quantitative Trait Loci (QTL) for subsequent marker-assisted selection (MAS). In the future, researchers will attempt to integrate MAS optimally with the conventional quantitative genetics approach to poultry breeding.
- Identification, localization, and cloning of useful candidate genes are prerequisites for their manipulation to produce transgenic chicken using the new DNA technology
- There has been considerable progress in development of background techniques for producing transgenic poultry. Application of these could enable dramatic gains in egg and meat productivity, disease resistance, and production of human proteins in eggs.

- Transgenic poultry would help to give new insights into many areas such as immunology, cancer biology, developmental biology, and physiology. The production of transgenic chicken will give scientists a unique opportunity to investigate gene expression and function within the complexity of a living organism.
- The time scale of progress in molecular biotechnology is largely proportional to the resources made available for the necessary research and development. In the case of poultry bio-technology, the resources have been minimal and need to be increased substantially.
- Poultry biodiversity, i.e. the set of genetically diverse poultry resources, must be preserved and conserved to sustain agricultural development.
- Blastodermal cells, PGCs, DNA, and spermatozoa can be preserved in the form of genome banks storing these at -196 0C in liquid nitrogen.

Poultry Health

- The application of molecular biotechnology to produce improved diagnostic kits and vaccines is now well established and will continue to grow as a major component of disease control in the years ahead.
- Increasing the innate resistance of birds to infections and parasites can increase disease control.
- Significant progress has been made in recent years on many aspects of the immune system and MHC-related basic studies that will ensure practical industrial applications in the near future.
- Low-cost thermostable vaccines and effective disease control of poultry in rural small-scale poultry production are required.
- Disease surveillance and forecasting systems need further strengthening.

Poultry Nutrition

- Basic research in nutritional biochemistry and physiology requires attention so that future nutritional technologies can be more science-based and less empirical.
- Alternative and cheaper ingredients for poultry feed must be developed, preferably locally.
- Production of genetically modified feeds with higher nutritive value for poultry should also be looked into more seriously.
- The definition of specific nutrient requirements for new and specific strains of poultry should become a regular feature of applied nutrition research.
- Low cost feed supplements should be developed based on local ingredients not used for human consumption.

Poultry Reproduction

- The poor reproductive performance of broiler breeder females should be given priority in poultry reproduction research. Solving the problem will depend on a deeper understanding of the basic neuroendocrine mechanisms involved.
- A further area of research likely to yield practical applications is that of the genetics of sex determination and the possibility of manipulating the sex ratio, i.e., to maximize female chicks in commercial layer strains or male chicks in commercial broiler strains.

General Consideration

- Cost effectiveness of various technologies should be evaluated.
- Collaboration among institutes and with NGOs and related agencies should be encouraged.
- Superior genetic stocks should be imported as and when required for improving efficiency of breeding programmes.
- Poultry science courses must be given more emphasis at graduate and postgraduate levels in all the veterinary colleges and universities.

CHAPTER 11
The Productivity of Goats

The goat is one of the most important species of livestock in India. It has short generation interval, high prolificacy, and is easily adaptable to a wide range of climatic conditions. These characteristics give it a greater relevance in the household economy of the poor, particularly in the marginal environments including arid, semi-arid, and mountain regions. In these environments rainfall is erratic and frequency of crop failure is high. The goat is capable of survivingon sparse vegetation and in extreme climates.

Goat meat is the most preferred meat in the country. Almost 95 per cent of the goat meat produced in the country is consumed locally; though per capita availability is far below the requirement. The goat produces a variety of other useful products and by-products including milk, skins, fleeces, and manure. In hilly regions, goats are valued for both meat and fine fibre (*pashmina*) production.

The productivity of goats in India is low. The average carcass weight is only 10 kg, lower than the world average of 12 kg. The milk productivity is also low. One of the main causes of low productivity is lack of adoption of scientific methods of production, and limited commercialisation of goat keeping.

Nevertheless, there is considerable potential to raise the productivity of goats and their economic and food security contributions, as India has a large number of important breeds of goat. This paper examines the population dynamics and contribution of goats, and identifies potential technologies for improving meat and milk productivity.

Goats constitute an important productive asset of the country that generates a flow of income and employment throughout the year, especially for the landless, marginal, and small landholders. These constitute about 85 per cent of all households, but occupy only one-third of the total land in India. On the other hand, the distribution of livestock wealth, including sheep and goats is more equitable. These households maintain about 71 per cent of the small ruminant population largely on common lands and harvested fields. Thus, they can beprofitably raised with low investment in extensive and semi-intensive systems.

The goat population in India has increased faster than all other major livestock species during the past two decades. From 1972-97, goats increased at an annual rate of 2.7 per cent, despite nearly 41 per cent of goats being slaughtered annually, and another 15.5 per cent dying of natural causes.

Density and Distribution

Due to the goat's adaptability to a variety of agroclimates, the goat population is distributed widely throughout India. Yet there are marked variations in its distribution and density across states . Livestock policy aimed to restrict the goat population to 40 million and increase the number of sheep to 70 million by A.D. 2000. Despite this, the population of goats rose to 115 million in 1992, whereas the population of sheep remained at 51 million. This reflects the socioeconomic relevance and wide adaptability of goats.

Their population is concentrated largely in Bihar and West Bengal in the East; Rajasthan, Maharashtra, and Madhya Pradesh in the West; and Uttar Pradesh in the North. The density of goats is highest in West Bengal (160 goats km^{-2}), followed by Bihar. In Assam, Kerala, Madhya Pradesh, Rajasthan, Tamilnadu and Uttar Pradesh there are 40-50 goats km^{-2}. The lowest density is in Jammu and Kashmir (8 goats km^{-2}), closely followed by Punjab.

Goats are often blamed for denuding the vegetative cover and causing desertification. If the density of goats is an indicator, the blame is unfounded. West Bengal and Bihar have the highest densities of goats, but there are no signs of desertification in these States. It is undoubtedly true that large populations of goats or any other livestock continuously grazing throughout the year in a small area would be extremely harmful to the growth of vegetation. Deforestation coupled with overgrazing by livestock will also have adverse consequences on the forests and wastelands. Therefore, in order to get the best from the system, the animals and common property resources (CPRs) must be properly managed.

Technologies for Enhancing Goat Productivity

The Central Institute for Research on Goats (CIRG), an off shoot of ICAR, is the main institute that conducts basic and applied research on goat production. The Institute has developed technologies and standardized methods for improving the productivity of goats. If effectively transferred to the goat farmers, these would go a long way in improving goat productivity. The rest of the paper deals with the technologies available for application in the field.

Genetic Improvement of Goats

There are twenty well-recognized goat breeds in India suited to different geographical and climatic conditions. Since 1971, systematic scientific efforts have been made to improve the genetic potential of goats in terms of increasing milk, meat, and fibre production. The superior germplasm, especially those of Barbari and Jamunapari breeds maintained at CIRG, could be used for breeding high-yielding animals.

Optimizing Survival of Goats

The well-managed goat is less likely to succumb to diseases. Those such as *peste des petits ruminants* (PPR), foot and mouth disease, brucellosis, and pustular dermatitis are widely prevalent in different regions. A number of research projects in the area of goat health have been successful to some extent in reducing mortality due to diseases. The CIRG has developed an annual goat health calendar for organized flocks. Implementation ofthis calendar could help check the mortality and production losses due todiseases up to 70 per cent.

Artificial Insemination

Limited access to good quality breeding bucks is one of the reasons for low productivity of goats. Artificial insemination, which has been standardized, could be used effectively as a breeding method for multiplication of superior quality animals. Semen production potentials have been worked out for breeds such as the Jamunapari, Baribari, Jhakrana, Kutchi, Marwari, and Sirohi. Studies have been conducted on sexual maturity and optimal age for semen production in different goat breeds. Bacterial load in buck semen has been worked out. A protocol for freezing buck semen has been developed that retains 50–55 per cent motility and 40 per cent fertility. The deep cervical insemination technique with freshly diluted semen has been standardized with a 75 per cent fertility rate in goats. A fertility rate of 50 per cent has been obtained with frozen semen using deep cervical insemination.

Structures and Appliances for Organised Goat Farms

Various structures and appliances for goat farms have been standardised that are essential for better management and the higher growth rate of goats. They also reduce contamination and wastage of feed.

Provision of optimum floor space in goat houses is essential for thecomfort of goats and to maintain higher survival rates and minimize disease incidence. Goats need covered as well as open space (paddock), and the requirement for the latter was found to be different for different age groups.

Ventilation Space

Proper ventilation provides enough oxygen for the animals, helps remove spent gases and moisture, and maintains a suitable vapour pressure in the shed. Ventilation also allows sufficient sunlight into the sheds. Ventilation of sheds affects the performance of goats and should be maintained at an optimum. Inhot dry periods a total ventilation space 70 per cent of the floor area should be provided. In hot humid regions, two facing sides of the wall should be kept totally open. During cool weather, 2–10 per cent ventilation is required, and during the rest of the year ventilation space should not be less than 25 per cent. A set of suitable feeders and watering mangers for goats of different age groups were developed for use in organized goat farms and villages to reduce contamination and wastage of feeds. Skilled and semi-skilled persons can fabricate this equipment in small workshops, using easily available materials such as angle iron, GI sheets, iron bars, and welding rods. The feeders and watering mangers were extensively tested and found suitable for use by both goats and sheep. The height of the feeding trough should be kept at theaverage shoulder point height of the animal for goats aged more than three months. For kids below three months the height should be 25 per cent less than the average shoulder point height. The feeders developed were suitable for feeding of concentrate, pelleted feed, dry fodder (straw), green fodder, and silage. The wastage of feed materials was reduced drastically using these, and there was no contamination by goat feces and urine.

Grazing and Carrying Capacity

As grazing resources are shrinking, tree fodder will be an important alternative for feeding goats. Harvested dried leaves could form part of a complete feed (pellets). Some of the promising feeds are:

1. 60 per cent Anni (*Chlorodendron phlomides*) leaves, and 40 per cent concentrate mixture (maize, barley, groundnut cake, sesame cake, mineral mixture and salt);
2. 40 per cent Heens (*Capparis horrida*) leaves, 20 per cent Arhar (*Cajanus cajan*) straw, and 40 per cent concentrate mixture; and
3. 40 per cent neem (*Azadirachta indica*) dry leaves (winter season), 30 per cent arhar straw, and 30 per cent concentrate mixture.

Urea treatment was found to be economical for improving poor quality straws. A complete ration was formulated using treated barley straw 47 per cent, barley grain 32 per cent, arhar straw 20 per cent and mineral mixture with salt one per cent, which can maintain adult goats. Twenty per cent subabul (*Leucaena* spp.) leaves in a complete feed yielded better growth and higher carcass production. Leaves of indigenousbabul (*Acacia nilotica*) at 15 per cent level in a complete feed were found to improve milk productivity. Subabul also has potential as feed for chevon production as it has no deleterious effect on various economic traits and carcass characteristics.

Value-added Products

Meat from Spent Goats

A nutrient dense shelf-stable dehydrated minced meat product (Chevon) has been prepared from spent (those animals that are no longer useful or productive) goats using 20 per cent split dehusked lentil paste. Good quality chevon pickle with better shelf life at ambient temperature could be prepared using mustard oil, acetic acid, dry and green spices, and cane sugar (flavour enhancer).

Curing and mechanical tenderizing of partially frozen meat chunks from spent goat carcasses helped overcome the problem of dark red color, strong flavor, and toughness. Good quality sausages with higher yield were manufactured from spent buck meat and have a shelf life of seven days under refrigeration.

Incorporation of 0.5 per cent phosphate mixture in *shami kabab* formulation resulted in an improvement of organoleptic scores, and yield and retention of the product's organoleptic traits on cold storage. The major cause of spoilage was visible surface mold growth. The product could safely be preserved for 14 days under refrigeration. Good quality Chevon *samosa* may be prepared from spent goat meat using 10 per cent cooked mashed potatoes. Goat stomach, often rejected by meat eaters, can be used to manufacture a crisp snack containing 55 per cent protein.

Goat Milk Products

Good quality *paneer* could be prepared from goat milk using citric acid (0.15% w/w) and fermented *paneer* whey as coagulants. *Paneer* packed in polypropylene bags could safely be preserved for three days under refrigeration (4+1°C). Addition of 2.0-2.5 per cent food grade gelatin was found beneficial for producing goat milk *shrikhand* of desired quality. The *shrikhand* could be preserved safely in glass containers for three days at ambient temperature and 30 days under refrigeration (4±1°C). Among the nonconventional milk coagulants used, *chhana* prepared using lactic acid was found superior to *chhana* prepared using hydrochloric acid solution, fermented *paneer* whey, and citric acid.

The technologies and methods discussed in this chapter have the potential to enhance the productivity and thereby the profitability of goats. Although both small and large goat farmers could use these, technologies befitting small farmers are needed for development of these systems. To ensure sustainable development of goat husbandry, the research and development efforts in the following areas should be given priority:

- Provision of good quality breeding bucks. Intensified efforts to prevent and control diseases, especially PPR and Johne's disease.
- Improvement of common grazing resources.
- Cessation of slaughter of underage animals.
- Commercialization and intensification of the goat enterprise.

CHAPTER 12
Domestication of the Chicken

The chicken (*Gallus gallus domesticus*) is a domesticated fowl, a subspecies of the Red Junglefowl. As one of the most common and widespread domestic animals, and with a population of more than 24 billion in 2003, there are more chickens in the world than any other species of bird. Humans keep chickens primarily as a source of food, consuming both their meat and their eggs.

The evidence suggests that domestication of the chicken was already under way in Thailand, Vietnam and the South East Asian jungles over 10,000 years ago, and spread into neighboring regions to the east such as China, and towards the west in India where it was conventionally thought to have been domesticated From India the domesticated fowl made its way to the Persianized kingdom of Lydia in western Asia Minor, and domestic fowl were imported to Greece by the fifth century BC. Fowl had been known in Egypt since the 18th Dynasty, with the "bird that lays every day" having come to Egypt from the land between Syria and Shinar, Babylonia, according to the annals of Tutmose III.

In the U.K. and Ireland adult male chickens are primarily known as *cocks*, whereas in America, Canada and Australia they are more commonly called *roosters*. Males under a year old are *cockerels*. Castrated roosters are called *capons* (surgical and chemical castration are now illegal in some parts of the world). Females over a year old are known as *hens*, and younger females are *pullets*. In Australia and New Zealand (also sometimes in Britain), there is a generic term *chook* (pronounced: rhymes with "book") to describe all ages and both sexes. Babies are called *chicks*, and the meat is called *chicken*.

"Chicken" originally referred to chicks, not the species itself. The species as a whole was then called *domestic fowl*, or just *fowl*. This use of "chicken" survives in the phrase "Hen and Chickens", sometimes used as a British public house or theatre name, and to name groups of one large and many small rocks or islands in the sea.

Chickens are omnivores. In the wild, they often scratch at the soil to search for seeds, insects and even larger animals such as lizards or young mice.

Chickens may live for five to ten years, depending on the breed. In commercial intensive farming, a meat chicken generally lives six weeks before slaughter. A free range or organic meat chicken will usually be slaughtered at about 14 weeks. Hens of special laying breeds may produce as many as 300 eggs a year. After 12 months, the hen's egg-laying ability starts to decline, and commercial laying hens are then slaughtered and used in processed foods, or sold as "soup hens". The world's oldest chicken, a hen, died of heart failure at the age of 16 according to the Guinness Book of World Records.

Roosters can usually be differentiated from hens by their striking plumage of long flowing tails and shiny, pointed feathers on their necks (*hackles*) and backs (*saddle*) which are typically of brighter, bolder colours than those of females of the same species. However, in some breeds, such as the Sebright, the rooster has only slightly pointed neck feathers, the same colour as the hen's. The identification must be made by looking at the comb, or eventually from the development of spurs on the male's legs (in a few breeds and in certain hybrids the male and female chicks may be differentiated by colour). Adult chickens have a fleshy crest on their heads called a *comb* or *cockscomb*, and hanging flaps of skin either side under their beaks called *wattles*. Both the adult male and female have wattles and combs, but in most breeds these are more prominent in males. A *muff* or *beard* is a mutation found in several chicken breeds which causes extra feathering under the chicken's face, giving the appearance of a beard.

Domestic chickens are not capable of long distance flight, although lighter birds are generally capable of flying for short distances, such as over fences or into trees (where they would naturally roost). Chickens may occasionally fly briefly to explore their surroundings, but generally do so only to flee perceived danger.

Chickens are gregarious birds and live together in flocks. They have a communal approach to the incubation of eggs and raising of young. Individual chickens in a flock will dominate others, establishing a "pecking order", with dominant individuals having priority for food access and nesting locations. Removing hens or roosters from a flock causes a temporary disruption to this social order until a new pecking order is established. Adding hens—especially younger birds—to an existing flock can lead to violence and injury.

Hens will try to lay in nests that already contain eggs, and have been known to move eggs from neighboring nests into their own. Some farmers use fake eggs made from plastic or stone (or golf balls) to encourage hens to lay in a particular location. The result of this behavior is that a flock will use only a few preferred locations, rather than having a different nest for every bird.

Hens can also be extremely stubborn about always laying in the same location. It is not unknown for two (or more) hens to try to share the same nest at the same time. If the nest is small, or one of the hens is particularly determined, this may result in chickens trying to lay on top of each other.

Skull of a chicken three weeks old. Here the opisthotic bone appears in the occipital region, as in the adult Chelonian. bo = Basi-occipital, bt = Basi-temporal, eo = Opisthotic, f = Frontal, fm = Foramen magnum, fo = Fontanella, oc = Occipital condyle, op = Opisthotic, p = Parietal, pf = Post-frontal, sc = Sinus canal in supra-occipital, so = Supra-occpital, sq = Squamosal, 8 = Exit of vagus nerve.

Roosters crowing (a loud and sometimes shrill call) is a territorial signal to other roosters. However, crowing may also result from sudden disturbances within their surroundings. Hens cluck loudly after laying an egg, and also to call their chicks. Chickens also give a low "warning call" when they think they see a predator approaching.

In 2006, scientists researching the ancestry of birds "turned on" a chicken recessive gene, *talpid* 2, and found that the embryo jaws initiated formation of teeth, like those found in ancient bird fossils. John Fallon, the overseer of the project, stated that chickens have "... retained the ability to make teeth, under certain conditions..."

Food Sharing and Courting

When a rooster finds food, he may call other chickens to eat first. He does this by clucking in a high pitch as well as picking up and dropping the food. This behavior may also be observed in mother hens to call their chicks and encourage them to eat.

To initiate courting, some roosters may dance in a circle around or near a hen ("a circle dance"), often lowering his wing which is closest to the hen. The dance triggers a response in the hen's brain, and when the hen responds to his "call", the rooster may mount the hen and proceed with the fertilization.

Breeding

Origins

The domestic chicken is descended primarily from the Red Junglefowl (*Gallus gallus*) and is scientifically classified as the same species. As such it can and does freely interbreed with populations of red jungle fowl. Recent genetic analysis has revealed that at least the gene for yellow skin was incorporated into domestic birds through hybridization with the Grey Junglefowl (*G. sonneratii*). It is believed by some that a single domestication event occurring in the region of modern Thailand created the modern chicken with minor transitions separating the modern breeds. Others believe that the intensive interbreeding which occurred in the past gave the modern chicken multiple origins in the jungles of South and Southeast Asia.

Researchers have found chickens' bones in unusual amounts and out of natural jungle range, thus denoting a breeding place. Bones of domestic chickens from about 6000-4000 BC have been found in Yangshao and Peiligan, China, from a time when the Holocene climate was not naturally suitable for the *Gallus* species. Archaeological data are lacking for Thailand and southeast Asia.

Later traces are found about 3000-2000 BC in Harappa and Mohenjo-Daro, Pakistan, and - according to linguistic researchers - in Austronesian populations traveling across southeast Asia and Oceania. A northern road spread chicken to the Tarim basin of Central Asia, modern day Iran. The chicken reached Europe (Romania, Turkey, Greece, Ukraine) about 3000 BC, and the Indus Valley about 2500 BC. Introduction into Western Europe came far later, about the 1st millennium BC. Phoenicians spread chickens along the Mediterranean coasts, to Iberia. Breeding increased under the Roman Empire, and was reduced in the Middle Ages. Middle East traces of chicken go back to a little earlier than 2000 BC, in Syria; chicken went southward only in the 1st millennium BC. The chicken reached Egypt for purposes of cock fighting about 1400BC, and became widely bred only in Ptolemaic Egypt (about 300 BC). Little is known about the chicken's introduction into Africa. Three possible ways of introduction in about the early first millennium AD could have been through the Egyptian Nile Valley, the East Africa Roman-Greek or Indian trade, or from Carthage and the Berbers, across the Sahara. The earliest known remains are from Mali, Nubia, East Coast, and South Africa and date back to the middle of the first millennium AD. Domestic chicken in the Americas before Western conquest is still an ongoing discussion, but blue-egged chicken, found only in the Americas and Asia, suggest an Asian origin for early American chickens.

A lack of data from Thailand, Russia, the Indian sub-continent, Southeast Asia and Sub-Saharan Africa makes it difficult to lay out a clear map of the spread of chickens in these areas; better description and genetic analysis of local breeds threatened by extinction may also help with research into this area.

Under natural conditions, most birds lay only until a clutch is complete, and they will then incubate all the eggs. Many domestic hens will also do this—and are then said to "go broody". The broody hen will stop laying and instead will focus on the incubation of the eggs (a full clutch is usually about 12 eggs). She will "sit" or "set" on the nest, protesting or pecking in defense if disturbed or removed, and she will rarely leave the nest to eat, drink, or dust-bathe. While brooding, the hen maintains the nest at a constant temperature and humidity, as well as turning the eggs regularly during the first part of the incubation. To stimulate broodiness, an owner may place many artificial eggs in the nest, or to stop it they may place the hen in an elevated cage with an open wire floor.

At the end of the incubation period (about 21 days), the eggs, if fertile, will hatch. Development of the egg starts only when incubation begins, so they all hatch within a day or two of each other, despite perhaps being laid over a period of two weeks or so. Before hatching, the hen can hear the chicks peeping inside the eggs, and will gently cluck to stimulate them to break out of their shells. The chick begins by "pipping"; pecking a breathing hole with its egg tooth towards the blunt end of the egg, usually on the upper side. It will then rest for some hours, absorbing the remaining egg yolk and withdrawing the blood supply from the membrane beneath the shell (used earlier for breathing through the shell). It then enlarges the hole, gradually turning round as it goes, and eventually severing the blunt end of the shell completely to make a lid. It crawls out of the remaining shell, and its wet down dries out in the warmth of the nest.

The hen will usually stay on the nest for about two days after the first egg hatches, and during this time the newly hatched chicks live off the egg yolk they absorb just before hatching. Any eggs not fertilized by a rooster will not hatch, and the hen eventually loses interest in these and leaves the nest. After hatching, the hen fiercely guards the chicks, and will brood them when necessary to keep them warm, at first often returning to the nest at night. She leads them to food and water; she will call them to edible items, but seldom feeds them directly. She continues to care for them until they are several weeks old, when she will gradually lose interest and eventually start to lay again.

Modern egg-laying breeds rarely go broody, and those that do often stop part-way through the incubation. However, some "utility" (general purpose) breeds, such as the Cochin, Cornish and Silkie, do regularly go broody, and they make excellent mothers, not only for chicken eggs but also for those of other species—even those with much smaller or larger eggs and different incubation periods, such as quail, pheasants, turkeys or geese. Chicken eggs can also be hatched under a broody duck, with varied success.

More than 50 billion chickens are reared annually as a source of food, for both their meat and their eggs. Chickens farmed for meat are called broiler chickens, whilst those farmed for eggs are called egg-laying hens. In total, the UK alone consumes over 29 million eggs per day. Some hens can produce over 300 eggs a year. Chickens will naturally live for 6 or more years, but broiler chickens typically take less than six weeks to reach slaughter size. For laying hens, they are slaughtered after about 12 months, when the hens' productivity starts to decline.

The vast majority of poultry are raised using intensive farming techniques. According to the Worldwatch Institute, 74 per cent of the world's poultry meat, and 68 per cent of eggs are produced this way. One alternative to intensive poultry farming is free range farming.

Friction between these two main methods has led to long term issues of ethical consumerism. Opponents of intensive farming argue that it harms the environment, creates human health risks and is inhumane. Advocates of intensive farming say that their highly efficient systems save land and food resources due to increased productivity, stating that the animals are looked after in state-of-the-art environmentally controlled facilities.

Incubation can successfully occur artificially in machines that provide the correct, controlled environment for the developing chick. The average incubation period for chickens is 21 days but may depend on the temperature and humidity in the incubator. Temperature regulation is the most critical factor for a successful hatch. Variations of more than 1°F from the optimum temperature of 99.5°F (37.5°C) will reduce hatch rates. Humidity is also important because the rate at which eggs lose water by evaporation depends on the ambient relative humidity. Evaporation can be assessed by candling, to view the size of the air sac, or by measuring weight loss. Relative humidity should be increased to around 70 per cent in the last three days of incubation to keep the membrane around the hatching chick from drying out after the chick cracks the shell. Lower humidity is usual in the first 18 days to ensure adequate evaporation. The position of the eggs in the incubator can also influence hatch rates. For best results, eggs should be placed with the pointed ends down and turned regularly (at least three times per day) until one to three days before hatching. If the eggs aren't turned, the embryo inside may stick to the shell and may hatch with physical defects. Adequate ventilation is necessary to provide the embryo with oxygen. Older eggs require increased ventilation.

Many commercial incubators are industrial-sized with shelves holding tens of thousands of eggs at a time, with rotation of the eggs a fully automated process. Home incubators are boxes holding from half a dozen to 75 eggs; they are usually electrically powered, but in the past some were heated with an oil or paraffin lamp.

Chicken eggs are widely used in many types of dishes, both sweet and savory, including many baked goods. Eggs can be scrambled, fried, hard-boiled, soft-boiled, pickled, and poached. The albumen, or egg white, contains protein but little or no fat, and can be used in cooking separately from the yolk. Egg whites may be aerated or whipped to a light, fluffy consistency and are often used in desserts such as meringues and mousse. Ground egg shells are sometimes used as a food additive to deliver calcium. Some people prefer to just have a female, and raise it for the eggs.

The meat of the chicken, also called "chicken", is a type of poultry meat. Because of its relatively low cost, chicken is one of the most used meats in the world. Nearly all parts of the bird can be used for food, and the meat can be cooked in many different ways. Popular chicken dishes include roasted chicken, fried chicken, chicken soup, Buffalo wings, tandoori chicken, butter chicken, and chicken rice. Chicken is also a staple of many fast food restaurants.

Chickens as Pets

Chickens are sometimes kept as pets and can be tamed by hand feeding, but roosters can sometimes become aggressive and noisy. Some have advised against keeping them around very young children. Certain breeds, however, such as silkies and many bantam varieties are generally docile and are often recommended as good pets around children with disabilities. Some people find chickens' behaviour entertaining and educational.

The meat of the chicken, also called "chicken", is a type of poultry meat. Because of its relatively low cost, chicken is one of the most used meats in the world. Nearly all parts of the bird can be used for food, and the meat can be cooked in many different ways. Popular chicken dishes include roasted chicken, fried chicken, chicken soup, Buffalo wings, tandoori chicken, butter chicken, and chicken rice. Chicken is also a staple of many fast food restaurants.

In Indonesia the chicken has great significance during the Hindu cremation ceremony. A chicken is considered a channel for evil spirits which may be present during the ceremony. A chicken is tethered by the leg and kept present at the ceremony for its duration to ensure that any evil spirits present during the ceremony go into the chicken and not the family members present. The chicken is then taken home and returns to its normal life.

In ancient Greece, the chicken was not normally used for sacrifices, perhaps because it was still considered an exotic animal. Because of its valor, the cock is found as an attribute of Ares, Heracles, and Athena. The alleged last words of Socrates as he died from hemlock poisoning, as recounted by Plato, were "Crito, I owe a cock to Asclepius; will you remember to pay the debt?", signifying that death was a cure for the illness of life.

The Greeks believed that even lions were afraid of cocks. Several of Aesop's Fables reference this belief.

In the New Testament, Jesus prophesied the betrayal by Peter: "Jesus answered, 'I tell you, Peter, before the rooster crows today, you will deny three times that you know me." (Luke 22:34) Thus it happened, and Peter cried bitterly. This made the cock a symbol for both vigilance and betrayal.

Earlier, Jesus compares himself to a mother hen when talking about Jerusalem: "O Jerusalem, Jerusalem, you who kill the prophets and stone those sent to you, how often I have longed to gather your children together, as a hen gathers her chicks under her wings, but you were not willing."

In many Central European folk tales, the devil is believed to flee at the first crowing of a cock.

In traditional Jewish practice, a kosher animal is swung around the head and then slaughtered on the afternoon before Yom Kippur, the Day of Atonement, in a ritual called kapparos. A chicken or fish is typically used because it is commonly available (and small enough to hold). The sacrifice of the animal is to receive atonement, for the animal symbolically takes on all the person's sins in kapparos. The meat is then donated to the poor. A woman brings a hen for the ceremony, while a man brings a rooster. Although not actually a sacrifice in the biblical sense, the death of the animal reminds the penitent sinner that his or her life is in God's hands.

The Talmud speaks of learning "courtesy toward one's mate" from the rooster. This might refer to the fact that when a rooster finds something good to eat, he calls his hens to eat first.

The chicken is one of the Zodiac symbols of the Chinese calendar. Also in Chinese religion, a cooked chicken as a religious offering is usually limited to ancestor veneration and worship of village deities. Vegetarian deities such as the Buddha are not one of the recipients of such offerings. Under some observations, an offering of chicken is presented with "serious" prayer (while roasted pork is offered during a joyous celebration). In Confucian Chinese Weddings, a chicken can be used as a substitute for one who is seriously ill or not available (e.g. sudden death) to attend the ceremony. A red silk scarf is placed on the chicken's head and a close relative of the absent bride/groom holds the chicken so the ceremony may proceed. However, this practice is rare today.

A cockatrice was supposed to have been born from an egg laid by a rooster, as well as killed by a Rooster's call.

An early domestication of chickens in Southeast Asia is probable, since the word for domestic chicken (*manuk*) is part of the reconstructed Proto-Austronesian language. Chickens, together with dogs and pigs, were the domestic animals of the Lapita culture, the first Neolithic culture of Oceania.

The first pictures of chickens in Europe are found on Corinthian pottery of the 7th century BC. The poet Cratinus (mid-5th century BC, according to the later Greek author Athenaeus) calls the chicken "the Persian alarm". In Aristophanes's comedy *The Birds* (414 BC) a chicken is called "the Median bird", which points to an introduction from the East. Pictures of chickens are found on Greek red figure and black-figure pottery.

In ancient Greece, chickens were still rare and were a rather prestigious food for symposia. Delos seems to have been a centre of chicken breeding.

The Romans used chickens for oracles, both when flying ("ex avibus", Augury) and when feeding ("auspicium ex tripudiis", Alectryomancy). The hen ("gallina") gave a favourable omen ("auspicium ratum"), when appearing from the left (Cic.,de Div. ii.26), like the crow and the owl.

For the oracle "ex tripudiis" according to Cicero (Cic. de Div. ii. 34), any bird could be used, but normally only chickens ("pulli") were consulted. The chickens were cared for by the pullarius, who opened their cage and fed them pulses or a special kind of soft cake when an augury was needed. If the chickens stayed in their cage, made noises ("occinerent"), beat their wings or flew away, the omen was bad; if they ate greedily, the omen was good.

Chickens were spread by Polynesian seafarers and reached Easter Island in the 12th century AD, where they were the only domestic animal, with the possible exception of the Polynesian Rat (*Rattus exulans*). They were housed in extremely solid chicken coops built from stone.

In 249 BC, the Roman general Publius Claudius Pulcher had his chickens thrown overboard when they refused to feed before the battle of Drepana, saying "If they won't eat, perhaps they will drink." He promptly lost the battle against the Carthaginians and 93 Roman ships were sunk. Back in Rome, he was tried for impiety and heavily fined.

In 161 BC, a law was passed in Rome that forbade the consumption of fattened chickens. It was renewed a number of times, but does not seem to have been successful. Fattening chickens with bread soaked in milk was thought to give especially delicious results. The Roman gourmet Apicius offers 17 recipes for chicken, mainly boiled chicken with a sauce. All parts of the animal are used: the recipes include the stomach, liver, testicles and even the pygostyle (the fatty "tail" of the chicken where the tail feathers attach).

The Roman author Columella gives advice on chicken breeding in his eighth book of his treatise on agriculture. He identifies Tanagrian, Rhodic, Chalkidic and Median (commonly misidentified as Melian) breeds, which have an impressive appearance, a quarrelsome nature and were used for cockfighting by the Greeks. For farming, native (Roman) chickens are to be preferred, or a cross between native hens and Greek cocks. Dwarf chickens are nice to watch because of their size but have no other advantages.

Per Columella, the ideal flock consists of 200 birds, which can be supervised by one person if someone is watching for stray animals. White chickens should be avoided as they are not very fertile and are easily caught by eagles or goshawks. One cock should be kept for five hens. In the case of Rhodian and Median cocks that are very heavy and therefore not much inclined to sex, only three hens are kept per cock. The hens of heavy fowls are not much inclined to brood; therefore their eggs are best hatched by normal hens. A hen can hatch no more than 15-23 eggs, depending on the time of year, and supervise no more than 30 hatchlings. Eggs that are long and pointed give more male, rounded eggs mainly female hatchlings.

Per Columella, chicken coops should face southeast and lie adjacent to the kitchen, as smoke is beneficial for the animals. Coops should consist of three rooms and possess a hearth. Dry dust or ash should be provided for dust-baths.

According to Columella, chicken should be fed on barley groats, small chick-peas, millet and wheat bran, if they are cheap. Wheat itself should be avoided as it is harmful to the birds. Boiled ryegrass (*Lollium* sp.) and the leaves and seeds of alfalfa (*Medicago sativa* L.) can be used as well. Grape marc can be used, but only when the hens stop laying eggs, that is, about the middle of November; otherwise eggs are small and few. When feeding grape marc, it should be supplemented with some bran. Hens start to lay eggs after the winter solstice, in warm places around the first of January, in colder areas in the middle of February. Parboiled barley increases their fertility; this should be mixed with alfalfa leaves and seeds, or vetches or millet if alfalfa is not at hand. Free-ranging chickens should receive two cups of barley daily.

Columella advises farmers to slaughter hens that are older than three years, because they no longer produce sufficient eggs.

Capons were produced by burning out their spurs with a hot iron. The wound was treated with potter's chalk.

For the use of poultry and eggs in the kitchens of ancient Rome see Roman eating and drinking.

Chickens in South America

An unusual variety of chicken that has its origins in South America is the araucana, bred in southern Chile by Mapuche people. Araucanas, some of which are tailless and some of which have tufts of feathers around their ears, lay blue-green eggs. It has long been suggested that they predate the arrival of European chickens brought by the Spanish and are evidence of pre-Columbian trans-Pacific contacts between Asian or Pacific Oceanic peoples, particularly the Polynesians and South America. In 2007, an international team of researchers reported the results of analysis of chicken bones found on the Arauco Peninsula in south central Chile. Radiocarbon dating suggested that the chickens were Pre-Columbian, and DNA analysis showed that they were related to prehistoric populations of chickens in Polynesia. These results appeared to confirm that the chickens came from Polynesia and that there were transpacific contacts between Polynesia and South America before Columbus's arrival in the Americas.

However, a later report looking at the same specimens concluded:

> A published, apparently pre-Columbian, Chilean specimen and six pre-European Polynesian specimens also cluster with the same European/Indian subcontinental/Southeast Asian sequences, providing no support for a Polynesian introduction of chickens to South America. In contrast, sequences from two archaeological sites on Easter Island group with an uncommon haplogroup from Indonesia, Japan, and China and may represent a genetic signature of an early Polynesian dispersal. Modeling of the potential marine carbon contribution to the Chilean archaeological specimen casts further doubt on claims for pre-Columbian chickens, and definitive proof will require further analyses of ancient DNA sequences and radiocarbon and stable isotope data from archaeological excavations within both Chile and Polynesia.

CHAPTER 13
Sheep Husbandry

Sheep husbandry is an important enterprise in the arid and semi-arid areas of India characterized by sparse vegetation, marginal land, and a high incidence of poverty. It is a low-investment sustainable enterprise yielding reasonably high rates of return. The sheep are valued for both mutton and wool production, although sheep productivity in terms of both is low. Wool yield in India is about 0.9 kg annum^{-1}, about 60 per cent less than the world average. The muttonyield is about 12 kg annum^{-1}, compared to a world average of 15 kg annum.

The reasons for low productivity of sheep in India are poor exploitation of genetic potential of native stock, inadequate feed resources, nutritional deficiency, heat stress, poor health monitoring, and inadequate marketing and credit support to sheep owners.

Various breeding strategies have evolved for improving body weight, and wool production and its quality. The emphasis has been on improving the production and quality of apparel wool. Limited efforts have been made to improve the production and quality of carpet wool or mutton production. A number of sheep strains have been evolved in India through cross-breeding of indigenous sheep with superior temperate breeds such as Dorset, Suffolk, Rambouillet, and Merino. The developed genotypes have demonstrated their production potential under experimental conditions. This Chapter attempts to document the technologies that can be employed gainfully under field conditions.

Sheep Biodiversity

India is a rich repository of sheep genetic resources and diversity. Sheep diversity is related basically to the geography of the region, production system, ecological and environmental variations, and the genetic constitution of breeds. India has the fourth largest sheep population in the world, accounting for 4.6 per cent of the global population. The country produces about 2 per cent of the world's sheep meat, 0.8 per cent of raw wool, and 1.1 per cent of scoured wool. It is estimated that India produces about 169 million kg of mutton, 42.7 million kg of wool, and 40 million skins annually. The national sheep flock is worth Rs. 24 billion producing an annual flow of outputs worth Rs. 8 billion. The sheep population remained almost static at about 40 million until the 1970s. In 1982, it increased to 49 million, and then declined to 45.7 million in 1987. In 1992, there was a subsequent increase to 51 million. The decline in 1987 was due mainly to widespread drought in the country, which resulted in a higher slaughter rate in that year.

The four distinct sheep breeding tracts in the country are North. Temperate (Himalayan region), Northwestern (Rajasthan, Maharashtra, Gujarat, Madhya Pradesh), Eastern (West Bengal, Bihar), and Southern Peninsular (Andhra Pradesh, Karnataka, Tamil Nadu). There are 57 breeds of sheep in India. Most of these are nondescript due to indiscriminate breeding and intermixing of breeds. They have evolved primarily through natural selection under the prevailing climatic conditions (usually harsh), migration, tropicaldiseases, poor nutrition, and shortage of drinking water. There are no breed societies or agencies that register animals of a particular breed, maintain flock books, or the purity of breed or type. The bulk of sheep is raised in the northwestern arid and semi-arid regions. In the north temperate regions sheep are mainly raised for apparel wool. Sheep are raised mainly for mutton in the southern peninsular region. Management, husbandry systems and breeds, ineach of these agroecological zones, are distinctly different.

Technologies for Improving Mutton Productivity

Several methods for increasing body weight of sheep have been tried by selection within the indigenous and cross-bred populations. In mutton production programmes, more emphasis has been given to six-month body weight than to greasy fleece. Since the characteristics related to mutton production (body weight gains, efficiency of feed conversion, and dressing percentage) are moderate to highly heritable, selection within indigenous breeds can bring about considerable improvement. Countries with developed sheep industriesmaintain special breeding flocks to supply superior germplasm to commercial flocks. The performance of Indian indigenous and cross-bred sheep with respect to growth, feed efficiency. Results on growth performance reveal that Malpura and Muzaffarnagari breeds of the northwestern region, and the Nellore and Mandya in the southern region have great potential for use as improver breeds for mutton production. New synthetics generally attain a live weight of about 30 kg at six months of age under intensive feeding conditions.

In cross-breeds, improvement in body weight up to six months of age over indigenous breeds is conspicuous. However, only marginal improvement is observed at 12 months of age. This indicates that cross-breeds/new synthetics require high levels of nutrition. If they are managed on the same feeding regime as the indigenous breeds, the differences that are conspicuous up to six months of age narrow gradually and become marginal at the age of one year.

Superior Germplasm for Mutton Production

Through selective breeding and intensive selection some of the important indigenous sheep breeds such as the Malpura, Sonadi, Muzaffarnagari, Madras Red, Mandya, Nellore, and Deccani have been improved.

Production of Fat Lamb

Production of fat lamb is a very promising commercial programme. The major advantage of this technology is that sheep owners need rear the animals only for about three months. Further, the profit earned after three months is on a par with or more than that earned after rearing lambs for 12 months under extensive grazing. After considering all the inputs required for raising the lambs to finishing weight, a net profit of about Rs. 316 per slaughtered lamb could be obtained. In addition, this technology would help avoid mortality risk and the unnecessary expense of rearing lambs for the whole year.

Malpura, an indigenous sheep breed, is well adapted to harsh climatic conditions with good mothering ability and sufficient milk to sustain lambs. An elite Malpura flock has been developed through intensive selection.

Technologies for Improving Wool Productivity

Wool production increased from 27.5 million kg in 1951 to 45.6 million kg in 1992-93. The sheep population in India constitutes 4.6 per cent of world population, but accounts for only 0.8 per cent of the world greasy and 1.1 per cent of the scoured wool production. About 65 per cent of wool is produced the northwestern region, followed by the southern peninsular region (20%).

The average wool production per sheep is only 0.9 kg against the worldaverage of 2.4 kg. The sheep of the northwestern region produce the highestyield (1.4 kg). The North Temperate region ranks next with an average yield of 1.3 kg. The sheep in the eastern and Southern Peninsular regions are poor yielders. The wool produced in the Northwestern and North Temperate regions is also of superior quality. As a result of poor productivity India imports about 50 million kg of wool (both apparel and carpet types) to meet the requirements of the industry. Efforts have been made to improve the genetic potential of sheep through cross-breeding of indigenous sheep with exotic breeds While it may not be possible to produce apparel wool in the required quantity, the carpet wool requirement can be met easily with suitable and progressive development programmes. India can make an impact on exports by marketing hand-knotted carpets, druggets, and hosiery items. Therefore, improving quantity and quality of carpet wool must be given due priority.

Carpet Wool Production

Almost all Indian wool types can be used for carpet manufacture if judiciously blended. However, the northwestern arid and semi-arid regions encompassing the states of Rajasthan, Haryana, Gujarat, Madhya Pradesh and plains of Uttar Pradesh, specifically produce good quality carpet wool. This region produces almost two-thirds of the total wool in the country. Excepting the wool produced from the Malpura and Sonadi breeds, the wool produced is of good carpet quality. Wool produced in the northern temperate region is suitable for apparel and finer carpets.

Indigenous Sheep Breeds

Research efforts have been made to improve wool yield and its quality among indigenous breeds through selective breeding and selection. Since the characteristics connected with carpet wool production (greasy fleece yield, fiber diameter, medullation, and staple length) are heritable, selection within the indigenous breed can bring about considerable improvement. Promising Indian sheep breeds that produce carpet wool are the Chokla, Magra, Nali, Patanwadi, Marwari, Jaisalmeri, Pugal, Bhakarwal, Gurez, Gaddi, and Rampur Bushair.

New Types

Avikalin: Much research has been conducted on improving carpet wool production and quality through crossing the extremely coarse and hairy Malpura breed with exotic fine wool breeds such as the Rambouillet. The halfbreeds from such a crossing yield about twice as much wool as the indigenousbreed, which is of excellent carpet quality. The Avikalin strain evolved from Rambouillet Malpura halfbreeds has been evaluated for its carpet wool quality the wool produced by this strain is superior to the carpet wool from allindigenous breeds.

Under field conditions, with the use of superior *Avikalin* rams, there was an increase of about 15-20 per cent in wool quantity in addition to an increase in body weight. The quality of wool was also better. Avikalin can be used as an improver breed for cross-breeding with the coarse wool breeds of sheep to increase carpet wool production. This breed is thus suitable as a dual-purpose type for carpet wool and mutton production.

Fine Wool Production

Attempts to cross-breed native sheep with exotic fine wool breeds for increasing wool production and quality were made even during the pre independence period. The major emphasis was to enhance fine wool production. As a result of cross-breeding experiments a few new fine wool sheep types were developed in the country and the wool.

Bharat Merino

The Bharat Merino breed was developed at the CSWRI, Avikanagar by crossing Rambouillet/Russian Merino with native Chokla, Malpura, Nali and Jaisalmeri ewes and stabilizing exotic inheritance at a level of 75 per cent. Thebreed produced annually 2.5–2.8 kg greasy fleece of 20ì fiber diameter,medullation of less than one per cent, and a staple length of 4–5 cm. Since 1987, a part of the flock is being performance tested under the subtemperate climate of the Kodai hills. The performance has been very satisfactory.

This is a promising substitute for fine wool sheep that are imported as improver breeds. The shorter staple length and lower greasy fleece weight under semi-arid conditions are attributed to climatic constraints and the inadequate availability of grazing and feed resources.

The performance of the Bharat Merino at the CSWRI regional station at Mannavanur has been encouraging. Since it has not been possible to get fine wool with desirable staple length from the higher crosses in the arid and semi-arid regions, apparel wool production can be intensified only in temperate areas such as the northern temperate hilly region and Nilgiri/ Kodai hills in the southern region.

In these areas three-fourth crosses of the Rambouillet or Merino, including the Bharat Merino can be propagated and annual clips obtained to meet the requirements for apparel manufacture.

Kashmir Merino

The Kashmir Merino breed was developed at the Government Sheep Breeding and Research Farm, Reasi (Jammu) using the foundation population produced by mating ewes of Kashmir valley, Gaddi, Bhakarwal, and Poonch breeds with exotic rams of Delaine Merino, Rambouillet and Soviet Merino breeds. The present population of this breed that has 75-82 per cent exotic genes exceeds one million.

This was achieved after sustained use of the genetic technique over 20 years. Inter se mating and rigorous selection has been followed for improving the fleece characteristics and body weights in Kashmir Merino. Due to the involvement of a number of native and exotic breeds, the Kashmir Merino sheep are highly variable in their morphological and production performance characteristics.

Feeding Management

There has been a continuous decline in availability of grazing areas for livestock due to increased population, urbanization, industrialization, and use of fallow lands for cultivation and other activities. It is, therefore, important to develop and use the remaining lands for pasture development and tree plantation.

The border areas under farms or defence artillery ranges can be developed as pasture and used for grazing sheep. Agroforestry, silvipasture, and hortipasture should be popularized. Forest areas, after initial protection for three years, could be used for controlled grazing. The system of extensive grazing should be modified to semi-intensive system. It may be possible to introduce the feedlot system in states such as Punjab, Haryana, and Andhra Pradesh where surplus broken grains and crop residues for feeding lambs are more readily available at competitive rates. Identification of new sources of protein or cheaper sources of compound animal feeds and fodder is also necessary. Utilization of byproduct and nonconventional feed resources and enrichment of low-grade feeds is desirable.

Health Management

Diseases in sheep adversely affect the production performance of the animals and, in turn, the net profit. Prophylactic health measures against prevalent diseases and antihelminthic drenching against internal parasites are the important health practices that must be strengthened in farmer's flocks to minimize losses and increase the productivity of sheep.

Effective vaccines in adequate quantities against diseases such as enterotoxemia, hemorrhagic septicemia, foot and mouth disease (FMD), and sheep pox.are essential.

Effective control measures against emerging diseases such as Blue Tongue and *peste de petite ruminantes* (PPR) must be developed. There should be effective arrangements for storage and transport of vaccines for which a proper cold storage infrastructure must be developed. It is important to control development of drug resistance. Hence, a proper drenching strategy must be developed to control this problem.

Conclusion

- Potential mutton-type breeds such as the Malpura, Sonadi, Muzzaffarnagari, Madras Red, Mandya, Nellore, Deccani, Mecheri, and Ganjam should be restricted to selective breeding by using superior rams for enhancing mutton production.
- Carpet wool producing breeds such as the Nali, Chokla, Patanwadi, Marwari, Magra, Pugal, Gaddi, and Jaisalmeri should be further improved through selective breeding by distribution of good quality rams of the respective breeds. Wool quality traits of these breeds better meet the carpet wool requirements of industry. Efforts should be made to introduce luster in indigenous carpet wool breeds to gain maximum returns through sale of quality carpet wool.
- Apparel wool production should be intensified only in temperate areas such as northern temperate hilly region and Nilgiri/Kodai hills in the South. In these areas three-fourth crosses of Rambouillet or Merino, including the Bharat Merino, could be propagated and annual clips obtained to meet the requirements for apparel manufacture.
- Cross-breeds could be tried in areas where adequate feed resources are available.

CHAPTER 14
Conservation of Farm Animals

The term 'sustainable management' has several definitions or connotations. The World Commission on Environment and Development defines sustainable management for development as a type of development that meets the needs of the present generation without jeopardizing its ability to meet the requirements of future generations. In the economic context, sustainable development means that the number of users and quantity of products/goods are maintained or made on some constant level, which is ecologically non-destructive or depletive over time. It should also meet at least the basic needs of all segments of the population.

At present, sustainable management is a subject of serious debate. One school of thought proposes that sustainability and continuous development are contradictory terms. The process of development involves an increase in entropy and therefore, cannot remain sustainable ad infinitum. Alternate resources or production systems must replace the original one after some time.

Exploitative production systems have depleted resources at an alarming rate in recent times. Modern production systems depend heavily on a few strains, breed types or crosses, in plants and animals. The local breeds or strains have therefore been neglected. Low economic viability has also contributed to endangerment and degeneration leading to extinction of certain forms of genetic resources.

Sustainable management assumes special importance with respect to domestic animals as they are vital sources of milk, meat, hides, fiber, draught power, and manure. With the application of biotechnology, genetic resources have been increasingly used for obtaining value-added products such as biochemicals, pharmaceuticals, and other genetically engineered substances.

Thus, sustainability should be determined on the holistic value of domestic breeds, though this is seldom done. Conservation in its broadest sense comprises judicious management of a resource to derive full benefits for the present and ensuring that it retains productivity potential so as to meet the needs of the future.

Although conservation of animal genetic resources is known to be essential, overriding economic considerations often jeopardize the attempts to preserve them. New biotechnological approaches have the potential for the conservation of genetic resources in the form of sperm, embryos, oocytes, isolated chromosomes, genomic DNA libraries, and isolated genes. Some of these technologies are still in the experimental stage but hold promise for the preservation of animal germplasm, which cannot be retained in situ due to poor production.

Conservation of Domestic Animal Biodiversity

Conservation of animal biodiversity is of the utmost importance because:

- Domestic animals are a part of global biodiversity and heritage of mankind and should be appropriately conserved and utilized.
- Human societies all over the world have developed social and cultural bonds with certain species or breeds of animals. Numerous religious rituals, festivals, and folklore are interwoven with native domestic animals. In some societies ownership of certain breeds is a status symbol.
- Animal production in the future will require new gene combinations. Only conservation of biodiversity can provide genetic variability and material for genetic engineering and developing more productive forms.
- Many minor breeds have not been exploited owing to their poor economic value and are rapidly decreasing in number. Minority breeds are also valuable reserves of genetic diversity and should be adequately recognized and exploited.
- Unplanned breeding has led to genetic erosion, dilution, and degeneration of some established breeds. Conservation becomes a vital necessity in such situations. Conserved germplasm can be used for reintroduction and revival of lost breeds.
- India is among the countries that have signed the 1992 Global Convention on Conservation of Biological Diversity. This places the onus for the conservation of all forms of biodiversity on the country of origin and use. Thus, conservation has become a national commitment. Barring sporadic studies on a few breeds reared on organised farms, domestic

animals have not been evaluated systematically for their total utility and economic viability. The production systems adopted by rural farming communities are radically different from those of organized farms.

Therefore, information on productivity of breeds in organized farms cannot be extrapolated to farmer's herds. Improved breeds with high production potential require special care and quality inputs for better performance. For native breeds, strategies for production improvement are urgently needed to ensure their conservation.

Population and Production Paradox

The animal genetic resources scenario in India is a strange paradox of prosperity and poverty. Farm livestock populations are exceedingly high in relation to the land area, while the productivity of the animals is much lower than in Europe, America, and Australia. The high livestock population density leads to diminished availability of inputs as well as poor maintenance, causing deterioration in the quality of animals. Thus, conservation in India should also include measures to prevent dilution in qualitative terms in livestock breeds.

Authentic information on population and status of various breeds of farm animals is scanty. Farm animals have been enumerated in each successive livestock census on the basis of species with no reference to breed. An attempt has been recently made to separately catalogue crossbred cattle. It is thus difficult to infer the status of a breed as threatened or endangered. The problem is further compounded by the fact that a number of breeds have not been accredited and characterized.

Dilution, Decline, and Degeneration

Between 60–80 per cent of farm animals fall into the nondescript category. Barring a few organized farms which still maintain small nuclear herds of pure breeds, there is unrestricted interbreeding. Furthermore, breeding plans recommended by central and various state governments are seldom followed rigorously.

Impact of Crossbreeding on Conservation

Breed substitution or modification by crossbreeding gained prominence in cattle and some other domestic species from the early 1960s. These strategies enhanced production but could not attain the established longtermgoals. Originally, it was envisaged that the advent of high yielding farm animals would include the concurrent elimination of low producers. It was hoped that the livestock population would stabilize and later decline with the increase of population of more efficient animals as in Europe and America.

However, this did not happen. Effects of these developments per se on native breeds have not been analyzed meticulously, but these are among the causal factors responsible for endangerment of native germplasm.

Process of Endangerment

The process of endangerment in livestock begins when the economic returns from a breed progressively decline or are not commensurate with the inputs. Effective and timely conservation measures can retrieve the breed from extinction. Incentives and subsidies for upkeep and alternate usage should be considered to address the problem. The eventual solution would lie in the improvement of production in the breed to make it sustainable.

Population Benchmarks

The International Union for the Conservation of Nature (IUCN) has given definitions for the rarity of species related to their chances of survival. However, considerable ambiguity exists in the terminology and population benchmarks for domesticated species for being declared endangered. In developing countries, the risk of population/breed loss due to disease, adverse climatic conditions, and drought are high. Therefore, population size of domesticated breeds of various species from the standpoint of vulnerability should be much higher than those suggested by various experts.

Survival Value of Breed for Conservation

Progressive improvement in the production potential over a period of time is an in-built security for the survival of breeds. It has been contended that exotic breeds with superior productivity or crosses are less adaptable than the indigenous breeds; yet they have better survival value in the production system owing to higher monetary return. The majority of indigenous livestock breeds have genetic attributes like better capacity to withstand drought, superior resistance to tropical diseases, and better capacity to utilize coarse forages. Despite this, low productivity diminishes their survival value necessitating conservation.

Herd Books of Animal Genetic Resources

The creation of herd books in the 1940s was the first meaningful attempt to register animals conforming to certain well-defined genetic attributes and production traits. The aim was to identify promising animals and ensure their optimal utilization particularly in improving the production level of the breed. So far, Haryana, Gir, Kankrej and Ongole cattle, and Murrah and Surti buffalo have been included in registration programmes. Additional breeds such as Rathi, Nagori, and Khillari cattle will soon be included. No scheme for other livestock breeds exists at present.

Participation of Farming Communities in Conservation

The Convention on Biological Diversity recognizes that the local communities are the real custodians of biological diversity and have vital stakes in conservation. They should thus be involved fully in conservation programmes. Farming communities should also share the benefits from sustainable utilization. At present, many financial institutions provide incentives and loans for the rearing of exotic or high-yielding crossbreeds, but do not provide similar assistance for indigenous stocks. Encouraging the propagation of native breeds will progressively increase their sustainability and they will be automatically conserved.

Legal Framework—A Gray Area in Conservation

The new patent laws and issues relating to intellectual property rights have neither been properly understood nor assessed in relation to their impact on domestic animal genetic resources. The laws on domesticated animals are inadequate and are not strictly observed in the absence of stringent punitive measures. These laws should cover all aspects of conservation such as benefit sharing, transfer, acquisition, accession, generation and sharing of information, and misuse and abuse of domestic animals. Currently, misuse, overexploitation, and non-judicious utilization of genetic resources are rampant. The following aspects require examination from the legal standpoint:

- Laws regarding trusteeship/ownership of animal genetic resources in gene banks outside the country.
- Laws prohibiting/permitting use of genetic resources/material, and punitive measures for infringements.
- Terms, conditions, rights, and obligations in such transactions involvingthird parties and further transfer of genetic resources.
- Transfer of genetic resources for commercial use and research—rights and obligations, and benefit sharing.
- Laws on the piracy and acquisition of classified data on animal genetic resources.
- Regulations on networking with global agencies.
- Legal guidelines on negotiations for bilateral agreements.
- Legal frameworks for the establishment and working of databanks.
- Laws regarding benefit sharing by parties and local communities.
- Rules and monetary obligations of non-governmental organisations (NGOs) handling animal genetic resource conservation programmes.
- Laws covering breed registration societies and other similar organisations.

Vistas of Conservation

The vistas of conservation and utilization in the Indian context aremultifaceted and complex. These should cover the following aspects:

- Judicious and scientific management of livestock breeds to progressively enhance their sustainability.
- Strategies for the preservation of less productive breeds with adequate genetic variability and distinctive characteristics as a part of genetic security.
- Development of technologies for enhancing sustainability. Alternate uses of the breed may at times ensure conservation.
- Establishment of in situ and ex situ gene banks.
- Establishment of informatics system having data banks with interactive networking with other organisations and global agencies.
- Development and progressive upgrading of software and hardware for computerized inventory systems.
- Building of regional level Livestock Conservation Boards/Conservation Units. Attempts should be made to enlist services of avid conservationists and committed NGOs in such ventures.
- Formulation of breeding policies with well defined objectives consistent with the economic conditions of the farmers, and ethos of conservation.
- Formulation of livestock population policy to ensure that animal populations are consistent with the carrying capacity and environmental management.
- Steps for people's participation in conservation programmes through Breed Societies, Associations, Breed Survival Trusts and NGOs.
- Enactment of laws pertaining to data banks, gene banks, transfer/ movement of genetic resources, patenting of genetic resources, prohibitive and punitive laws for preventing abuse, and misuse.
- Development of financial and institutional mechanisms that are mandated to support conservation of domesticated animals.

It is obvious that sustainable management, coupled with enhancement of the economic returns are key elements for conservation. However, less viable breeds should be supported being a part of the genetic heritage of mankind as well as to maintain genetic diversity.

CHAPTER 15

Improving Livestock Productivity

Adequate nutrition is important for maintenance, growth, and reproduction of animals. Indian livestock are underfed and under nourished. India is short of dry fodder by 31 per cent, green fodder by 23 per cent, and concentrate feeds by 47 per cent. This is due per se to the huge numbers of animals in relation to available feed and fodder resources. Animals largely derive their feed requirements from crop by-products and grazing on common lands.

Further, a majority of livestock is owned by small land-holders and the landless, who often face acute shortage of feed and fodder.

Animal science research has yielded a number of biochemical and mechanical technologies that, besides improving the nutritional quality of feed, also help avoid wastage of these resources. The efficacy of many of these techniques has been proved, yet their adoption has remained restricted and sporadic due to a number of operating constraints. This paper describes different nutritional technologies and attempts a subjective assessment of their adoption and impact.

Chopping Green Fodder

Chopping of green fodder and unthreshed straws/stovers is a simple but effective technology. This has developed gradually from use of various handoperated chaffing blades to power-operated mechanical mega-chaff cutters of varying capacities. Residues of crops such as rice, millets, and maize are long and need chopping before being fed to livestock.

Ruminants reduce feed particle size by chewing. Energy spent onchewing reduces the amount of metabolizable energy (ME) used for production, and can thus have a substantial negative effect on productivity. Feeding of chopped roughage reduces the energy wasted while chewing.

Chopping green fodder, straws and stovers helps in adopting strategic supplementation, improves the palatability of less-preferred roughages by mixing with highly palatable fodder, improves digestibility, and reduces wastage. The net biological value of the feed also improves. Chaffing of all varieties of green fodder including sugar tops, straws, and stovers such as rice, maize, pearl millet (*bajra*), and sorghum (*jowar*) is practiced in most of northern India.

Wetting and Soaking

Wetting and soaking of roughage and concentrates is also a simple and age-old technology. The straws, stovers, and concentrates (ingredients or mixtures) are either soaked in water or moistened just prior to feeding. This hydration of the particles facilitates their digestion in the rumen.

Soaking of concentrate mixtures or ingredients is a common practice followed in most parts of the country. Soaking or wetting of straws and stovers is however not as common. During the hot-dry periods in some parts of the country the wheat straw (*bhoosa*) is soaked / wetted before feeding to ruminants.

Addition of soaked concentrate mixture or ingredients such as cakes, bran, chuni, and flour to chopped straws and stovers improves theirpalatability and the total dry matter intake of basal diets comprising dry roughage. Mixing of high density concentrates and low density roughages results in even distribution of nutrients and facilitates better microbial and enzymatic action in the rumen.

Soaking or wetting of straws helps remove some of the undesirable elements such as excess oxalate in rice straw. Soaking roughage and concentrate is common where animals are fed a gruel. Soaking of straws orstovers for long periods however may result in the loss of some soluble nutrients, so care must be taken that the soaking is only for very short periods.

Grinding and Pelleting

Grinding and pelleting involve physical treatment that enhances the utilization of fibrous feed stuffs by ruminants. Grinding decreases particle size and increases the bulk density of leaf and stem fraction of forages. Ground roughage is further processed by pelleting or cubing before feeding to the animals. Pelleting helps increase the bulk density and decrease dustiness. This is a common practice wherever concentrates are fed.

Commercial feed-manufacturing mills/factories pellet the concentrate mixture for different species of livestock. Preparation of a complete feed comprising of concentrate and roughages has not been adopted by commercial feed manufacturers mainly because of the high processing costs.

Grinding and pelleting of roughages increase feed intake and reduce feed:gain ratio. Digestibility of ground and pelleted roughages is generally low compared to the original material fed in either long or chopped forms due to a reduction in fiber digestion. However, grinding and pelleting of forages dramatically reduces the time that ruminants spend on chewing the long coarse material, resulting in the increased availability of digestible energy for production. Although the performance of animals improves with processed feeds, net energy (NE) content of poor quality roughages still remains poor. Furthermore, the process of grinding and pelleting is energy dependent and, hence, the technology has not received much attention.

Conservation of Feeds and Fodder

Seasonal feed deficits can be reduced considerably or overcome through conservation and storage of feed resources during surplus seasons for use in lean periods. During the monsoon, plenty of green fodder is available in fields, on bunds, roadsides, and under forest covers. These can be profitably conserved for feeding. The surplus fodder can be conserved as hay in a dry form or as silage in a wet form.

Haymaking

This involves reducing the moisture content of green forages to less than 15 per cent, so that they can be stored without spoilage or further nutrient loss. Green forages with 80-85 per cent dry matter preserve most of their nutrients. Crops with thin stems and more leaves are better suited for haymaking as they dry faster than those with a thick, pithy stem and small leaves. Leguminous fodder crops should be harvested at the flower initiation stage or when crown buds start to grow, while grasses and other fodder crops should be harvested at the preflowering stage. They should preferably be harvested when air humidity is low. The harvested forage is spread in the field and raked a few times for quickdrying. The dried forage is then collected and baled when the moisture concentration is low (<15%) which helps storage and requires less space.

Crops with thick and juicy stems are dried after chaffing to speed up the drying process and to prevent loss of nutrients. Field curing is conducted during bright sunny weather but may result in bleaching of the forage and loss of leaves due to shattering. To avoid this,drying can be done in barns by passing hot air through the forage. Although artificial drying produces hay of good quality, it is expensive and beyond the reach of small and marginal farmers. The technology of haymaking is fully standardized and can be easily applied under favourable conditions. However slight carelessness could result in loss of quality or even complete spoilage. Conservation of fodder is not undertaken routinely by the average Indian farmer.

The reasons for the low adoption of this technology are:

- Lack of knowledge of the benefits of fodder conservation.
- High losses due to incorrect harvesting time and weather conditions.
- Lack of interest and skills for proper preservation and storage.
- Losses due to shattering and dropping of leaves, especially in legumes.
- Losses of soluble nutrients due to leaching caused by rain during the drying period.
- Storage of hay with high moisture content resulting in mold growth.
- Extra expenditure in terms of labour and materials for the processing of green fodder.

Haymaking is one of the best methods of preserving forages. Feeding hay to livestock helps reduce the amount of concentrate feeding, and thereby, the cost of feeding. The low moisture content of hay considerably reduces costs and efforts involved in transportation and handling. The surplus green grasses available during the monsoon in the forest go unused and could be put to the best possible use by this process.

Silage Making

Silage is the product of controlled fermentation of green fodder retaining high moisture content. Naturally produced organic acids, chiefly lactic acid, preserve the green fodder. Silage making involves selecting crops and plant materials rich in soluble sugars with dry matter concentration of about 15-30 per cent. The material is stored in pits under anaerobic conditions. Chaffing of the material for ensiling increases the compactness. The silo should be airtightafter filling. Fermentation begins within hours of closing the silo and accelerates in the next two to three days. Molasses or jaggery is added to increase the fermentation. Organic acids (primarily lactic and acetic acid), ethanol, and gases such as carbon dioxide (CO_2), methane (CH_4), and ammonia (NH_3) are produced during the fermentation process. The pH of the biomass is reduced to below 4.0, resulting in the termination of all biological activities. The material remains conserved. This method preserves the forage material for a long period with minimal nutrient loss.

Crops rich in soluble carbohydrates, such as maize, oats, sorghum, pearl millet, and cultivated grasses are most suitable for ensiling. During abundant green fodder availability they can be converted to silage and stored for use in times of scarcity. The crops should contain about 30-35 per cent dry matter at the time of ensiling. Sorghum and oats should be harvested at the flowering stage while maize has to be harvested at the milk stage.

Large quantities of sugarcane tops rich in soluble carbohydrates are available in sugarcane growing areas during the crushing season. Only 30 per cent of the available sugarcane tops is used for animal feeding as fresh feed and the rest is partly used as fuel. Conversion of these to silage would provide sufficient wet fodder during summer.

Tall varieties of rice are grown in some traditional rice-growing areas in India. They are susceptible to lodging under conditions of high fertilization, to avoid which, one-third of the top portion is removed during the vegetative stage. Fresh straw of many dwarf varieties is quite succulent at maturity and contains about 50-65 per cent moisture at harvest, making it suitable for ensiling.

Silage making is not an established practice in most parts of India due to reasons such as:

- Lack of surplus forage during the rainy season.
- Labour requirement for cutting, raking, collecting, chopping, pit construction, and materials (polyethylene, molasses) are a problem in some areas.

Some of these problems may be overcome if the milk cooperatives and state animal husbandry departments prepare large silos. Preparing silage near reserve forest areas by harvesting the forest grasses at a proper stage and ensiling them, rather than drying and burning, would be useful.

Urea-Ammoniation of Straws

Urea treatment of straws is so far the most accepted chemical treatment. Urea (fertilizer grade) available in all parts of the country is relatively safe, easy to store, and dissolves easily in water. Urea treatment is more feasible in tropical climates because it breaks down quickly into ammonia under higher ambient temperatures. The treatment is quite flexible, as it can be adapted to localconditions and preferences. Of all treatments the economics of urea treatment is best understood.

The treatment process is simple, and 4 kg urea is the optimal amount to treat 100 kg of air-dried straw. Water is essential as it helps in the hydrolysis of urea and also acts as a carrier for the ammonia to penetrate the cell walls of the plant material. The moisture level is not very critical to the process but a 30-40 per cent moisture level gives the desired effect. The total cost for treating one tonne straw is Rs. 800. Feeding livestock with urea-treated straw can result in saving of concentrates to the extent of 1.5 kg animal^{-1} day^{-1}.

The key factor that determines the economics and practicality of ureatreatment is the method of storage. Cemented storage structures are ideal but not practical in the field. Pits or mud structures may also be used. Covering the stack is important and can be achieved by using polythene sheets, empty urea bags stitched together, or even dried grass/leaves to keep it airtight.

This technology is most likely to work when:

- Plenty of dry, slender straw is available.
- Straw is cheap compared to other feeds.
- There is a shortage of grasses or other green fodder.
- Water is freely and conveniently available.
- The price of urea is not prohibitive.
- The cost of polythene covering is low.
- Labour is easily available

Microbial growth in the rumen depends on the nitrogen supply, rumen digestible energy, and sources of phosphorus and sulfur. The efficiency of microbial production depends on the amount of microbial biomass produced per unit of adenosine triphosphate (ATP) during fermentation of carbohydrates in the rumen to volatile fatty acids (VFAs). Cell wall carbohydrates are the major source of energy for rumen microbes on a straw diet. Insufficient energy from cell wall-rich crop residues is often a limiting factor to ruminant productivity in the tropics. Urea ammoniation, apart from being a source of nitrogen for microbial synthesis, also provides additional energy due to the weakening/loosening of the lignocellulose bonds in the treated straw.

Urea-treated straw feeds save on concentrate feeding, increase milk yield by 1-2 litres animal^{-1} day^{-1}, reduce the land area required for green fodder production, and offer better economic returns to the farmer. Treated straw can be fed to growing, lactating, and pregnant cattle and buffalo. The feedback from farmers who have adopted this technology indicates:

- Increase in straw consumption.
- Better growth performance.
- Improvement in health.
- Increase in milk yield ranging from 0.5-1.5 litres animal^{-1} day^{-1}.

Despite acknowledging the benefit of the technology during demonstrations, farmers have not enthusiastically continued urea treatment. The most important reason for this is that in most cases the returns are marginal. Other constraints are:

- Production of sticky dung complicates the preparation of dung cakes.
- Pungent smell of ammonia.
- Spoilage of straw in open stacks.

Urea-Molasses Treatment

Molasses is used to improve the palatability of the basal feed or as a source of readily fermentable energy, which may stimulate microbial fermentation in the presence of other nutrients such as nitrogen (urea) and phosphorus (phosphoric acid). Spraying of straw with 10 per cent molasses and 2 per cent urea is found to improve intake and digestibility of the basal roughage. Urea provides an additional source of nitrogen.

A urea-molasses-mineral block (UMMB) has been developed recently, which contains soluble and fermentable nitrogen from urea, highly fermentable energy from molasses, and essential minerals. Natural protein sources such as groundnut extract and cottonseed extract have also been added to provide preformed peptides and amino acids.

The field application of urea-molasses by spraying is limited owing to difficulty in handling of the mixture and toxicity in cases of uncontrolled intake. The high cost of molasses is also a limiting factor. The method is particularly useful in situations where there is plenty of straw, medium to low animal production, and limited access to other supplements.

The UMMB technology has been tested on-farm in Gujarat and was more popular with farmers maintaining buffalo. Modifications have been made to improve the nutrient balance and consistency for better acceptance by farmers. Supple-mentation of UMMB has been found to improve the dry matter intake of the basal roughage and the feed digestibility. The nutrients from the block are well utilized by the animals and UMMB supplementation improves reproductive performance of cows due to enhanced availability and utilization of nutrients, particularly micronutrients.

Calf Starter/Milk Replacer

Calf starter is a balanced concentrate mixture fed to calves from the 10th day of age to supplement the nutrients and raise them on a limited milk intake. This provides a balanced diet to the calf and cuts down the cost of milk feeding. Generally 16 per cent digestible crude protein (DCP) and 70 per cent total digestible nutrients (TDN) in the calf starter are sufficient for a satisfactory growth. The protein quality is important during the pre-ruminant stage. The calf starter should contain a major proportion of grains to provide readily soluble carbohydrates, protein-rich sources such as cakes, fat sources, and mineral mixture. The constituents of the calf starters can be altered according to the feed availability. Ingredients such as barley/oats/millet grains, groundnut cake/linseed oil meal/soybean oil meal, wheat bran/rice bran, fishmeal, and mineral supplements can be used to make a good quality calf starter. Good quality hay or leguminous green fodder given in addition to calf starters has been found to encourage the early development of rumen functions. The adoption of this technology has been limited because of the following reasons:

- The farmer feels that he is unethically depriving the calf of milk.
- There is a lack of awareness of the technology.
- There is a (wrong) perception that the health of the calf would be affected.

Bypass Nutrients

Bypass nutrients are fractions of the nutrients that are fermented to a comparatively lower degree in the rumen. They then become available intact at the lower part of the gastrointestinal tract for subsequent digestion and absorption. The approach envisages minimization of ruminal fermentation losses and better utilization of the nutrients after their digestion and absorption in the small intestine. There are three types of major nutrients that could bypass rumen fermentation to a certain degree. These are proteins/amino acids, starch/glucose, and fats/fatty acids. Slowly degradable or bypass nutrients may occur in feeds in their natural form. Alternatively, feeds that are highly degradable in the rumen can also be manipulated to restrict their degradation.

Bypass Proteins

A high proportion of the soluble plant protein from roughage-based diets is deaminated and lost as ammonia during digestion in the rumen. This is because the rate of protein degradation is faster than the utilization of nitrogen for microbial growth. Thus, if part of the protein is not degraded in the rumen it can be utilized more efficiently in the small intestine. Several feed ingredients have been screened for their bypass protein value. Some of them such as cottonseed cake, fishmeal, solvent-extracted coconut cake, subabul leaf meal, soybean extract, sunflower extract, and maize gluten meal have bypass characteristics in their natural form. However feeds such as groundnut cake, wheat bran, gingelly cake, and horse gram have to be manipulated to reduce their rumen degradability for optimization of ratios between degradable and nondegradable fractions in the diet.

Chemical—or heat treatments are the main methods used for protecting proteins. Heat treatment of groundnut cake at 130°C for two hours or formaldehyde treatment at 1 per cent of crude protein (CP) significantly increases the bypass protein of the cake (up to 50%).

Feeding bypass protein to high yielding animals (about 10 litres day-1 or more) and fast growing calves (500 kg day^{-1}) would offer better economic returns to farmers by way of increased milk production/growth rate. Lactating cows yielding 8 litres and above require about 50 per cent of CP in the feed in the form of bypass protein particularly when fed on straw based diets. The economic returns of feeding bypass protein to animals are quite substantial because of increased production (1.5 kg animal^{-1} day^{-1}).

Use of bypass protein feeds by farmers is limited. Lack of awareness is a major constraint. In some parts of the country the farmers use natural high bypass protein sources and even heat treatment to a limited extent.

Bypass Starch and Bypass Fat

Starch can be protected from ruminal hydrolysis with formaldehyde or ammonia treatment. Encapsulating fats/lipids with formaldehyde-treated protein is an effective method of protection against ruminal hydrolysis and biohydrogenation of lipids. However, the method has its limitations due to the use of formaldehyde. A simpler approach is the conversion to calcium salts of free fatty acids removed from edible oils during refining. These are protected against rumen degradation.

Feeding bypass starch reduces excess production of lactic acid in the rumen, which otherwise inhibits digestion of fiber. The starch left unfermented in the rumen is digested in the small intestine, producing glucose which, after absorption, is more efficiently used as an energy source by the animals. Feeding protected fats to high-yielding animals that receive low fat density diets increases milk yield and also efficiency of energy utilization.

Providing higher fat supplements without protection affects the utilization of fiber in the rumen. Providing bypass fat is necessary to meet the energy requirements of high-yielding cows, especially in early lactation.

Both the technologies are useful only for high yielding animals and thus have limited level of adoption. The technology is being commercialized.

Mineral Supplementation

Although minerals are required in only small quantities, mineral deficiency can have a marked effect on productivity, reproductive performance, and health. Under farming systems, where straws/stovers form the major source of roughage, the role of minerals becomes more pertinent as these roughages are low in many minerals and contain certain antinutritional factors such as oxalates, tannins, and silica, which may affect mineral utilization. Mineral imbalances depend on the type of feed and where it is grown. Mineral needs depend on animal output and supplements are particularly important for highyielding animals.

Feeding of formulated mineral mixtures or pure ingredients, althoughsimple, is not a cost-effective method. Besides, the bioavailability of minerals is greater from organic than inorganic sources. Selection is therefore based on the biological availability or release and absorption coefficient.

In areas of acute mineral deficiency or where animals exhibit chronic symptoms of deficiency, providing chelated organ-omineral complexes with high bioavailability is a better approach. Providing region-specific mineral supplements based on mineral mapping is an alternative cost-effective approach. The best way of providing mineral supplements is through the feed or fodder/top feed sources, which are rich in minerals, without affecting the feeding practices followed by the farmers. Few farmers use mineral supplements, except on the advice of a veterinarian. Supplementation of the diet with a mineral mixture is an effective way ofovercoming most reproductive problems such as repeat breeding, low fertility, infertility, delayed postpartum estrus, and silent heat. It is also essential for optimum level of production whether it be milk, meat, egg, or wool production.

Strategic Supplementation

Feeding only straw does not provide sufficient nutrients to maintain theanimals, although coarse straws (millets, sorghum, maize) give better results than slender straws (rice, wheat, barley). Feeding straw for a short period may be good for survival or for dung production, but to achieve higher levels of milk, meat, or draught power, straw must be either treated or supplemented with better feeds. Supplementation can be made with concentrates, roughage or both.

Supplementation of straws with deficient nutrients such as nitrogen and minerals to improve straw intake and digestibility is called catalytic supplementation. Use of small amounts of concentrate supplements, licks, kitchen waste, or green fodder may achieve this objective. Supplementation for increased straw intake is achieved through improved rumen function. The amount of supplement is small in this case, since higher levels of supplementation decreases straw intake through a substitution effect, which may be inevitable when feeding high-producing animals as the level ofsupplement required is very high. Farmers generally feed cakes/bran or grass to their productive stock along with straw. This technology is viable and sustainable and does not greatly interfere with the existing farming system. Technical information available onthe nutritive value of supplementary diets and strong extension support are required for increased adoption of this technology.

For an animal to maintain body weight and produce 2-3 litres of milk day^{-1} catalytic supplementation (provision of urea, small amounts of cake, bran, or green fodder) is recommended. For higher levels of productivity supplementation with concentrates, green forages, or compound feeds is required. The level and type of supplementation depend on the availability of supplements, their prices, and the desired level of production. For supplementation to be economically attractive, the value of increased output has to be greater than the cost of the supplement.

The addition of small amounts of supplements increases the intake of poor quality roughage. Supplements such as urea, oil cakes, or green fodder improve the intake of crop residues by providing a more favourable rumen environment. Straw sprayed with two per cent urea improves straw intake by about 10 per cent; just enough for an animal to achieve maintenance. Groundnut cake fed at a rate of 20 per cent of straw dry matter intake (finger millet straw-based diets) improves dry matter intake and digestibility.

Diet of finger millet straw and wheat bran (75:25) with groundnut cake improves nutrient digestibility. Use of legumes or top feeds (*Sesbania, Gliricidia, Leucaena*) which supply nitrogen and minerals increases straw intake. Mixing local grasses/top feeds/green fodder with straw during chopping will enhance intake and digestibility and also helps in producing good quality dung. This technology is suitable where straw is cheap, supplements are expensive, and where only low production/growth is achievable.

Probiotics/Growth Promoters

Antibiotics and antimicrobials when used in low quantities (subtherapeutic) as growth promoters, increase feed and reproductive efficiency, and reduce mortality. However, their use has created much controversy on the possibility of drug residues in animal products that may be toxic to humans. The antibiotics are pure chemical compounds and are absorbed in the digestive tract. They improve growth and feed efficiency but can cause mutation of other microorganisms.

Most probiotics are specific in their action and are used to improve feed utilization, uptake of nutrients, or feed efficiency by altering the rumen fermentation and/or improving feed conversion efficiency. The most commonly used probiotics are yeast cultures (*Saccharomyces cerevisae* and *Aspergillus)* and bacteria (*Lactobacillus* spp., *Bacillus subtilis, Streptococcus* spp.), which are available commercially in the form of water-soluble powders, liquids, or as feed additives. In addition to bacteria and yeast, some enzyme cultures are also being used as additives for improving the nutritional efficiency of feedstuffs.Some enzymes when added to the feed increase the availability ofpolysaccharides (starch) and proteins, partially hydrolyze viscouscarbohydrates (beta-glucans, arabinoxylans) present in some grains,supplement the animal's endogenous enzymes, and hydrolyze fibrous materials that are not hydrolyzed by the endogenous enzymes.

These effects are generally more evident in young animals whose digestive systems are not completely developed. Several manufacturers are now adding probiotics to their compound feed. The use of probiotics by farmers themselves is negligible due to prohibitive cost, lack of awareness, and inconsistent results.

Manipulation of the Rumen Ecosystem

Increasing digestion of fiber by manipulating rumen microbes is being experimentally tested. The types and numbers of fiber-degrading microorganisms in the rumen have been identified under varying feeding conditions. Knowledge of the genetic diversity and number of these organisms at the species and strain level is lacking.

The identification of specific populations of rumen microorganisms in their natural environment is likely to improve due to molecular techniques based on 16S rDNA sequences that canphylogenetically identify these organisms. Further studies may alsodemonstrate the possibility of ascribing activity to organisms on a phylogenetic basis.

The enzymes reintroduced into the dominant rumen bacteria have been primarily cellulases, xylanases, and more recently, esterases. However mechanisms involved with the binding and presentation of rumen bacteria and enzymes to cellulose (e.g. cellulosome complex) are still poorly understood, impeding the ability to manipulate a rate-limiting step in the kinetics of ruminal fiber digestion. Recent studies have demonstrated that the genus *Ruminococcus* is very diverse in both genotype and fiber-digesting ability and may therefore be amenable to manipulation. The technology has not been perfected so far and efforts in this direction are continuing. Non-genetic manipulation of the protozoa in the rumen by chemical andbiological means has been tried.

Although the balance of nutrients available to the animal may improve, treatment of ruminants with defaunating agents to remove ciliate protozoa from the rumen had a secondary effect on population of rumen fungi and bacteria. This technology has thus not been accepted as an effective approach.

Genetic Manipulation for Improvement in NutritiveValue of Straws/Stovers

The nutritive value of crop residues can be improved by genetic manipulation. Genetic manipulation has been used to increase grain production, resistance to disease, and drought resistance in crops. Some of the attributes incorporated in this process might adversely affect the quality of crop residues. High silica and lignin for example could be protective for the plant but adversely affect the nutritive value of crop residues. Genetic manipulation for improvement in quality and/or quantity of straws and stovers, without negatively affecting the grain yield, could resolve many problems in mixed crop-livestock farming systems.

Not much emphasis has been laid in the past on genetic manipulation of crops for improvement in quality and/or quantity of straws and stovers. Recombinant DNA technology is being used to produce transgenic subterranean clover (*Trifolium subterraneum*) and lucerne with increased concentrations of proteins that are resistant to rumen degradation and are hydrolyzed rapidly by intestinal proteases. These forage legumes have been transformed with genes encoding for the sulfur amino acid-rich proteins sunflower albumin and ovalbumins, which are degraded slowly by rumen microorganisms. Improving forage protein quality through genetic manipulation is promising but progress is relatively slow. The adoption of this technology does not require much effort. However, the relative contribution of genetic and environmental effects needs to be better studied. This requires a coordinated approach by the plant breeders, geneticists, animal nutritionists and physiologists. Controlled experiments leading to a better understanding of the effects of environmental factors on plant physiology and straw quality such as leafiness, translocation of cell solubles from stem to grain, hemicellulose cellulose ratio, lignification of cell walls, and digestibility need to be conducted.

The ultimate decision to adopt a particular technology depends to a great extent on the farmer's perceptions about the technology attributes and their socioeconomic relevance. There is a growing concern among researchers, extension personnel, and policy makers to include farmers' perceptions in generation and adoption of technology. Lack of coordination among various agencies has often resulted in delay or failure in the accomplishment of thegoals. There is an urgent need to work out possible feed options, utilizing feed resources available to farmers in different agroecological zones of the country, to match the nutrient requirements of the animals. This is a gigantic but necessary task that should not be delayed any further.

CHAPTER 16
The Livestock Revolution

Population growth, urbanisation and income growth in developing countries are fuelling a substantial global increase in the demand for food of animal origin, while also aggravating the competition between crops and livestock (increasing cropping areas and reducing rangelands).

The livestock revolution is stretching the capacity of existing production, but it is also exacerbating environmental problems. Therefore, while it is necessary to satisfy consumer demand, improve nutrition and direct income growth opportunities to those who need them most, it is also necessary to alleviate environmental stress.

Conventional agriculture is known to cause soil and pasture degradation because it involves intensive tillage, in particular if practised in areas of marginal productivity.

Technologies and management schemes that can enhance productivity need to be developed. At the same time, ways need to be found to preserve the natural resource base. Within this framework, an integrated crop-livestock farming system represents a key solution for enhancing livestock production and safeguarding the environment through prudent and efficient resource use.

The increasing pressure on land and the growing demand for livestock products makes it more and more important to ensure the effective use of feed resources, including crop residues.

An integrated farming system consists of a range of resource-saving practices that aim to achieve acceptable profits and high and sustained production levels, while minimizing the negative effects of intensive farming and preserving the environment. Based on theprinciple of enhancing natural biological processes above and below the ground, the integrated system represents a winning combination that:

(a) Reduces erosion.

(b) Increases crop yields, soil biological activity and nutrient recycling.

(c) Intensifies land use, improving profits.

(d) Can therefore help reduce povertyand malnutrition and strengthen environmental sustainability.

Advantages and Main Constraints

Advantages

In an integrated system, livestock and crops are produced within a coordinated framework. The waste products of one component serve as a resource for the other. For example, manure is used to enhance crop production; crop residues and by-products feed the animals, supplementing often inadequate feed supplies, thus contributing to improved animal nutrition and productivity.

The result of this cyclical combination is the mixed farming system, which exists in many forms and represents the largest categoryof livestock systems in the world in terms of animal numbers, productivity and the number of people it services. Animals play key and multiple roles in the functioning of the farm, and not only because they provide livestock products (meat, milk, eggs, wool, hides) or can be converted into prompt cash in times of need.

Animals transform plant energy into useful work: animal power is used for ploughing, transport and in activities such as milling, logging, road construction, marketing, andwater lifting for irrigation.

Animals also provide manure and other types of animal waste. Excreta has two crucial roles in the overall sustainability of the system:

(a) *Improving nutrient cycling:* Excreta contains several nutrients (including nitrogen, phosphorus and potassium)and organic matter, which are important for maintaining soil structure and fertility. Through its use, production is increased while the risk of soil degradation is reduced.

(b) *Providing energy:* Excreta is the basis for the production of biogas and energy for household use (e.g. cooking, lighting) or for rural industries (e.g. powering mills and water pumps). Fuel in the form ofbiogas or dung cakes can replace charcoal and wood.

Crop residues represent the other pillar on which the equilibrium of this system rests. They are fibrous by-products that result fromthe cultivation of cereals, pulses, oil plants, roots and tubers. They are a valuable, low-cost feed resource for animal production, and are consequently the major source of nutrients for livestock in developing countries. The overall benefits of crop-livestock integration can be summarized as follows:

- Agronomic, through the retrieval and maintenance of the soil productive capacity.
- Economic, through product diversification and higher yields and quality at less cost.
- Ecological, through the reduction of crop pests (less pesticide use and better soil erosion control).
- Social, through the reduction of ruralurban migration and the creation of new job opportunities in rural areas.

This system has other specific advantages:

- It helps improve and conserve the productive capacities of soils, with physical, chemical and biological soil recuperation. Animals play an important role in harvesting and relocating nutrients, significantly improving soil fertility and crop yields.
- It is quick, efficient and economically viable because grain crops can be produced in four to six months, and pasture formation after cropping is rapid and inexpensive.
- It helps increase profits by reducing production costs. Poor farmers can use fertilizer from livestock operations, especially when rising petroleum prices make chemical fertilizers unaffordable.
- It results in greater soil water storage capacity, mainly because of biological aeration and the increase in the level of organic matter.
- It provides diversified income sources, guaranteeing a buffer against trade, price and climate fluctuations.

Constraints

- Nutritional values of crop residues are generally low in digestibility and protein content. Improving intake and digestibility of crop residues by physical and chemical treatments is technically possible but not feasible for poor small farmers because they require machinery.
- Crop residues are primarily soil regenerators, but too often they are either disregarded or misapplied.
- Intensive recycling can cause nutrient losses.
- If manure nutrient use efficiencies are not improved or properly applied, the import of nutrients in feeds and fertilizers will remain high, as will the costs and energy needs for production and transportation, and the surpluses lost in the environment.

- Farmers prefer to use chemical fertilizer instead of manure because it acts faster and is easier to use.
- Resource investments are required to improve intake and digestibility of crop residues.

Mixed farms are prone to using more manure than crop farms do. Manure transportation is an important factor affecting manure use.

Challenges

- Develop strategies and promote croplivestock synergies and interactions that aim to;
  - *(a)* integrate crops and livestock effectively with careful land use;
  - *(b)* raise the productivity of specific mixed crop-livestock systems;
  - *(c)* facilitate expansion of food production;
  - *(d)* simultaneously safeguard the environment with prudent and efficient use of natural resources.
- Devise measures (for instance, facilitating large-scale dissemination of biodigesters) to implement a more efficient use of biomass, reducing pressures on natural resources; and develop a sustainable livestock manure management system to control environmental losses and contaminant spreading.

Key Principles

- *Cyclic:* The farming system is essentially cyclic (organic resources – livestock – land – crops). Therefore, management decisions related to one component may affect the others.
- *Rational:* Using crop residues more rationally is an important route out ofpoverty. For resource-poor farmers, the correct management of crop residues, together with an optimal allocation of scarce resources, leads to sustainable production.
- *Ecologically sustainable:* Combining ecological sustainability and economic viability, the integrated livestock farming system maintains and improves agricultural productivity while also reducing negative environmental impacts.

Some Lessons Learned and Recommendations

- The maintenance of an integrated croplivestock system is dependent on the availability of adequate nutrients to sustain animals and plants and to maintain soil fertility. Animal manure alone cannot meet crop requirements, even if it does contain the kind of nutrients needed. This is because of its relatively low nutrient density and the limited quantity available to small-scale farmers. Alternative sources for the nutrients need to be found.

- Growing fodder legumes and using them as a supplement to crop residue is the most practical and cost-effective method for improving the nutritional value of crop residues. This combination is also effective in reducing weight loss in animals, particularly during dry periods.
- Given their traditional knowledge and experience, local farmers are perfectly able to apply an integrated system. In practice, however, relatively few adopt this system, mainly because they have limited access to credit, technology and knowledge. The crop-pasture rotation system is complex and requires a substantial capital outlay for machinery and implements. Associations of grain and livestock producers are useful for filling these gaps and can promote the adoption of a croplivestock system;
- Veterinary services are generally unable to reach poor small farmers in remote areas. Therefore, for livestock production to beimproved, more attention needs to be paid to making veterinary care accessible, particularly in terms of prevention.
- Better livestock management is needed to safeguard water. Livestock water demand includes water for drinking and for feed production and processing. Livestock also have an impact on water, contaminating it with manure and urine. All of these aspects need to be given due consideration.
- Intensification of agriculture through appropriate incorporation of small livestock has the potential to decrease the land needed for agricultural production and relieve the pressure on forests.
- Key issues and questions for project design.
- The increase in demand for livestock products presents opportunities for small farmers who can increase livestock production and benefit from related income.

However, in terms of environmental impact, the growing number of livestock and the increase in livestock processing can have anegative impact on natural resources unless actions are taken to identify farming practices that are economically and ecologicallysustainable. Thanks to the dynamic interaction of its various components, the highly improved integrated crop-livestock system can guarantee more sustainable production and therefore constitutes a valid new approach.

Experience in the use of this system has shown that:

(a) Adopting sustainable management practices can improve production while preserving the environment.

(b) Residues, wastes and byproductsof each component serve as resources for the others.

(c) Poor farmers have the traditional knowledge needed to integrate livestock and crop production, but because of their limited access to knowledge, assets and inputs, relatively few adopt an integrated system.

The challenge for development practitioners is to ensure that poor small farmers can increase the productivity of traditional farming systems, adopting an effective integrated system that produces usable biomass while conserving natural resources, and can therefore be sustainable in the long term.

Within this framework some key questions for project design are:

- How can livestock production increase to meet the growing demand for livestock products, using methods that the resource base can sustain?
- Do the strategies devised for raising productivity in integrated crop-livestock systems take into account the stage of development of the target population with respect to the nature of crop-livestock interactions?
- Do the farmers concerned have the right skills, knowledge, capital and technology to set up this system?
- Are the roles and responsibilities of men and women given sufficient consideration?
- How can additional needed nutrients be obtained? And, can the productivity of the system be increased without stressing the environment?
- Is enough good-quality feed available to sustain animals, especially during the dry season?
- Are nutrients that are relocated from grazing areas to croplands efficiently recovered?
- Are the different components of the farming system (crop, livestock and, eventually, fish) efficiently integrated?

CHAPTER 17
Profitability of Animal Agriculture

Improving efficiency of feed use is critical to raising the productivity and profitability of animal agriculture. The cost of feed accounts for 50-60 per cent of the total cost of production in ruminants and 65-80 per cent in nonruminants under intensive production systems. The significant impact of improved nutrition on animal productivity in the developing countries has repeatedly been highlighted. Crop residues and other cellulosic materials are staple ruminant feeds in India. The low nitrogen and mineral content, alongwith high lignin and silica contents of roughage, lead to its low digestibility.

To achieve productive levels in the animal consistent with their genetic make-up, the straw-based rations need protein-rich oilseeds and oil cakes as supplements. This is important in countries such as India that have enormous livestock populations and shortages of feed in relation to requirements.

The objective of this paper is to assess the oil cake availability for feed use and its contribution towards improving the nutritional security of livestock by examining various oil cakes for their nutritional attributes.

Oilseeds: As Meals and Cakes

India is the third largest producer of oilseeds after the USA and China. It accounts for 8.8 per cent of world oil seed production and 7 per cent of world oil meal production). It has about 27 thousand ha under oilseeds, producing about 25000 tonnes of oilseeds. The major oilseeds cultivated in India are groundnut, rapeseed-mustard, soybean, sunflower, sesame, linseed, castor, and niger.

The yield level of most of these oilseeds is below the world average. For some crops such as soybean, sunflower, rapeseed-mustard, and linseed the yield levels are about 50 per cent of the world average. Oilseed meals are rich in protein and other valuable feed nutrients for livestock. Oil is extracted from oilseeds by using pressure to force out the oil, or by using an organic solvent, usually hexane, to dissolve oil fromthe seed. Seeds such as groundnut, cottonseed, and sunflower have a thick coat or husk, rich in fiber and of low digestibility, which lowers the nutritive value of the material. This husk may be completely or partially removed by cracking and riddling, the process being known as decortication. Removal of the husk lowers the crude fiber content and improves the apparent digestibility of the other constituents. Generally, the residual oil content of the cakes is higher in screw-pressed cakes than in solvent-extracted meals.

India also has many unconventional oilseeds of which only a small proportion is presently exploited. They are also rich sources of protein and other nutrients, but their use in the livestock industry is limited by the presence of one or more undesirable nutritional factors.

These, however, can be used in concentrate mixtures in varying proportions depending on their chemical composition. The quality of a protein in a particular oilseed is relatively constant, but may vary in the cake or meal, depending on the technique employed for the extraction of the oil. As mentioned earlier, generally, the residual oil content of the cakes is generally higher in screw-pressed cakes than in solvent-extracted meals. High temperatures and pressures of expeller processing may result in the lowering of the nutritive value. For ruminants, such denaturation may be beneficial, owing to an associated reduction in degradability. High temperatures and pressures also degrade some deleterious substances such as gossypol.

Solvent extraction does not involve pressing, temperatures are comparatively low, and protein value of meals is almost the same as that of the original seed. The oilseed cakes may make a significant contribution to the energy content of the diet, particularly when the oil contents are high.

Anti-nutritional Factors

Some oil meals contain certain antimetabolites or other anti-nutritional factors which when consumed may be toxic to animals. Table 17.1 shows some of the important antinutritional factors found in different oilseed cakes/ meals. These factors may affect the absorption of dietary nutrients in the digestive tract as a result of toxic action on some organ or tissue, or production traits. Detoxification of some factors is possible by treating a particular ingredient. Some of these treatments are simple whereas others are cumbersome. It is, however, necessary that whenever such ingredients containing toxic factors are mixed in the feed, their inclusion levels should be such that an animal can tolerate them. Toxic factors can be of two types, intrinsic and extrinsic.

Table 17.1: Antinutritional Factors in Oilseeds/Plant Protein Meals

Meals	Antinutritional Factors
Soybean	Protease inhibitors*, allergins*, oligosaccharides, phytin, lipoxygenase*, lectins* saponin, hemagglutinins, citrinin
Rapeseed	Erucic acid, glucosinolates, sinapine, tannins, pertins, oligosaccharides
Canola	Glucosinolates, sinapine, pectins, oligosaccharides
Cottonseed	Gossypol, tannins, cyclopropenoid fatty acids
Sunflower	Chlorogenic acid, high fibre, achratoxin
Groundnut	Mycotoxins, tannins, oligosaccharides, protease inhibitors*
Copra	Fibre, mannans
Palm kernel	Fibre and sharp shells, galactomannans
Sesame	Phytase, oxalate
Sal seed	Tannins
Linseed	Prussic acid

* Destroyed by heating.

Intrinsic factors are usually of plant origin such as tannins, trypsin inhibitors, goitrogens, cyanogenetic glucosides, saponins, hemagglutinins, gossypol, lathyrogens, and nimbin and its derivatives. Extrinsic factors are those produced by the attack of pathogens on feed ingredients, e.g. *Aspergillus* spp., causing aflatoxicosis.

Amino Acid in Oilseed Meals

Oilseed cakes and extractions are the most important sources of essential amino acids. In general, oilseed proteins have low cysteine and methionine content and a variable but low lysine content. As a result, these cannot adequately supplement the cereal proteins with which they are commonly used.

The gross protein value of some oilseed such as cotton, groundnut, and soybean is high; their chemical composition does not favour their greater use. Cottonseed meal also has the disadvantage of a low cysteine, methionine, and lysine contents, with lysine being the first limiting amino acid.

Different oilseed meals are degraded at varying rates in the rumen of livestock. Since high-yielding dairy cattle and fast-growing goats and sheep need higher levels of undegradable dietary protein, it is possible to select desirable components of protein meals and formulate rations for differential levels of productivity. The problem of aflatoxins in animal feeds is being debated at length.

Table 17.2: Important Limiting Amino Acid Contents of Commonly-used Oil Meals

Source	Arginine	Lysine	Tryptophan	Methionine	Cysteine
	....	....	%	....	....
Groundnut	4.4	1.3	0.4	0.6	0.7
Soybean	3.0	2.6	0.5	0.8	0.7
Sesame	3.7	1.2	0.6	1.4	0.4
Safflower	3.8	2.0	0.6	1.6	0.7
Cotton seed	3.4	1.4	0.5	0.8	1.0

Limitations

The use of groundnut meal, which is very susceptible to fungal infection and aflatoxin contamination, has drastically decreased recently despite the superiority of its proteins. Improper harvesting, transport, processing, and storage all contribute to aflatoxin contamination. Preventive measures during crop production and postharvest handling of seeds would greatly reduce the level of contamination in feeds. Creating an awareness among farmers about aflatoxins would helpincrease groundnut meal use in animal feeds. While soybean meal is not normally found to contain detectable amounts of aflatoxins, the incidence of these metabolites has been on the rise recently.

Sunflower meal is very rich in many essential amino acids, but its use has been restricted owing to its high fiber content. Decorticating the sunflower seeds prior to expelling/solvent extraction produces oil with less gum content, better clarity, and a meal with lower fibre. However, the economic viability of the process has yet to be established. Similar problems limit the use of other meals such as safflower meal, and niger seed meal in animal feeds.

CHAPTER 18

Improving the Productivity of Grasslands

India is a country with tropical monsoon climate where most of the rains occur between June and September. Thus, the active growth period in rainfed areas is 3-4 months. In this climate the native vegetation comprises different types of woodl and. Seminatural grazing lands grow only on clearing of the wood bunds. Grazing lands are controlled by the degree of grazing. Pastures are not maintained due to the prevalent ecoclimate and exist only at high altitudes in the Himalayas beyond the tree line.

The total area of grazing lands in India is about 86 million ha. This, together with crop residues and by-products, supports India's entire livestock population. The total arable land in the country is about 147.4 million ha. Assuming that croplands donate one-tenth of production as fodder, the total arable land supporting livestock feed would be about 14.7 million ha, thereby increasing the potential grazing area to about 100 million ha. Taking the average potential above-ground net primary productivity as 500 gm^{-2} yr^{-1} the total fodder production is 501.5 million t of dry fodder yr^{-1} for 239 million animals, excluding sheep, goats, horses, camels, and donkeys. Also, assuming that a normal healthy cow consumes 7 t dry herbage yr^{-1}, the annual consumption is 1673 million t yr^{-1} . The net primary production level of Indian grasslands is thus far below the total requirement. The overgrazing and continuous degradation of grazing lands, along with loss of fertility, is further decreasing their productivity.

The problems of grazing lands are related to ecological and socioeconomic causes. In arid areas water is the limiting factor; in semi-arid areas improper land utilization and excessive grazing are the main problems;

and in the high rainfall zones the low nutritive value of the herbage is a constraint. Another serious problem is the low legume component of the grasslands.

Present Scenario

Over the past 62 years while the net area sown increased by about 20 per cent, the gross cropped area increased by over 40 per cent, implying an increase in the cropping intensity from 1.1 in 1950–51 to 1.3 in 1992-93. Although the areaunder forests shows an increase, the area under the tree canopy has decreased drastically. The area under pastures, cultivable waste, fallow, and barren lands has also decreased. Thus, common grazing lands have declined in area, both quantitatively and qualitatively.

The fodder demand and supply position has always been considered in relation to the grazing animal population and the area under forage crops. Estimates show a deficiency of feed and fodder. A different feeding strategy and feed quality are required for different animal species. Buffalo and cattle require stall feedng. Small ruminants need a greater fodder supply from tree leaves besides grazing/browsing in forests. Also, thereare large areas facing land degradation, which progressively reduces the productivity of the grasslands.

Types, Production and Potential of Grasslands

A survey of the grasslands of India conducted between 1954 and 1962 revealed five major grass covers. These were *Sehima-Dichanthium*, *Dichanthium-Cenchrus-Lasiurus*, *Phragmites-Saccharum-Imperata*, *Themeda-Arundinella*, and Temperate Alpine associations.

Sehima-Dichanthium

This cover type spreads over the whole of peninsular India, including the Central Indian Plateau, the Chhota Nagpur Platéau and the Aravali Ranges with a potential coverage of approximately 1.74 million km^2. It is represented by dominant perennial grasses such as *Dichanthium annulatum*, *Sehima nervosum*, *Bothrichloa pertusa*, *Chrysopogon fulvus*, *Heteropogon contortus*, *Iseilema laxum*, *Themeda triandra*, *Cynodon dactylon*, *Aristida setacea*, and *Cymbopogon* spp. Important associated species are *Apluda mutica*, *Bothrichloa intermedia*, *Arundinella nepalensis*, *Desmostachya bipinnata*, *Eragrostis*, and *Eragrostiella* spp.

Dicanthium-Cenchrus-Lasiurus

This type is associated with subtropical arid and semi-arid regions comprising the northern part of Gujarat, the whole of Rajasthan, excluding the Aravalli Ranges in the south, western Uttar Pradesh, Delhi, Punjab, and Haryana with a potential area of more than 0.44 million km^2. The principal perennial grass species are *Cenchrus ciliaris*, *C. setigerus*, *Dicanthium annulatum*,

Cymbopogon jwarancusa, Cynodon dactylon, Eleusine compressa, Lesiurus sindicus, Sporobolus marginatus, Dactyloctenium sindicum, and *Desmostachya bipinnata.*

Important associated species are: *Chloris dolichostachya, Heteropogon contortus, Saccharum bengalense,* and *Vitevaria zyzanioides.*

Phragmites-Saccharum-Imperata

This association occurs throughout the Gangetic Plain and the Brahmaputra Valley and extends into the plains of Punjab. The area covers approximately 2.8 million km² in the northeastern states, West Bengal, Bihar, Uttar Pradesh, Punjab, and Haryana. The principal perennial species in drier regions are: *Imperata cylindrica, Saccharum arundinaceum, S. spontaneum, Phragmites karka,* and *Desmostachya bipinnata.* Other important species are *Bothrichloa intermedia, Vitevaria zizanioides, Imperata cylindrica, Chrysopogon aciculatus,* and *Panicum notatum.*

Themeda-Arundinella

This association occurs in the entire northern and northwestern mountain tract, in an approximate area of 230 thousand km² in the northeastern states, West Bengal, Uttar Pradesh, Punjab, Haryana, Himachal Pradesh, and Jammu and Kashmir. This type is associated with undifferentiated forest and hill soils, and also with undifferentiated forest submountain regional soils. The principal grass vegetation is represented by *Arundinella bengalensis, A. nepalensis, Bothrichloa intermedia, Chrysopogon fulvus, Cymbopogon jwarancusa, Cynodon dactylon, Heteropogon contortus, Themeda anathera, Eulaliopsis binata,* and *Ischaemum barbatum.* Associated perennial species are: *Apludamutica, Arundinella khaseana, Pennisetum flaccidum,* and *Chloris dolichostachys.*

Temperate Alpine

These grasslands occur on the high hills of Uttaranchal, Jammu and Kashmir, Himachal Pradesh, West Bengal, and the northeastern regions. They differ from the *Themeda-Arundinella* type in that they essentially occur at higher elevations beyond the tree line, approximately above 3000 m in the west and above 2000 m in the east. The principal perennial species are: *Agropyron conaliculatum, Chrysopogon gryllus, Dactylis glomerata, Danthonia cachemyiana, Phleum alpinum, Carex nubigena, Poa pratensis,* and *Stipa concinna.* Associated species are: *Poa alpina, Festuca lucida, Eragrostis nigra,* and *Bromus ramosus.*

Research on Grassland Improvement

Grassland improvement is possible through various ecological approaches such as protection of grassland for recovery of vegetation, removal of unwanted bushes, reseeding, application of fertilizers, and better management. These improvement techniques are discussed below:

Protection from Grazing

Overgrazing results in degradation of grasslands with sparse vegetation and dominance of unpalatable and noxious vegetation. Increased protection through fencing can improve vegetation recovery. Grazing lands can be protected with barbed wire/chicken wire or chain links supported by angle iron/cement/stone/wooden poles or by fencing with unpalatable bushes.

A review of the efficacy and cost effectiveness of various kinds of fencing indicated that living fences were most cost effective for protecting large areas. Species suitable for live hedges are: *Pithecelobium dulce, Carissa carandas, Agave sisalana, Agave Americana, Opuntia ficusindica, Zizyphus nummularia, Jatropha curcas, Parkinsonia aculeata,* and *Lawsonia inermis.* For grazing lands in the hills. Effective fencing for 5 years with no improvement measures could increase herbage yield from 0.9-3.0 t ha^{-1} Closing these grazing lands not only improves forage quantity but also its quality . A stone wall (1 m high and 45 m wide) supported by live hedges of *Agave americana, Barberis,* and *Yucca* sp. was found to be economically and ecologically viable.

Studies revealed an increase in the herbage yield from 0.1 to 3.5 t ha^{-1} within 3 years of protecting degraded grazing lands. The plant population of desired perennial grasses increased from 11 plants m^{-2} to 397 plants m^{-2} and that of undesirable forbs decreased from 444 plants m^{-2} to 33 plants m^{-2} during a period of five years on semi-rocky land. After two years of protection, the forage yield increased by 148 per cent in 'poor', 92 per cent in 'fair', and 116 per cent in 'good' condition classes of rangelands in tropical arid regions with sandy to sandy loam soils.

Bush Clearing

Heavy infestation of bushes in grazing lands adversely affects the availability of open space for growing grasses and forage. Studies conducted at the Indian Grassland and Fodder Research Institute (IGFRI), Jhansi, and elsewhere in arid regions, reveal the adverse effect of high bush density on forage yield. The standard practice of bush clearing involves either manual or mechanical felling and removal of stumps, or application of selective herbicides on the cut stumps to prevent them from coppicing. Those trees providing fodder, however, should be maintained in the grazing lands as feed reserves.

A certain ratio could be maintained between the bush cover and the grass cover. Researcher recognized three density classes of the bushes of *Zizyphus nummularia* in the grazing lands of the Indian deserts, where yields of grass and leaf fodder are influenced by varying densities of bushes. A medium density level of 14 per cent of the land area covered by shrubs is considered optimal for high forage and leaf production.

Reseeding

To improve the productivity of deteriorated rangelands, low-yielding annual grasses must be replaced by reseeding with high-yielding perennial grasses adapted to the prevailing conditions. Tropical grasslands usually have grasses of lower quality (low in protein content) than temperate grasslands. Introduction of suitable pasture legumes rectifies this to some extent. Studies have shown that planting legumes can add 40-50 kg N ha to grassland soils. Legumes also influence total dry matter production and crude protein yield.

Cenchrus ciliaris is the most suitable grass for arid and semi-arid zones, *C. setigerus* for sandy loam soils, *Chrysopogon fulvus* for red-gravelly/sloping lands, *Lasiurus sindicus* for extreme arid conditions, *Panicum turgidum* for sand dunes, *Dichanthium annulatum* for moist loamy soils, and *Iseilema laxum* and *Panicum maximum* for clay soils with higher moisture contents. In sandy or sandy loam soils with rainfall up to 750 mm, suitable legumes are *Stylosanthes hamata, Alysicarpus rugosus,* and *Lablab purpureus.*

Fertilizer Application

Application of nitrogen can considerably improve forage production and quality of grasses in terms of crude protein. Application of 40-60 kg N ha^{-1} and 20-30 kg P ha^{-1} could increase pasture production by 50-100 per cent.

Increases in pasture production due to the application of P_2O_5 are of a lower order compared to nitrogen application. No significant effect on pasture production is observed due to potash application. However, potassium is important for the long-term maintenance of pastures. In northwest Himalayan grazing lands have shown increase in forage yield on application of N and P The use of nitrogenous fertilizers on grasslands is expensive. Therefore, introduction of legumes into native grasslands is a cheap alternative due totheir nitrogen-fixing capacity.

Cutting Management

The ultimate objective of pasture management is to provide maximum digestible dry matter per unit area per growing season through a series of harvests. Harvesting at 60 day intervals at 15 cm above the ground level gave the highest forage yield. However, crude protein content has been found to be higher at shorter cutting intervals.

Grazing Management

The greatest single factor responsible for deterioration of grasslands is overgrazing. While grazing, animals tend to favor certain grasses and avoid others. Desirable species thus become depleted much faster than species that are less palatable. Most perennial grasses utilize the reserve food material stored in the underground parts to produce new shoots. When overgrazing occurs the reserve food material is lost faster, and perennial grasses are unableo regenerate due to a continuous drain on food reserves. A certain period of rest is thus essential for perennial grasses to recuperate and rejuvenate. Based on these considerations the following types of grazing systems are recommended:

- Continuous grazing.
- Deferred grazing.
- Rotational grazing.
- Deferred-rotational grazing.

In the continuous grazing system the grassland is not divided in to compartments or paddocks and animals are free to move in the whole area. Continuous grazing with high stocking rates can lead to a deterioration in composition and production of good forage grasses and an increase in unpalatable ones. It also affects soil fertility levels and exposes the area to run off and soil loss. In the deferred system, the grazing area is divided in to compartments and at least one of these is rested until seed setting. In rotationalgrazing compartments are grazed in rotation for a specific duration.

The deferred rotational grazing system is a mix of the latter two types and is considered the best system of grazing because

1. The same grassland supports a greater number of grazing days.
2. Proper vegetation composition is maintained through self seeding.
3. Health of the sward is maintained as the optimum utilization of biomass takes place and a period of rest is available to grasses.
4. Soil fertility is maintained.
5. Potential erosion hazards are avoided.

In *Sehima*-dominated grasslands, the deferred rotational grazing system is superior to the continuous system. For arid rangelands, there was an increase of 22 per cent in dry matter yield of *Cenchrus* species under deferred-rotational grazing and an increase in carrying capacity from 0.49 to 0.73 sheep ha^{-1}. Under continuous grazing only 0.53 sheep ha^{-1} were carried. In the *Lasiurus*-dominated grasslands in western Rajasthan, the deferred-rotational grazing system is superior to the continuous grazing system in terms of average body weight gain of Tharparker heifers. The calving rate was also higher (26%) under a deferred-rotational grazing system compared to the continuous system.

Animal Production

Animal production based on pastures and the silvipastoral system has been less studied. Two grass species were compared for growth and milk production under grazing conditions, but found no significant differences. Other studies have shown that animal productivity can be sustained with proper management with improved vegetation in a multi-tier system.

Silvipastoral Systems

The silvipastoral systems involve the establishment of multipurpose trees in existing pastures/grazing lands or waste lands, with grasses, legumes or cereals planted between the lines of trees. The pastures are used for cut and carry or in situ grazing. During the initial years of tree establishment and growth, the grasses and legumes are harvested as hay, and the area is maintained as aseasonal hay plot followed by grazing in a rotational or deferred rotational grazing system. The technique seems simple but the land area, soil type, topography, natural vegetation, local socioeconomic conditions, stocking rates, rainfall, temperature, and wind are some of the important factors that determine its success.

Forage Production

Depending upon the land capability, soil type, and its fertility, forage production rises from the first year and peaks in the 2nd or 3rd year. Forage production of up to 7.9 and 7.4 t ha^{-1} could be easily harvested depending on the choice of grass. The canopy of different trees did not make a significant difference to grass growth. Thus, depending upon the soil moisture and nutrients, yield differences of 2–10 t ha^{-1} yr^{-1} could be obtained from the grasses.

Firewood

Four to six t ha^{-1} yr^{-1} of firewood can be expected from short rotation species on degraded lands at a tree density of 500 plants ha in a 10 year cycle. Annual lopping when trees are 6-7 years old has been found to give 2.3-3.5 t ha^{-1} fodder and 4.5-6.5 t ha^{-1} firewood. Thus, combining the forage and top feed yield, the system could easily produce 5.3-9.5 t ha orage and 5 t ha^{-1} firewood or 10-14.5 t ha^{-1} total biomass. With the correct plant species, geometry, and management it might be possible to raise this to12-15 t ha^{-1} yr^{-1}.

Grazing

The stubble after the grass harvest can be grazed by different species of animals from the fourth year onwards between December and June. The productivity of grasses during the next monsoon is not affected. The leaf litter of the trees, the legume component in the pasture, and occasional lopped tree leaves provide a balanced ration.

Seed Production

The production of grass, legume, and tree seeds is a profitable enterprise. On slightly better sites, in a rotation of 5-6 years at the time of system renewal a crop of pigeon pea or cowpea could be obtained. Good production of these crops has been obtained in many situations.

Hortipastoral System

Dryland fruit crops such as *Zizyphus mauratiana*, custard apple, and *Emblica officinalis*, when grown in a hortipastoral system with grasses and legumes, provide early income from fruits, firewood from prunings, and forage from the grasses and legumes. These systems have been found to provide an annual forage yield of 4-6 t ha^{-1}. The presence of *Stylosanthes hamata* helps to increase fruit production.

Techniques and Choice of Species for Different Types of Degraded Lands

The techniques and choice of species for rehabilitating different types of degraded lands to optimize land productivity. Species such as *Acacia nilotica* and *Dalbergia sissoo* account for 86 per cent and 84 per cent interception of seepage. Trees inter-planted with Napier grass are more efficient at intercepting seepage.

Grasses and legumes can provide early colonization of mine overburdens. Species such as *Stylosanthes hamata*, *Clitoria ternata*, and *Macroptilium atropurpureum* produce poor root/shoot ratios but are desirable as colonizing and nitrogen-fixing species. Grasses such as *Bothrichloa intermedia*, *B. pertusa*, *Cenchrus setigerus*, and *Chrysopogon fulvus* colonize early with high production but poor root/shoot ratios.

Soil Productivity

Six years after silvipasture establishment, nitrogen, phosphorus, organic carbon, and potassium levels have been found to increase with time even when grasses are harvested and removed every year.

Socio-economic Implications of Silvipastoral Systems

Privately owned land improves and appreciates when managed well. However, common property resources are highly susceptible to degradation due to a lack of responsibility sharing. In such situations, institutional arrangements to suit local/regional problems and policies are required to protect and improve the degraded resources. Production-related activities having direct impact onnatural resources need to be analyzed in an economic framework including non-monetary costs. The production from degraded lands has been analyzed financially.

The merit of silvipastoral and hortipastoral systems indicating the high benefit/cost (B/C) ratios with higher employment potential and environmental benefits. In another study on the sub-Himalayan boundary degraded lands, Scientists reported a B/C value of 3.43 under *Acacia catechu* plantation with bhabar grass (*Eulaliopsis binata* (Retz) Hubbard). They observed that silvipasture or silviculture of fast-growing species in ravines was the best option with a B/C ratio of 1.9. They observed that on good lands, hortipastoral systems gave a B/C ratio of 3.2, while on highly degraded lands silvipastoral systems gave a B/C ratio of 1.8. On highly degraded rocky and gravelly areas or ravines in the central Indian semi-arid zone, silvipastoral, energy plantations, and hortipastoral systems provided the most viable option of land use and land cover. Several studies reported very high B/C ratio and internal rates of return (IRR) on energy plantations and silvipastoral systems.

Future Thrust Areas

- The grassland cover survey carried out during 1954 needs updating.
- Changing land use and land cover demands reinvesting in proper land use decisions for degraded lands where silvipastoral systems are most ideal. Habitat-specific studies are required to optimize forage supply from such lands.
- System synthesis for producing diversity in the components, and designs for optimizing yields are needed for different types of degraded lands. Research and development emphasis is required on high altitude pasture management systems.
- Grazing management is needed to sustain productive grasslands and improved animal productivity.
- Grass densification (baling), storage, and improved transport efficiency to deficit zones in the country during adverse weather.
- Socio-economic analysis and interventions for optimizing pasture productivity and sustenance through participatory management on common property resources, and through Joint Forest Management, need urgent attention.

Free Range Grazing to Managed Feeding

The study examines technological and institutional issues in conversion of free range grazing to managed feeding in the semi-arid Bundelkhand region of central India. The region is spread over 72,000 km^2 and supports a population of 12 million humans as well as 10 million cattle and buffalo. Growing human and animal populations have resulted in an increased pressure on the land, which has in turn led to a decline in the productivity and availability of grazinglands (natural grasslands, wastelands, and forests).

The region thus suffers from a serious shortage of livestock feed for most of the year, leaving many farmers with little option but to allow their animals to graze freely. Such practices damage cropped fields and discourage farmers from growing crops inthe summer season.

The intensification of livestock production is often considered a solution to the problems arising from free-range grazing. The farmers may replace their current large numbers of free grazing, low-productivity animals with smaller numbers of stall-fed, more productive animals. In an effort to stimulate this change, technologies have been developed for fodder production from irrigated, rainfed, and rehabilitated lands; the latter including grasslands, wastelands, and forests. Although technically sound, most of these technologies have not been adopted by the local farmers. This study is anattempt to address such issues. The study was conducted in 1998 with the specific objectives of:

- Determining the reasons for the persistence of free grazing.
- Identifying constraints and opportunities for conversion from free grazing to managed feeding systems.
- Identifying context-specific and client-oriented technologies required for managed feeding systems.

The traditional view of technology transfer is that it is a linear process, from research institute to extension department to farmers. The feedback, if any, is limited and informal and thus, researchers have limited contact with the farmers. This approach focuses only on the technology without considering the socioeconomic environment in which the farmer lives and works. The study uses Agricultural Research for Development (ARD) approach which is wider in perspective, focuses on participatory technology development, and takes into account the indigenous knowledge of farmers and their requirements.

The steps followed during the research period are:

- Reconnaissance surveys to understand the geographical, social and economic context in which free grazing operates.
- Analysis of block level secondary data to identify criteria for zoning.
- Zoning of the Bundelkhand region to identify relatively homogeneous subareas with regard to factors or criteria relevant to the study, and select sites for an in-depth study.
- In-depth study of eight selected villages in four blocks using Participatory Rural Appraisal (PRA) methodology employing tools such as semistructured interview, transect walks, social and natural resource mapping, seasonal calendars, analysis of agricultural knowledge and information system (AKIS), and problem identification and ranking.

The villages were selected based on the probability of existence of free grazing/managed feeding systems. Ghisauli, Bajni and Guraiya villages had a watershed project in each. Baghavali and Bajni had Joint Forest Management (JFM) projects. These villages were selected to see if these projects had any influence on the feeding systems being followed in the village. Simariya was avillage where the villagers realized the ill-effects of free grazing and were making conscious efforts to arrest the practice. Gorakaranpur and Virasani fell in the area that was supposedly following a high degree of managed feeding.

Menpaani had a large buffalo population and there was a high degree of stallfeeding, with all the feeds being bought.

Conditions that Favour Free Range Grazing or Managed Feeding

Free range grazing and managed feeding were not mutually exclusive but were found to coexist at zonal, village, and house-hold/herd level. However, the relative importance varied at different levels. At block level, the relative importance of free range grazing or managed feeding depended mainly on the availability of fodder from crop residues versus fodder from natural grasslands, wastelands, and forests.

The major factors that influenced the relativeimportance of free grazing or stall-feeding included:

- Cropping intensity: In zones and villages with high cropping intensities, the amount of crop residues was high, while natural grazing resources were limited. In these areas, stall-feeding was relatively important. The reverse held for zones and villages with a low cropping intensity.
- Proximity to forests, wastelands, and fallow lands: Villages nearer to these areas had a high proportion of free range grazing.
- Access to land: Smallholders and the landless practiced free range grazing even in irrigated (high fodder producing) areas.
- Access to markets for milk and fodder: Villages with access to milk and fodder markets had a higher proportion of stall feeding than those in remote and inaccessible areas.

Economic Rationale for Free Grazing or Managed Feeding

Before designing or recommending new technologies, it is important that scientists understand the farmer's viewpoint. Stall-feeding is assumed to be economically better than free grazing. This is because stall-fed animals are usually of better genotype, and produce more milk than free grazing animals. In this sense, improved breeds are considered to be more productive.

On the other hand, the decisions of farmers are based on the output per unit of capital (and labour), and influenced by their resource endowments, and the constraints/opportunities existing in the surroundings. For example, an investment of Rs. 20 thousand to buy 20 local cattle that are free grazed at limited labour costs may well be only as productive as spending the equivalent amount on the purchase of one buffalo. Although the latter yields more milk per head than the local breed, it may not be as profitable as 20 local cows.

Farmers may practice free grazing only because they have the opportunity to do so. They are not interested in more productive animals except for a few that they can feed with their home-produced crop residues.

Low productivity becomes a problem when local animals can no longer be free grazed, and farmers are forced to stall-feed them. The breed then does not perform well enough and farmers replace these animals with buffalo.

Stall-fed, high-producing breeds are not necessarily always more profitable economically than free range grazed, local breeds. Farmers might opt for a system with a high degree of stall-feeding because it is economically more productive than free grazing (a positive choice) or because the circumstances preclude the option of free grazing (a negative choice). Also, farmers who practice free grazing might do so because they have no other option (a negative choice), or because they have nothing to gain from converting to a stall-feeding regime (a positive choice for free grazing).

The labour requirement for the livestock subsector shows considerable variation between villages and households where free range grazing prevails and those where stall-feeding is predominant. In free grazing, labour is required for supervision of grazing during the winter and monsoon seasons and is usually drawn from the family. One person can supervise a large herd. In the villages and households practicing stall-feeding one of the setbacks of the system is that labour is required on a continuous basis. Children are sometimes kept away from school to keep up with the high labour requirements. A detailed partial budgeting analysis was carried out with three types of farmers practicing various degrees of stall-feeding to examine the profitability of free grazing *vis-à-vis* stall-feeding. These three types were:

1. *A farmer with a herd of six cows and buffalo and an irrigated land area of 9 ha.* The grazing practice varied according to the season. During summer, all animals were on unsupervised grazing for the whole day. In winter, nonlactating animals were grazed under supervision in the morning and evening. In the monsoon, all animals grazed unsupervised in the farmer's grassland during the morning and evening. In the afternoon, they were grazed under supervision on the common lands. The farmer gave a concentrate mixture of linseed, cotton seed cake, barley flour, and gram flour to both lactating and dry cows and buffalo three times a day during winter and summer. Only the lactating buffalo were given concentrates during the monsoon. The herd was fed with wheat straw

every day during summer and winter. The farmer used 30 man-days of hired labour and 16 man-days of family labour animal^{-1} yr^{-1}.

2. *A system where there was no land available for grazing and a system of dairying largely based on stall feeding with purchased inputs and minimal free grazing.* Wheat straw was provided to the animals for 10 months. Concentrates were fed for eight months (during the lactation period). On average, a farmer used nine man-days of family labour animal yr Replacement of stock was done every three years. The herd size ranged from 4–60 ruminants per household.
3. *A commercial, peri-urban dairy farmer with an average herd of six cows and 10 buffalo practicing a totally stall-fed system without any grazing.* All inputs were purchased and wheat straw and concentrates provided to animals throughout the year. Twenty-six man-days of hired labour and 11 man-days of family labour animal^{-1} yr^{-1} were used. Stock was replaced every two years.

The best estimates of major variables were used to determine the gross margin. These estimates were based on information collected from the farmers, direct observations, the literature, and expert knowledge.

The best estimates of the gross production value, gross costs, and gross margins for the above three systems as well as a completely free grazing system on a per animal basis, and an estimate of the cash inflow and outflow. The latter excludes the imputed costs incurred in milk production or 'costs' that do not require cash payments, such as the imputed values of farm-produced fodder and crop byproducts, interest on own capital, and family labour. The tables also show household cash income from the different systems under varying assumptions of herd sizes. The household cash income was based on herd size × cash flow peranimal, minus the value of home-consumed milk at 0.6 l day^{-1}. For large herd sizes (that exceeded the number that could be fed with the crop residues of a large nine ha farm, or that could be managed with family labour of 547.5 man-days per year), the additional costs of fodder and labour were also deducted from the herd size × cash flow per animal to obtain the net household cash income.

The cash flow figures for the free grazing and mixed systems are based on the best estimates ofproduction value and gross cash costs, whereas the cash flow for the two stall-fed systems are based on maximum estimates of production value, and best estimates of gross cash costs. Only then do the latter two systems seem to produce a positive cash flow. The assumption seems justified, moreover, that these stall-feeding systems yield closer to the maximum estimates than mixed feeding systems.

Analysis of the results suggests that:

- In real economic terms, i.e., when all the costs (including costs that do not require cash payments, such as the imputed values of farm produced fodder and crop by-products, imputed interest on own capital, and family labour) are taken into account, free grazing would be the only viable system. All other systems would produce negative gross margins.
- The positive household cash incomes for the mixed and stall-fed systems would only be obtained when imputed costs of household labour, capital involved, and crop residues are not considered. The comparison of the household cash income for the two herd sizes (3 cattle + 1 buffalo *vs.* cattle + 3 buffalo) of the mixed system suggests that, in areas where thereis no land for free range grazing, increasing the herd beyond the size that can be supported by farm-produced crop residues is not an economically viable option.

This comparative economic analysis suggests that, if economic costs are considered but environmental and social costs to the community ignored, free grazing is the only system that gives a positive gross margin. Stall-feeding is only sustainable when farmers disregard the cost of own labour, capital, and crop residues. The analysis suggests that gross margins and cash flows drop dramatically when herd sizes are extended beyond the numbers that farmers can feed with their own crop residues, and they have to purchase fodder tocover the deficit.

The economic analysis suggests that farmers who practice free range grazing may do so because it is the best allocation of their capital, while those who practice complete stall-feeding or mixed systems (involving some purchased inputs) may only do so because there is not enough land to graze their animals.

The potential for further intensification of livestock production and thetechnologies required must, therefore, be looked at in relation to the resource availability at zonal, house-hold, and village level. At current prices, a high dependence on stall-feeding is unlikely to become a viable option unless the quality and quantity of homegrown crop residues can be increased substantially on a year-round basis at low or no additional cost, and the conversion efficiency of animals considerably increased through low-cost genetic improvements.

Marketing Systems

Market access is necessary for the application of systems involving a high degree of stall-feeding. The fodder market found in the region had three features:

- In most of the villages studied, the most readily available fodder consisted of crop by-products, especially wheat straw. The price of fodder fluctuated considerably, i.e., low immediately after harvesting and increasing as the season advanced. The highest price was during winter. The farmers in Gorakaranpur reported that they bought dried wheat straw from their neighbors at Rs. 100 to Rs. 150 per 100 kg. Farmers who could afford it and had storage space usually bought fodder just after the harvesting season.
- Farmers living in villages with Joint Fodder Management (JFM) activities did sell some of the fodder harvested from the protected forests. They did this due to lack of storage space or because it was a means of earning some ready cash.
- Some buyers of fodder guaranteed their supply through an arrangement where a farmer raised a fodder crop on their request. The purchaser collected fodder and weeds from the designated plot. This was supposedly cheaper than purchasing the fodder from the market. However, when comparing the costs incurred this seemed doubtful. The buyer got about 500 kg of green sorghum from a plot of 46.45 m2 at a cost of Rs. 900, while 100 kg of green fodder could be bought in the market for Rs. 100. The only advantage was that the farmer could collect other grasses and weeds from the field as well. The same field produced 350 kg of *Berseem* during winter.

Knowledge and Information System

Zonal variations must be taken into account when developing technologies. Links between farmers and technology sources tend to be limited. Farmers who want to use forest resources without restriction often clash with the Forestry Department, which has a legal enforcement role.

The JFM is a more viable alternative as it creates opportunities for better collabouration. Farmers should be made aware of the long-term benefits of the approach instead of looking only at short-term benefits such as free fodder and employment intrench digging.

Furthermore, farmers are not interested in taking an active role in the sustainable use of natural resources, if these do not belong to them and they do not have a stake in the benefits. Farmers appreciate contacts with extension staff. However, the technological training of the latter is limited to technology transfer, and they are rarely capable of providing organisational and leadership training to farmers.

The researchers have even less contact with farmers. Due to the absence of good mechanisms for dissemination, the technologies do not reach the farmers, leaving a big gap in terms of flow of information and feedback from both researchers and farmers. Nongovernmental organisations are other potential collabourators in the dissemination of technologies. They have the advantage of a more appropriate approach in mobilizing people.

Policy Influences

Central and state government policies also influence the choice of free grazing or stall-feeding. Agriculture is a state subject, yet the central and state governments have control over various issues related to forest and wastelands. Different governments control different categories of land e.g. revenue land, and protected/unprotected forests. The lack of co-ordination among various agencies is a hindrance to implementing the wasteland development projects. Some issues in this regard are now mentioned.

Land Ceiling Act

The ceiling of irrigated land in Uttar Pradesh and Madhya Pradesh is 7.3 ha for two crops a year, and 10.9 ha for one crop a year. The ceiling for dry land is 18.3 ha in Uttar Pradesh and 21.9 ha in Madhya Pradesh. Many large landowners do not want to opt for a second crop, as that will reduce the amount of land they can own. According to government officials this failure or reluctance to have a second crop leaves a lot of land area uncultivated and promotes free grazing. However, the Ceiling Act is not a major factor, as only a few farmers possess more than 7.3 ha of land. Irrigation facilities have been designed for *rabi* (dry season) crops only. Another reason is failure to popularize short duration *kharif* (wet season) crops. The lack of fodder in summer due to non-production of *zaid* (summer) crop is mainly due to a lack of irrigation. At present, only small areas of vegetables are grown during summer, which do not provide any crop residues.

Forests and Wasteland Policy

Increasing the productivity of wastelands and forests, which are categorized as revenue lands, protected, unprotected, and grazing lands is complex as different government departments and ministries control these. Grass plantations can be harvested legally by community organisations in the absence of formal lease deeds. Various authorities are permitted to lease out different categories of lands. Lack of coordination and information on land ownership often causes delays in obtaining the lease. For example, a District Collector in Rajasthan leased some revenue land to a tree growers' cooperative. Five years into the project it was realized that the land was reserve forest, which can only be leased by the central government. The deed was cancelled and the project had to be rolled back. Due to encroachment, and state government policy to distribute common lands to landless people, the area under village common land in the country has been reduced by 41–55 per cent. Before the New Forest Policy of 1988, the community rights forownership of pasture and share of forest produce were not recognized.

The Government of India issued guidelines in 1990 for participation of the people in the management and sharing of forest produce, with emphasis on nontimber forest products. This concept is in its pilot phase and, presently, does not induce true participation.

Fodder Policy

The National Commission on Agriculture emphasized that feeding is of crucial importance. The NCA recommended identification of grass species suitable for wastelands and development of technologies for improving productivity of such lands. The Commission observed that highyielding nutritious fodder crops should compete favorably with any food or cash crop.

This policy was not coupled with similar suitable policies (such as credit facilities and provision of bulls in the villages for crossing) in other departments for replacement of unproductive livestock by high-yielding breeds. The government put much emphasis on artificial insemination programmes to produce high-yielding animals, but farmers refuted the programme for many valid reasons. The NCA did not at the time realize the importance of crop residues that can be used for fodder.

Grazing Policy

There is presently no national grazing policy, although it is in the process of formulation. Madhya Pradesh has a grazing policy, which imposes several restrictions and grazing fees, but does not discuss pasture development. In the absence of a grazing policy, only forest regulations cover grazing restrictions, and these often contradict the fodder policy. All these factors lead to an imbalance between grazing pressure and carrying capacity of grazing lands.

Industrial Policy

The significant influence of industrial policy on free grazing was observed in Jalaun district. A multinational soybean-processing company popularized soybean cultivation in the area, distributed minikits and bought back the soybeans at good prices. Farmers accepted the technology because of its profitability. Now, many farmers grow soybean as a second crop during the *kharif* season. However, the free grazing is restricted. In some of these villages, farmers now use soybean straw as fodder.

Technology Needs and Recommendations

A number of technologies have been developed to address the issues of fodder shortages and overgrazing. Approaches have included wasteland rehabilitation schemes coupled with grassland/silvipasture development, development of improved varieties of fodder grasses and legumes, and identification of species resistant to grazing pressure. The main aim has been to provide farmers with sufficient fodder for managed feeding systems (which may include stall feeding as well as rotational grazing), thereby reducing the widespread degradation of forest and grasslands due to free range grazing.

The wide range of farm types in the region means that solutions need to be tailored differently depending on whether the farmers own large or small holdings, or are landless. The landless animal owner, for example, would benefit from the increased employment opportunities and the increased fodder availability provided through wasteland rehabilitation and grassland management schemes. Provision of improved fodder crop varieties and improved cropping schemes (fodder/food intercrops), and improved animals could be targeted at large-scale farmers. The smallholder would benefit from dual-purpose (food and fodder) crop varieties, enabling maximum use of the limited land available.

Availability of water can solve the problem of free grazing, as it is the main reason for the severe shortage of fodder, especially during the summer months.

This problem affects on-farm crop production and also the productivity of forests and grasslands. In areas where water conservation methods are used, the land is more productive; the grasses produced often being 'cut and carried' for use in stall feeding systems. Water conservation schemes need to be coupled with grassland management projects.

A major problem faced by small farmers in the study area was the shortage of land for crop production. Farmers with access to irrigation andthus the potential for high crop yields, tended to grow only food crops. Less than one per cent of the land was put to fodder cultivation. The development of dual-purpose crops (food/fodder) is almost certainly the only practical solution to the fodder shortages of the area.

A number of watershed projects in the area, although technically sound, failed to adequately involve the local people. For example, in Guraiya and Ghisauli villages, watershed projects were seen more as an employment opportunity than for the increased land productivity. This was because the people did not have a sense of project ownership, nor were they fully aware of the advantages of sustaining the project once the implementing agency had left.

This shows that technological experiments need to be conducted incombination with social experiments to find the most suitable match of technology and the form of organisation to manage a common property. Parallel or separate experiments may not be successful as social organisational constraints may well rule out the use of certain technologies despite their relative merits. For example, it may prove that cut and carry is the only technology that can be controlled or managed, given the constraints of the organisation concerned, although other technologies (rotational grazing or deferred rotational grazing) may well produce higher quantities of biomass.

The technical optimum is not necessarily the most feasible social solution. Research should then focus on optimizing cut and carry systems, despite the lower biomass production of this technology.

CHAPTER

19 The Growth in Dairying

The importance of the dairy subsector in the Indian economy is reflected by the fact that it is the second largest contributor to the gross value of output of the agricultural sector, after rice. Milk production has grown at an annual growth rate of 4.1 per cent between 1980-81 and 1998-99. The annual per capita availability of milk in the country has increased at an average annual growth rate of 2.5 per cent during this period. As a result, India's import dependence hasreduced. At present, almost the entire milk demand is met through domestic supplies.

Various agencies such as the National Dairy Development Board (NDDB), Dairy Cooperatives, National Dairy Research Institute (NDRI), and other research and developmental institutions have contributed to this phenomenal growth.

The remarkable growth in dairying achieved over the last few decades needs to be sustained in an efficient and economic manner so as to ensure adequate returns to investments at farm and industry levels, and the continued availability of milk and milk products at economical rates to consumers. This would be possible by developing vertical linkages between producers and consumers with the processing sector in between. This paper first examines the prospects of value addition to milk and then identifies efficient value added technologies.

Prospects for Value Addition

Of the total milk produced in the country, about one-third is retained by the producers for personal consumption, and the rest finds its way to the market. There is little information on the utilization pattern of milk; yet the bulk is consumed as whole milk and/or as ghee and curds. Available statistics indicate that only about one-fifth of the total milk produced is processed into productssuch as cheese, butter, whey, and sweetmeats. This is due to the lack of processing and associated infrastructures. Nevertheless, there isa huge potential for development of the market for processed milk food.

Several factors underline this proposition. First, India's huge population itself is a source of demand for processed milk products. However, the effective demand is constrained due to the low per capita income of the majority of the population.

The rapid growth in per capita income in recent years indicates the gradual emergence of an upwardly mobile middle class, which because of its nouveau riche behavior, is expected to be a great source of demand for processed foods. Second, a large part of the demand comes from the urban population, which has been growing rapidly in recent decades. Third, India's present share in world exports of dairy products is miniscule. This is because of higher domestic demand for milk and lack of competitiveness in the world market due to high levels of support to producers, industry and exporters of milk and milk products in Europe and the USA. With the implementation ofthe WTO agreement the cost of milk production, as well as processing, is expected to rise in major exporting countries. This is to the advantage of many developing countries including India. Furthermore, processing costs in India are also high for a number of reasons. The application of improved processing technologies would help reduce processing costs.

Dairy Production Technologies

Improving Quality of Raw Milk Lactoperoxidase

System for Preservation of Raw Milk

Refrigeration of raw milk in rural areas is difficult because of the inadequacy and frequent breakdown of power supply, voltage fluctuations, and high cost of refrigeration equipment. Thus, an alternative method for preservation of milk, known as the lactoperoxidase (LP) system, has been developed.

The advantages of this method are:

- LP is a naturally occurring antimicrobial agent in bovine milk, which can be harnessed for effective preservation of raw milk.
- LP can be activated with an exogenous dose of thiocyanate and hydrogen peroxide within 2-3 hours of milk production.
- Milk remains in a good condition up to 30 hours at 37°C.
- The cost of preservation is low.

Technologies for Process Upgradation of Traditional Milk Products

The sector engaged in the preparation of a wide range of indigenous milk products lacks organization and requires modernization. Intensive scientific, research/development (R&D), and financial inputs are necessary to develop industrial manufacturing and packaging systems. Significant work has been done to this end; some of the new processes are discussed here.

Khoa Powder

Khoa cannot be stored for more than five days at room temperature withoutspoiling. Addition of preservatives to *khoa* is illegal in India. Thus, in many parts of the country, *khoa* production is banned during summer.

Unfortunately this is the time when the demand for *khoa* is invariably at its peak. The cost of packaging and transportation of *khoa* is also high due to its bulk. The technology developed for manufacture of *khoa* powder would help eliminate these problems. Standardized buffalo milk is vacuum concentrated to the desired level and heated to accentuate flavour prior to drying. Antioxidants and free-flowing agents are added to improve the chemical and physical properties.

The advantages of the new process are:

- About 14 kg of *khoa* powder is obtained from 100 liters of standardized buffalo milk. On reconstitution with water, this quantity produces about 21 kg of *khoa*.
- *Khoa* powder can be used directly for the preparation of various sweets (*burfi, milk-cake, kalakand,* and *gulab jamun*). The quality of sweets made from *khoa* powder is highly acceptable.
- With appropriate preservative techniques *khoa* powder can be stored up to 10 months at 30°C.

Instant Kulfi Mix Powder

Kulfi is a popular frozen milk product. The chemical and organoleptic qualities of commercially sold *kulfi* vary and tend to be of inferior microbial quality. A technology has been perfected for the manufacture of *kulfi* mix powder by spray drying. The mix is formulated from milk fat, milk solid not fat (MSNF), sucrose, and isabgol (*Plantago psyllium)* husk.

The concentration of solids in the mix is adjusted and only 25 per cent of the total sugar required addedbefore drying. The mix is homogenized and heat-treated in a tubular heat exchanger, then spray dried. The remaining sugar is powdered, dry blended with the mixture, and packaged in tin cans. The approximate chemical composition of *kulfi* mix powder is: fat 25.4 per cent, MSNF 37.0 per cent, isabgol 0.5 per cent, sugar 34.7 per cent, and moisture 2.5 per cent.

The advantages of the new process are:

- The product has a shelf life of seven months at 30ºC in tin cans.
- The cost of production of *kulfi* mix powder at current prices works out to Rs. 90 per kg; much lower than that from regular processes.
- *Kulfi* mix powder can be instantly reconstituted and frozen to get *kulfi* of consistently good quality throughout the year at an affordable price.

Gulab Jamun Mix Powder

Gulab Jamun is traditionally prepared from a mixture of *khoa*, bleached wheat flour (*maida*), and baking powder. There are wide variations in the chemical composition flavour, and texture of *khoa*; these affect the final quality of *gulab jamun*. The shelf life of traditionally prepared *Gulab Jamun* is about one week at ambient temperatures. Refrigeration adversely affects its texture and quality. The instant *Gulab Jamun* mix powder overcomes these problems, with several additional benefits.

Gulab Jamun mix powder is formulated from milk powder, vanaspati oils, *maida*, semolina, baking powder, and ground cardamom. Two different formulae have been developed for spray and roller-dried skimmed milk. Theproduct can be packed and sold in a metallized polyester laminate.

The steps involved in *Gulab Jamun* preparation such as making the dough, deep fat frying, and soaking of balls in sugar syrup were standardized for the mix powder. One kg mix powder yields about 150 *gulab jamuns* of average size (25 g each).

The advantages of the new process are:

- *Gulab Jamun* mix powder packaged in metallized polyester laminates without preservatives remains fit for use for up to eight months at 30°C.
- The cost of *Gulab Jamun* mix powder formulated from roller dried skimmed milk is estimated to be Rs. 70 per kg; the spray-based mix formulation is slightly costlier (Rs. 75 per kg).
- The technology is simple and the product convenient to use.

Instant Kheer Mix

Kheer is a dessert popular throughout India, but has limited life even under refrigeration. In the past, several unsuccessful attempts have been made to extend the shelf life of *kheer*. Rice *kheer* produced in a dry form suitable for ready reconstitution has overcome the problem of a limited shelf life.

The process for an instant rice-based *kheer* mix consists of separate instantization of the milk and rice phases of the product employing two-stage spray-bed and fluid-bed drying systems. Appropriate compositional and process manipulations ensure a high product quality. The two-phase product comprising powdered liquid/milk fraction and a particulate (rice) fraction is packaged bag-in-bag, a small polyethylene pouch of rice being carried in a bigger bag containing the powder. The mix packaged in metallized polyester/LDPE pouches has a shelf life of at least six months at 37°C. Reconstitution involves rehydration of instant rice in boiling water for 10 minutes followed by dispersal of the powder into the rice-water mixture. The reconstituted product can be suitably flavoured and enriched with dry fruits if desired, and is very close to conventional *kheer*.

The advantages of the new process are:

- The shelf life of *kheer* is enhanced to six months compared to 1-2 days for the conventional product.
- It is of considerable convenience to consumers–no sourcing of raw materials is required.
- Cooking time is reduced to 10 minutes as compared to one hour in conventional process, therefore there are savings in terms of fuel.
- The cost of manufacture is low.

Paneer and Related Products

Paneer is prepared by acid and heat coagulation of milk. Traditionally, small dealers or the consumers themselves have produced it in very small quantities.

Commercial production of *paneer* helps dairies utilize surplus milk during the flush season and provides an outlet for relatively inferior quality milk. The limitations of *paneer* production on a large scale are lack of improved technology of manufacture and limited shelf life.

The advantages of the new process using buffalo milk are:

- Higher yield and improved rheology achieved by incorporation of hydrocolloids.
- Improved rheological characteristics by proper pH and temperature control.
- Economical production through use of low cost un-conventional coagulants.
- Savings in energy and water requirement.
- The simplified manufacturing technique makes the process more suitable for mechanization.

UF–Paneer: Membrane technology has been used for the manufacture of *paneer*. The process involves standardization and heating of milk followed by ultrafiltration (UF) whereby lactose, water, and some minerals are removed. The concentrated mass is cooled, acidified, and then placed in suitable containers. This is followed by texturization using microwave technique. The resulting product has typical characteristics of normal *paneer*. The process also helps increase the shelf life.

The advantages of this technique are:

- Uniformity of production.
- Improved shelf life and increased yield.
- It is a nutritionally improved product.

Long Shelf-life Paneer in Retort Pouches: The traditional technology is suitable for batch operations and handling of milk from 5 to 10 thousand liters in batches, but has certain limitations. Nearly half the milk solids are lost in whey. It has a limited shelf life and production is labour intensive. Proper packaging and quality assurance systems are lacking. The new process achieves the in-package sterilization and texturization of *paneer* in retort pouches.

The advantages of the new process are:

- The product yield is almost doubled.
- Whey solids are retained in the product and there is no problem of whey disposal.
- The product has a shelf life of three months at 30°C.
- Various unit operations are integrated fully with mechanized energyefficient equipment.
- An appropriate packaging system is available.
- Cost of manufacture is low.

Technologies for Manufacture of Cheese and Related Products

Accelerated Ripening of Cheese

The traditional process of manufacturing ripened varieties of cheeses such as Cheddar and Gouda takes a long time to yield the product. The long-time curing is cumbersome, labour intensive, energy consuming, and expensive. This problem is aggravated further in the case of cheddar cheese production from buffalo milk. Technologies have been developed that accelerate the ripening process of cheeses, thus saving on refrigeration and labour.

The new process involves standardization of buffalo milk, relatively higher heat treatment, addition of a higher rate of starter culture and microbial rennet, and cooking at lower temperature. Supplementing the starter culture with adjunct bacteria, addition of exogenous free enzymes, such as lipase and protease, and microencapsulated enzymes, and partial curing of cheese at elevated temperatures accelerates the rate of ripening.

Supplementation of buffalo milk with goat milk also improves the flavour, and the development of body and texture.

The advantages of the new process are:

- Buffalo milk can be used to manufacture good quality Cheddar cheese.
- Supplementation with goat milk provides a profitable outlet for using goat milk.
- The process saves a considerable amount of labour, space, and energy and curtails the amount of money tied up in cold storage.
- It reduces the total ripening costs to about 20-27 per cent of the original.

Cheddar Cheese Flavour Base

A process technology for Cheddar Cheese Flavour Base (CCFB) in a paste and spray-dried form has been developed. This form has 15 to 20 times more intensity of flavour and is a cheap and convenient substitute for matured natural Cheddar cheese, which is used conventionally for flavouring different food products.

The CCFB is made by incubating young cheese slurry and exogenous enzymes at elevated temperatures under controlled reaction conditions. Cheddar cheese flavour develops within hours. All the critical control points of the process are standardized to obtain a uniform product. The flavour components are retained during spray drying using micro-encapsulation techniques. The shelf life of spray dried CCFB packed in metallized polyester laminate pouches is more than eight months at 15°C. The advantages of the new process are:

- Production costs are reduced by as much as 40-80 per cent.
- Production capacity is increased and product stability enhanced
- There is improved consistency and batch-to-batch product uniformity.
- There is better control in the development of new products.

Technologies for Manufacture of Fermented Milk Products

Mishti Dahi

Mishti dahi is a popular traditional fermented milk product from eastern India. Since the manufacturing conditions are not controlled, the quality of each lot of *mishti dahi* is different. A standard method has now been developed, which is also suitable to large-scale production.

Skimmed milk is concentrated into known total solids employing avacuum process. Cream is added to adjust fat in the partially concentrated milk. The standardized concentrated milk is heated and homogenized, followed by addition of sugar. The sweetened milk is heated to generate the characteristic caramel flavour, cooled to 30°C, and inoculated with LF-40 starter culture (1% by weight of milk). It is then filled in pasteurized polystyrene cups and incubated at 30°C for seven hours.

UF-Shrikhand

Shrikhand is an indigenous fermented milk product presently being manufactured by conventional methods. The conventional method allows the whey proteins to drain along with whey during *chakka* (curd cheese) making. The yield of skimmed milk *chakka* is about 18 per cent by the conventional method. A new method of skimmed milk *chakka* manufacture has been standardized that gives 23 per cent extra yield (due to the recovery of whey proteins) using an UF technique. The quality of *shrikhand* made from UF-*chakka* has been found to be excellent.

Coagulated skimmed milk is concentrated by ultrafiltration using amineral membrane module so as to recover whey proteins in the form of UFretentate (*chakka*). Cream and sugar are added to the retentate. The minimum shelf life of the product is two weeks under refrigeration.

Technologies for Manufacture of Formulated Foods

Bifidus-containing Infant Formula

Existing infant formulae being marketed currently in India do not offer the bioprotective features essential to protect the health of bottle-fed babies. Higher instances of diarrheal diseases are reported among bottle-fed babies.

The advantages of the new technology are:

- The ratio of whey protein: casein: fat: carbohydrate: mineral is similar to that of human milk.
- Essential nutrient and caloric content conform to WHO/FAO, *Codex Alimentarius* Commission standards.
- The product contains 1.2 × 105 cfu per gm of *Bifido-bacterium bifidum* suitable for intestinal implantation in babies.
- Nutritional/biological adequacy has been established through feeding trials carried out under pediatric supervision.
- The cost of manufacture is 40 per cent lower than that of conventional formulae.

Low Fat Spread

Butter is one of the most consumed dairy items. However, very few of those who would like to eat butter can afford to buy it. When refrigerated, butter becomes har and brittle and loses its spreading consistency. When left at ambient temperature, it loses its plasticity.

It is therefore necessary to provide a product that is accept-able in all respects including spreadable consistency at ambient and refrigerated temperatures. An attempt was made to develop a low-fat, low-cholesterol, and low-cost spread, which could serve as a substitute for butter. Low fat spreads usually have about 40 per cent moisture content.

Consequently, its shelf life is slightly less than that of conventional butter that has only 15-16 per cent moisture. The butter-flavoured spread is prepared with skimmed milk powder, a blend of hydrogenated fat and refined soybean oil, carrageenan, trisodium citrate, common salt, diacetyl, glycerol monostearate, and annatto butter colour. The cheese-flavoured spread can be prepared in the same way except that part of the skimmed milk powder is replaced with ripened Cheddar cheese to impart the typical flavour.

The advantages of the new process are:

- Butter-flavoured spread packaged in polystyrene cups (100 g) can be stored for six weeks at 5°C.
- Butter-flavoured low-fat spread costs only 58 per cent the price of conventional butter, whereas the cheese-flavoured product is slightly more expensive being 70 per cent the cost of butter.

Low Lactose Milk

Per capita consumption of milk, which is low in India, is expected to rise with an increase in milk production in the near future. Nearly 62 per cent of the Indian population cannot digest lactose in milk. The incidence of lactose intolerance varies from region to region. The problem can be overcome by conversion of the lactose in milk into glucose and galactose by the enzyme ß-galactosidase.

Since lactose in milk is converted into these monosaccharides in the human body following ingestion of milk, consumption of low lactose milk prepared by treatment of milk with ß-galactosidase will overcome lactose intolerance without any side effects. The critical factor in preparation of low lactose milk is the enzyme

β-galactosidase. A number of microorganisms have been screened and identified as suitable sources for the enzyme. Strains of the yeast *Kluvyeromyces fragilis* and bacterial strains of *Streptococcus cremoris*, *S. thermophilus*, *Lactobacillus bulgaricus*, and *Leuconostoc cremoris* are all suitable for production of the enzyme. Whey (a by-product of the cheese industry) supplemented with a nitrogen source serves as the medium for the propagation of the organism.

The enzyme is also commercially available. The quantity of the enzyme is expressed in terms of enzyme units; one unit being equivalent to hydrolysis of 1.0 ìmole of lactose into glucose and galactose in one minute. The advantage of the new process is that low lactose milk has the same shelf life as nonhydrolyzed milk.

Technologies for the Manufacture of Dairy By-products

Whey Powder

Whey is the by-product obtained during the manufacture of cheese, *paneer*, *chhana*, casein, and other coagulated products. The growing demands for cheese and increasing industrial production of casein and other coagulated products have generated enormous quantities of whey. On average, about 800 million kg of whey are produced annually as a byproduct, with about 52 million kg of nutritious whey solids. Unfortunately most of this goes waste.

Besides being nutritious, whey solids possess excellent functional attributes such as solubility, emulsifying and foaming property, gel-formation, water binding property, flavour, and viscosity. Whey is rich in organic matter. The BOD (Biological Oxygen Demand) of whey is as high as 35-50 thousand mg O_z L^{-1} Disposal of untreated whey can therefore be harmful to the environment and human health.

Thus, recovery of whey solids offers dual advantages. A technology has been developed for the manufacture of whey powder, whey protein concentrate, and lactose using membrane technology, which is less energy intensive and more cost effective. The method of production of whey powder involves clarification of whey, its partial concentration employing reverse osmosis, followed by vacuum concentration, precrystallization of lactose using alpha-lactose monohydrates as seeding material, and finally spray-drying and packaging.

Whey Protein Concentrates

Whey protein concentrates (WPC) are used mainly as ingredients in non-dairy products, but also to some extent in dairy products such as infant and weaning foods. Additionally, they can be utilized for designing speciality food products, such as health food, hospital meals, fruit juices, and beverage mixtures. The process for WPC manufacture involves pretreatment and ultrafiltration of whey, followed by spray drying of the UF-retentate. The pH of whey obtained from buffalo milk Cheddar cheese is adjusted to 7.2 prior to heating. Whey is cooled to 50°C before ultrafiltration. The retentate is spray dried using 180°C inlet and 80°C outlet temperatures. Whey protein concentrate powder thus obtained is cooled to room temperature, and packaged in polyethylene or metallized polyester laminates.

The advantages of the new process are:

- Energy requirements of membrane processes are low compared to evaporation processes.
- Adoption of membrane technology has distinct advantages in terms of improved yield and enhanced nutritive value.
- The product is stable for six months at room temperature.

Acido Whey – A Whey Drink

A process has been developed to prepare a palatable soft beverage utilizing whey that has been named 'Acido-whey'. Acido-whey is a noncarbonated drink, fermented with a selected strain of lactic acid bacteria and retaining all the nutrients of the whey intact. No preservative or synthetic colour is added. It is highly refreshing, therapeutic in nature, and costs less compared to other beverages. The process is commercially feasible and economical to those dairy industries that are engaged in simultaneously processing fluid milk and manufacturing *paneer* and cheese.

Technologies for Use of Probiotics in Dairy Products

Probiotic Cheese

The tremendous growth of the market for probiotic food in Japan, Europe, the USA, and Australia are indicative of a trend that could be emulated by the dairy industry in India. A process was standardized for manufacturing Edam cheese containing an adequate number of viable cells of the probiotic microorganism *Bifidobacterium bifidum*. This cheese was comparable to the conventional product in its organoleptic and physicochemical characteristics. The efficacy of the probiotic characteristics imparted to the cheese was demonstrated through animal bioassays, i.e. intestinal implantation, antagonism towards colonic coliforms, and reduction in β-glucuronidase activity. The cheese also contains physiologically active peptides that augment its functional value. It is expected that the implantation of this health-promoting strain in the human intestine will lead to the manifestation of the probiotic attributes in the human system. This needs to be further investigated through clinical trials.

The advantages of the new process are:

- Product diversification and value addition.
- Added therapeutic and physiological benefits in the cheese.
- Distinct anticarcinogenic properties besides antagonism towards enteric coliforms, thus reducing the risk of gastrointestinal diseases.

Technologies for Manufacture of Dairy Equipment

Continuous Butter Melter

The melting of butter is an important unit operation that precedes the use of the continuous ghee-making system. Butter is received from cold storage in the form of large slabs normally at 4°C, and melts in jacketed tanks very slowly due to poor heat transfer coefficient. The melting operation has to be startedin advance to keep the system in operation. The handling of large bricks of butter is also difficult. Continuous butter melters are not manufactured in India.

The continuous butter melter consists of a tank type heat exchanger with a rotor comprised of three components: a cutter, a conveying and turbulence generator, and a retainer disc to disintegrate butter lumps.

The advantages of the new process are:

- Quick operation: The melting capacity of 600-1000 kg/h is obtained with aheat-transfer surface area of only 0.72 m^2. The initial temperature of butter is 12-14°C and temperature at the outlet is 55-65°C.
- It is a safe and convenient way of handling butter.
- The heat transfer coefficients are high.
- Less energy is required compared with that in the jacketed kettle. Approximately 50 kJ kg^{-1} butter can be saved.

Continuous Ghee-making Machine

Ghee is currently manufactured by a batch process, which suffers from many disadvantages:

- A low heat transfer coefficient and unhygienic method of operation.
- An excessive strain on the operator due to the heat and humidity.
- Problems of severe scaling and foaming leading to inefficient utilization of the heat transfer surface and product loss.
- A high energy requirement. A new process has been designed on the principle of heat transfer and hydrodynamicsin a horizontal thin film-scraped surface-heat exchanger with a specific rate of water evaporation of 75 kg at 3.5-4.0 atm. steam pressure.

Continuous Khoa Making Machine

Khoa is an important ingredient in the manufacture of milk-based sweets. Presently, *khoa* is made primarily in jacketed kettles, which have the following disadvantages:

- They are unhygienic to operate.
- The heat transfer cannot be controlled and optimized
- An excessive strain on the operator due to the heat and humidity.
- Handling of large volumes is cumbersome.A cascade system comprising two horizontal straight-sided thin filmscraped surface-heat exchangers has been fabricated to manufacture *khoa* from standardized buffalo milk. The rotor of the first heat exchanger isprovided with four variable clearance blades and rotated at 3.3 rps. In this heat exchanger, milk is concentrated to about 40 per cent total solids, which then flows into the second heat exchanger by gravity. The rotor of this heat exchanger has two helical conveying ribbons in addition to two variable clearance-scraping blades rotated at 2.5 rps.

The advantages of the new process are:

- The heat transfer rates are high.
- Cleaning is easy due to the absence of fouling.
- There is a negligible hold-up volume as the product remains in the form of a thin film.
- The product is of uniform quality.

India has undoubtedly made tremendous progress in dairying, but this is more quantitative than qualitative. What India now requires is a qualitative improvement in the entire food chain so that the country can establish itself as a reliable supplier of dairy products conforming to international standards and the quality assurance systems as envisaged under WTO agreements. Fast urbanization, increased purchasing power, nutritional awareness, and demand for region-specific milk products require new technologies to be developed for tailor made products.

Bibliography

Council for Agricultural Science and Technology. 1999. Animal Agriculture and Global Food Supply. In *Task Force Report*, no. 135. Ames, Iowa: CAST.

Delgado, C., M. Rosegrant, H. Steinfeld, S. Ehui and C. Courbois. 1999. *Livestock to 2020: The Next Food Revolution*. Food, Agriculture and the Environment Discussion Paper 28, Washington, D.C.: International Food Policy Research Institute.

Food and Agriculture Organisation of the United Nations 2000 Small Ponds Make a Big Difference: Integrating Fish with Crop and Livestock Farming. Rome: FAO.

Food and Agriculture Organisation of the United Nations. 2001. *Mixed Crop-Livestock Farming: A Review of Traditional Technologies based on Literature and Field Experience*. Animal Production and Health Papers 152 Rome: FAO.

Food and Agriculture Organisation of the United Nations. 2003. *Integrated Livestock - Fish Farming Systems*. Rome: FAO.

Food and Agriculture Organisation of the United Nations. 2007. Tropical Crop-Livestock Systems in Conservation Agriculture. The Brazilian Experience. Rome: FAO.

Food and Agriculture Organisation of the United Nations and World Bank Group. 2001. Farming Systems and Poverty: Improving Farmers' Livelihoods in a Changing World. Rome: FAO.

International Fund for Agricultural Development. 2008. *Improving Crop-Livestock Productivity through Efficient*. Nutrient Management in Mixed Farming Systems of Semi-arid West Africa.

International Fund for Agricultural Development, 2005. Integrated Crop-Livestock Farming System, Burkina Faso. Rome: IFAD.

International Fund for Agricultural Development. Undated. Community Approach to the Development of Integrated Crop/Livestock Production in the Low Rainfall Area.

International Livestock Centre for Africa, 1998. *Crop-Livestock Interactions. A Review of Opportunities for Developing Integrated Models*. Llangefni, United Kingdom: Stirling Thorne Associates.

International Livestock Research Institute, 1996. *Nutrient Cycling in Integrated Rangeland/Cropland Systems of the Sahel*. Niamey: ILRI, Sahelian Centre.

Keftasa, D. and International Livestock Centre for Africa. 1988. Role of Crop Residues as Livestock Feed in Ethiopian Highlands. In *Proceedings of the Third Workshop at the International Conference Centre*. Arusha, United Republic of Tanzania, 27-30 April 1987. Addis Ababa: ILCA. Preston, T.R. and E. Murgueitio. 1992. Sustainable Intensive Livestock Systems for the Humid Tropics. *World Animal Review* 72:2-8.

Index

E

F

G